The God

OF

Jesus

The God

_OF_

Jesus

A Comprehensive Examination of the
Nature of the Father, Son and Spirit

David A Kroll

WESTBOW
PRESS
A DIVISION OF THOMAS NELSON

ISBN: 978-1-4497-7285-7 (sc)
ISBN: 978-1-4497-7286-4 (e)

Library of Congress Control Number: 2012921892

WestBow Press books may be ordered through booksellers or by contacting:

WestBow Press
A Division of Thomas Nelson
1663 Liberty Drive
Bloomington, IN 47403
www.westbowpress.com
1-(866) 928-1240

TABLE OF CONTENTS

PREFACE

Most Christians believe God is a Trinity. It is believed God is co-eternal, co-equal and con-substantial (of the same essence) Persons of Father, Son and Spirit. These three Persons are believed to be the same in every respect short of being each other. There is no separation or subordination seen in the Triune God. The Persons of the Trinitarian God are seen as indwelling each other and always acting together as a single Being. The Trinitarian God is seen as having no beginning or end and eternally existing as Father, Son and Spirit.

This doctrine of God began to develop in the fourth century A.D. from theological discourse regarding the relationship between the Father and the Son. This led to formulation of the Nicene Creed at the Council of Nicaea in A.D. 325. The Nicene Creed states the following:

We believe in one God, the Father Almighty, Maker of all things visible and invisible. And in one Lord Jesus Christ, the Son of God, begotten of the Father [the only-begotten; that is, of the essence of the Father, God of God], Light of Light, very God of very God, begotten, not made, being of one substance with the Father; by whom all things were made [both in heaven and on earth]; who for us men, and for our salvation, came down and was incarnate and was made man; And in the Holy Ghost.

This Creed identifies Jesus Christ as being of the essence of the Father, being of one substance with the Father and being "very God of very God." Therefore, Jesus Christ is identified as being God in every way the Father is God short of being the Father. The Son is seen as becoming God in the flesh in the person of Jesus. Jesus is seen as simultaneously being God and man in what is designated as the doctrine of the incarnation.

The Nicene Creed was updated at the Council of Constantinople in A.D. 381 to include the Holy Spirit as proceeding from the Father and worthy of worship as is the Father and the Son. Thus was established a Trinitarian concept of God.

In the pages that follow, I provide a systematic and comprehensive examination of the orthodox Christian doctrines of the Trinity and incarnation. My investigation takes into account the historical development of this theology and the manner in which Biblical scholars and theologians use the Scriptures to support these two mainstream Christian beliefs. In doing the research for this book, I have made every effort to accurately represent the Trinitarian/Incarnational position as commonly taught.

My initial goal in studying the doctrine of the Trinity and incarnation was to identify how these doctrines are supported by the Biblical Scriptures. It is here where I discovered these doctrines to be problematical. In studying the Scriptures and the scholarly material that relates to the doctrine of the Trinity and incarnation, it became apparent that Scripture is often taken out of context and exegesis is done based on assuming the thing to be proved, that God is a Trinity and Jesus is God incarnate. In carefully examining the many Scriptures that pertain to these doctrines, it became apparent to me that when these Scriptures are studied within the greater context of the whole of the Biblical narrative, they lead to a different perspective as to the nature of the Father, Son and Spirit from what is commonly taught within mainstream Christianity.

In looking at the nature of the Father, Son and Spirit in the context of the whole of Scripture, I was forced to reconsider orthodox doctrine and compelled by the evidence to understand that the Father is the one and only Supreme God over all reality. Jesus is not "God of very God" as the Nicene Creed proclaims. Jesus is the Father's human agent to facilitate salvation for mankind and, in so doing, was glorified by the Father and elevated to a position of great power and authority at the right hand of the one and only God. The Holy Spirit is the mind and power of God whereby He creates and sustains all things.

The first twenty-two chapters of this book will be devoted to discussion of the Father and the Son. Chapter Twenty-Three will deal with the nature of the Holy Spirit and Chapter Twenty-Four will provide a summery of what has been presented. All Scriptural quotations will be from the New International Version (NIV) unless otherwise indicated. I have inserted most of the Scriptures I reference right into the narrative. My hope is that this will enable readers to easily see the correspondence between what I write and what the Scriptures reveal.

I have chosen not to use footnotes within the body of this material. I do reference some resources in the narrative as I go along and provide a partial list at the end of this book of the many resources I used in preparing this material. Also provided is a list of the Bible translations I reference and quote from.

I titled this book *The God OF Jesus* because Jesus plainly taught the one and only true God is the Father and it is the Father who is His God. Apostles Paul and John, along with the other authors of the New Testament, teach the same thing. Trinitarianism teaches God is Father, Son and Spirit and therefore Jesus is God as the Father and the Spirit is God. In the following chapters, we will comprehensively examine the dynamics of this issue and carefully examine what the Scriptures teach as to the nature of the Father, Son and Spirit.

I encourage readers to approach this discussion with an open mind and not draw any conclusions until carefully and objectively considering all the material presented.

David Kroll

Chapter One

The God _Of_ Jesus

It is commonly believed the Son and Spirit of God is God in every way the Father is God short of being the Father. It is instructive, however, that the phrase "God the Son" or "God the Spirit" is not found in Scripture. We only see the phrase "God the Father" and other phraseology identifying the Father as the one and only God. Orthodox Christianity teaches Jesus is the incarnate Son of God. As such, Jesus is seen as God in the flesh. Jesus, however, clearly teaches the Father is the one and only God. Jesus tells us the Father is greater than He and is the source of His life. Jesus consistently relates to the Father as <u>the only</u> God.

John 5:43-44: I have come in my Father's name, and you do not accept me; but if someone else comes in his own name, you will accept him. How can you believe if you accept praise from one another, yet make no effort to obtain the praise that comes from <u>the only God</u>?

In the Greek the phrase "only God" is "<u>one</u> and only God" and is so rendered in other English translations such as the New American Standard Version (NASV). Jesus clearly identifies His Father as being the "one and only God." There is absolutely nothing in Jesus' statement to suggest He sees Himself and the Spirit included in the reality that is the one and only God. Jesus sees God as the Father with no hint of God being anything but the Father. In John 17:3, Jesus, in speaking to the Father, is quoted as saying to the Father that the Father is the only true God.

John 17:3: Now this is eternal life: that they may know you, <u>the only true God</u>, and Jesus Christ, whom you have sent.

Jesus sees Himself as being sent by the only true God who is the Father. There is no indication Jesus includes himself in the designation "only true God." There is no indication Jesus considers Himself co-eternal, co-equal and con-substantial with the one who sent him. Nothing in what Jesus said suggests He is an indwelling distinction of the one and only true God and is God of very God as the Nicene Creed proclaims.

Trinitarians believe when Jesus says the Father is the one and only true God, Jesus is seeing the Father as the one God within an indwelling relationship of Father, Son and Spirit. Therefore, to see the Father as the one and only true God is to also see the Son and Spirit as the one and only true God. This argument is based on the belief that God is indwelling co-eternal, co-equal and con-substantial distinctions of the single Being called God. Therefore, Trinitarians believe anyone of these three distinctions can be seen as the one and only God because they include the other two.

The Scriptures, however, never speak of God the Son or God the Spirit. The Scriptures only speak of God the Father. If God is Father, Son and Spirit, we would expect to see references to God the Son and God the Spirit in addition to the many references we see to God the Father. You will not find such references in Scripture.

Furthermore, the Scriptures consistently speak of the Son of God and the Spirit of God but never speak of the Father of God. If God is Father, Son and Spirit, we would expect to see references to the Father of God in addition to seeing references to the Son and Spirit of God. If God is an indwelling union of Father, Son and Spirit, we should expect the Father to be identified as being of God as much as the Son and Spirit are identified as being of God. Nowhere do we see this in Scripture. What we do see in Scripture are references to the Son and Spirit proceeding from the Father who is the only individual consistently identified as being

God. Here is what Jesus said about where He and the Spirit proceed from.

John 8:42: Jesus said unto them, If God were your Father, ye would love me: for I proceeded forth and came from God; neither came I of myself, but he sent me (KJV).

John 15:26: But when the Comforter is come, whom I will send unto you from the Father, even the Spirit of truth, which proceedeth from the Father, he shall testify of me (KJV).

In John 8:42, Jesus says He proceeded forth from God whom he identifies as the Father. In John 15:26, Jesus shows the Spirit proceeds from the Father. Trinitarianism teaches God is indwelling distinctions of Father, Son and Spirit. If this is the case, Jesus and the Spirit should be seen as proceeding from God and not just the single distinction of God called the Father. Yet the Scriptures teach the Son and Spirit proceed from the Father who Jesus said is the one and only God. Therefore, it should be evident when Jesus speaks of the Father being the one and only God and the Scriptures speak of the Son and Spirit being of God and proceeding from God, it is the Father who is clearly identified as the one and only God from whom the Son and Spirit proceed.

Trinitarians argue that because the Son and Spirit proceed from God the Father, the Son and Spirit are God in every respect the Father is God short of being the Father. They analogize this to humans born of humans being humans, dogs born of dogs being dogs and so forth. This analogy, however, does not reflect the Trinitarian concept of God. The Trinitarian God is seen as an un-separated single Being of indwelling distinctions of Father Son and Spirit. Humans born of other humans and dogs born of other dogs don't indwell each other and they are separate individuals. While humans

3

share a number of common characteristics, they often exhibit differences in will and purpose. Trinitarians teach there is no separation or difference of will or purpose in the Trinitarian God. Therefore, this analogy does not apply.

The God that the Son and Spirit are of and proceed from is the Father. In Trinitarian theology, God is Father, Son and Spirit. These three indwell each other and constitute the one God. Trinitarianism teaches there is no separation or subordination in the Triune God. Father, Son and Spirit are all equally God. If God is a tri-unity of Father, Son and Spirit, it would be this Triune God that the Son and Spirit are of, and proceed from. The Son and Spirit could not proceed only from the Father if there is no separation in God. Yet, Scripture reveals that the Son and Spirit are of and proceed from the Father alone. The Scriptures teach the Son and Spirit proceed from a single, undifferentiated Being identified as the Father who alone is God. Scripture identifies God as the Father and the Father as God.

Jesus identifies the Father as the one and only God. Jesus clearly dispels any notion of Him being equal to the Father when He plainly says His Father is greater than He.

John 14:28: You heard me say, `I am going away and I am coming back to you.' If you loved me, you would be glad that I am going to the Father, for the <u>Father is greater than I</u>.

Here Jesus clearly teaches His Father is greater than He. This statement makes it evident Jesus, as the Son of the Father, is not co-equal with the Father as is taught within Trinitarianism. Some argue Jesus is seeing the Father as greater than He purely from a human perspective. It is believed John 14:28 refers to Jesus relating to the Father in what is believed to be His "incarnated human state of being" and not in his eternal state of being. It is believed Jesus made this statement within the context of His "incarnate identity," not His "eternal identity." Since it is assumed Jesus is both God and man, anything Jesus said during His ministry that appears to picture him as separate and subordinate to the Father is seen as Jesus speaking within the context of His humanity, not His Divinity.

Others believe all Scriptural statements that show the Father to be superior to the Son must be viewed as Jesus being eternally begotten by the Father within the relational structure of the Trinity where the Son relates to the Father as the source of His existence. The Son is seen as generated by the Father and yet ontologically one with the Father and the Spirit (equal in Being with the Father and Spirit). Even though the Son is said to originate from the Father, He is not seen as separate from the Father but as being equal with the Father in all things short of being the Father.

In John, chapters 14 through 16, Jesus begins an extensive discussion with His disciples by saying, **"Trust in God, Trust also in me" (John 14:1).** Jesus clearly distinguishes between Himself and God whom He identifies as the Father throughout John 14-16. This discussion takes place shortly before His crucifixion where He reveals he will soon leave this world and go to the Father. It is in this context He says the Father is greater than He. Throughout these three chapters, Jesus shows how everything He does is from the Father and will continue to be from the Father after He ascends to the Father. Jesus' entire discussion gives evidence to the Father being greater than Jesus not only in relation to Jesus' physical existence on earth but also after He ascends to the Father following His resurrection from the dead.

As already discussed, Jesus clearly identifies the Father as the one and only God. In saying the Father is greater than He, Jesus is essentially telling His disciples that although He is the unique Son of God, has been given great power and authority by His God and will be ascending to His God, He is not at the same ontological level (level of Being) as God. He is separate in level of Being from that of the Father. Now let's look at Mark 13:32.

Mark 13:32: No one knows about that day or hour, not even the angels in heaven, nor the Son, but only the Father.

If Jesus was at the same ontological level as the Father, He would have the same level of knowledge, understanding and wisdom as the Father. Yet, Jesus clearly shows this not to be the case when He says that only the Father knows the day and hour of the eschatological events described in Mark 13. It is interesting that in the Matthew 24:36 parallel account of this passage, the phrase "nor the Son" is missing in a number of ancient Greek manuscripts. Some scholars believe this phrase was deleted by scribes who believed Jesus was God and were troubled by the implication that Jesus didn't know what God knew. Fourth century Trinitarian theologian Athanasius did not include this phrase in his rendering of Matthew 24:36.

Jesus plainly reveals it is the Father who has life within Himself (intrinsic life). It is from the Father that Jesus receives His life. Jesus did not have intrinsic life. If Jesus was an incarnation of an indwelling distinction of the eternal God, He would not need for the Father to grant life to Him. He would have intrinsic life as the Father does. Yet Jesus says He receives His life from the Father.

John 5:26: For as the Father has life in himself, so he has granted the Son to have life in himself.

Jesus reveals it is the Father alone who has immortal life in Himself and gives of this life to the Son. The context of John 5 shows it is eternal life being discussed. Although Jesus' physical life comes from the Father as is true with all humans, Jesus is not talking about God granting Him His physical life in this passage. The context of John 5 is eternal life. If the Son (Jesus) is co-eternal with the Father, He would have eternal life in Himself as does the Father and would not have to be granted such life by the Father. Jesus was given eternal life through resurrection from the dead as will be made clear as we progress with this discussion. Scripture consistently shows Jesus to relate to the Father as <u>His</u> God. This is clearly shown in a statement Jesus made to Mary following His resurrection.

John 20:17: Jesus said to her, "Do not cling to Me, for I have not yet ascended to My Father; but go to My brethren and say to them, `I am ascending to My Father and your Father, and to <u>My God</u> and your God."

In this statement made to Mary shortly after His resurrection, Jesus clearly identifies the Father as God and more specifically as <u>His</u> God. Some argue that when Jesus says "to My Father …and to My God," He is simply recognizing the Father as a distinction of the Triune God. Since Jesus consistently speaks of God as His Father during His ministry, it is believed He is telling Mary He is ascending to the person of the Father who is God as one of three distinctions in a Trinitarian relationship of Father, Son and Spirit.

Some Trinitarian thinkers believe "Father" is being used in a two-fold way in this passage and throughout the New Testament (NT) Scriptures. It is believed "Father" is used to identify God as the Creator and Lord of and over all things and in some separate sense as the God and Father of Jesus. Therefore, when Jesus says to Mary He is ascending to His Father and God and her Father and God, it is believed He is telling Mary He is ascending to the Being she knows as the unbegotten, unoriginate source of all there is. On the other hand, Jesus is seen as ascending to the Being He knows as His God and Father within the Trinitarian relationship of Father, Son and Spirit. This apparently was the position taken by fourth century theologians Athanasius and Gregory Nyssen relative to John 20:17.

The problem with this perspective is that Jesus made it clear during His ministry the Father is the <u>one and only</u> God (John 5:43-44 and 17:3) with no hint of He also being this God. Jesus' statement to Mary is totally consistent with what He previously stated about the Father being the one and only God. Jesus provides no hint of God being a plurality of Father, Son and Spirit. In John 20:17 Jesus speaks of ascending to His Father <u>and His</u> God. If Jesus is God in all attributes that define God except that of being the person of the Father or the person of the Spirit, why does Jesus speak in terms of ascending to <u>His</u> God when He is the God He is ascending to? Why is the Father seen as the God <u>of</u> Jesus if Jesus is God in every way except that of being the Father? This issue is addressed in more detail in Chapter Twelve where the concept of "eternal begettal" is discussed.

Just before Jesus died on the cross He cried out, "My God, My God, why have you forsaken me?" This is another example of Jesus relating to God as His God. Trinitarians see this as Jesus relating to God strictly as an expression of his human nature. Yet if the Son is an indwelling distinction of the one God who is Father, Son and Spirit, it appears He would have addressed the distinction called the Father rather than address God in making His plea. If Jesus is an indwelling distinction of God, by addressing God, Jesus is virtually addressing Himself. He is making a plea to Himself.

It is much more consistent with Jesus' own proclamations regarding who God is to conclude when Jesus addresses God with His plea, He is addressing His Father who, during His ministry, He identified as the one and only God.

How is God identified by the Apostles?

Like Jesus, Apostle Paul identifies the Father as being the only God.

Romans 3:29-30: Is God the God of Jews only? Is he not the God of Gentiles too? Yes, of Gentiles too, since <u>there is only one God</u>, who will justify the circumcised by faith and the uncircumcised through that same faith.

Romans chapter three shows God facilitates salvation for both Jews and Gentiles through the death and resurrection of Jesus. Is Paul teaching that God facilitates salvation through God the Son who is the one God as is the Father and Spirit? The overall context of Romans 3 shows Paul using the word God as synonymous with the Father who he identifies as the only God. Therefore, when Paul says there is only one God, it is the Father He sees as the one God. This one and only God is seen as justifying both Jews and Gentiles by faith in the man Jesus who this one and only God has presented as a sacrifice of atonement.

Romans 3:25a: God presented him (Jesus) as a sacrifice of atonement, through faith in his (Jesus') blood.

There is nothing in this passage to suggest Paul is saying God the Father has presented God the Son as a sacrifice of atonement. It should be evident Paul is saying God the Father, who Paul identifies as the one and only God (verse 30), has presented His supernaturally begotten human Son as a sacrifice for sin. The begettal of Jesus will be discussed in detail in Chapter Twelve.

A review of NT Scriptures reveals repeated references to God being the God and Father <u>of</u> Jesus. God is seen as the Father of Jesus and the God of Jesus. How then can Jesus be seen as being the same God He looks to as <u>His</u> God? In the following Scriptural passages, it can be seen that God is identified as not only the Father of Jesus but the God of Jesus.

Romans 15:5-6: May the God who gives endurance and encouragement give you a spirit of unity among

yourselves as you follow Christ Jesus, so that with one heart and mouth you may glorify the <u>God and Father</u> of our Lord Jesus Christ.

2 Corinthians 1:3a: Praise be to the <u>God and Father</u> of our Lord Jesus Christ.

2 Corinthians 11:31: The <u>God and Father</u> <u>of</u> the Lord Jesus, who is to be praised forever...

Ephesians 1:3a: Praise be to the <u>God and Father</u> <u>of</u> our Lord Jesus Christ.

Ephesians 1:17: I keep asking that the <u>God of</u> our Lord Jesus Christ, <u>the glorious Father</u>, may give you the Spirit of wisdom and revelation, so that you may know him better.

1 Peter 1:3: Praise be to the <u>God and Father</u> <u>of</u> our Lord Jesus Christ! In his great mercy he has given us new birth into a living hope through the resurrection of Jesus Christ from the dead.

James 1:1: James, a servant of God <u>and of</u> the Lord Jesus Christ, To the twelve tribes scattered among the nations: Greetings.

Revelation 1:5b-6: To him who loves us and has freed us from our sins by his blood, and has made us to be a kingdom and priests to serve <u>his</u> <u>God and Father</u>—to him be glory and power for ever and ever! Amen.

Trinitarians argue that when the writers of Biblical Scriptures use the phrase "God and Father," they are referring only to the person of the Father in the Trinitarian relationship that is the one God who is Father, Son and Spirit. Therefore, when Jesus speaks of we serving his God and Father in Revelation chapter one, it is believed He is speaking of serving the person of the Father in the tri-union of Father, Son and Spirit which is God. This notion, however, is contrary to the plain and straightforward language in the foregoing Scriptures and this notion is clearly dispelled by Apostle Paul in His first letter to the Corinthian Christians where he addresses the issue of eating foods sacrificed to idols.

1 Corinthians 8:4-6: So then, about eating food sacrificed to idols: We know that an idol is nothing at all in the world and that there is no God but one. For even if there are so-called gods, whether in heaven or on earth (as indeed there are many "gods" and many "lords"), yet for us there is but one God, the Father, from whom all things came and for whom we live; and there is but one Lord, Jesus Christ, through whom all things came and through whom we live.

Apostle Paul emphatically writes there is no God but one and identifies this one God as the Father. It is instructive that he does not say there is one God the Father and the Son. He does not say there is one God who is Father, Son and Spirit. He does not say there is one God the Father and one God the Son. Paul never uses the phrase God the Son or God the Spirit. It is always God the Father.

Paul identifies Jesus Christ as Lord. Trinitarians argue that to say Jesus is Lord is to say Jesus is God because in the Old Testament (OT) "Lord" is used as a synonym for *YHWH*. *YHWH* is the name by which the one God identifies Himself to Israel. Therefore, it is believed Paul is saying there is one God/ Lord (*YHWH*) who is Father and Son. The designation "Lord" is seen as equivalent in meaning to the Greek *Theos* which is translated "God" In the NT. It is believed Paul is seeing both the Father and the Son as *YHWH* God.

As will be seen as we proceed with this discussion, *YHWH* God is identified as Father in the OT. Nowhere is *YHWH* identified as being Father plus others. The name *YHWH* is rendered LORD (all caps) in some English translations of the Hebrew Scriptures. In addition, the authors of the Hebrew Scriptures often used the Hebrew *Adonai* as a synonym for *YHWH* which is translated into English as Lord (capitol L followed by lower case letters). The NT uses just one word for "lord," the Greek *kurios*. The Greek *kurios* is used in association with the word God and the words Father and Jesus in a variety of ways in the NT. This requires strict attention to context in order to properly determine how *kurios* is being used. For example, in the following passages, *kurios* is used twice to identify the Father and once to identify Jesus.

Luke 10:21a: At that time Jesus, full of joy through the Holy Spirit, said, "I praise you, Father, Lord (*kurios*) of heaven and earth"

Acts 17:24: The God who made the world and everything in it is the Lord (*kurios*) of heaven and earth and does not live in temples built by hands.

Acts 2:36: Therefore let all Israel be assured of this: God has made this Jesus, whom you crucified, both Lord (*kurios*) and Christ.

Jesus identifies the Father as Lord of heaven and earth (Luke 10:21). Apostle Paul identifies God as Lord of heaven and earth (Acts 17:24). Since Jesus identifies the Father as Lord of heaven and earth, it is reasonable to conclude when Paul says God made the world and everything in it and is Lord of heaven and earth; it is the Father he is speaking of. Peter instructs that God made Jesus Lord and Christ (Acts 2:36). Here we see God appointing Jesus as Lord. If God makes Jesus Lord, how can Jesus be the same Lord God is?

The Hebrew Scriptures clearly identify *YHWH* as the one and only LORD God. *YHWH* is also called *Adonai* (Lord). Are

Paul and the other NT authors, when speaking of Jesus as *kurios* (Lord), equating Him with the *YHWH* (LORD) and *Adonai* (Lord) of the OT? As will be seen in Chapter Three, the OT Scriptures identify *YHWH* (LORD) and *Adonai* (Lord) as the one and only Supreme Most High God while identifying the Son of this God as *adoni* (lord) which means a servant of the one and only Supreme, Most High God. While the Greek *kurios* (Lord) is used as a designation for both the Father and the Son in NT Scripture, God the Father is seen as the One and Only Most High LORD (*YHWH*) over all reality. Jesus, the Son of God, is *YHWH's* begotten, appointed and anointed Lord to facilitate *YHWH's* salvation. This will be made very plain as we proceed with our discussion. Now let's look at how Apostle Paul further distinguishes between God and Jesus.

Ephesians 4:4-6: There is one body and one Spirit-- just as you were called to one hope when you were called-- one Lord, one faith, one baptism; one God and Father of all, who is over all and through all and in all.

Romans 16:25-27: Now to him who is able to establish you by my gospel and the proclamation of Jesus Christ, according to the revelation of the mystery hidden for long ages past, but now revealed and made known through the prophetic writings by the command of the eternal God, so that all nations might believe and obey him-- to the only wise God be glory forever through Jesus Christ! Amen."

To the Ephesians we see Paul speaking of the one Lord, who he identifies in 1 Corinthians 8:6 as Jesus Christ. As Paul did with the Corinthians, he identifies the one God as the Father. To the Romans Paul speaks of glorifying the eternal and only wise God through Jesus Christ. The eternal and only wise God is distinguished from Jesus. We know from the context of Paul's writings that when he uses the word God he means the Father. When Paul says, "to the only wise God" he is identifying the Father as the one and only God.

We are to glorify the one and only God through Christ. Trinitarians see Paul saying we glorify God through God the Son in the Trinitarian union that is Father, Son and Spirit. Paul, however, never speaks of God the Son or God the Spirit. Paul consistently writes of the Father being the one and only God. As we move through this material, it will become evident the Son is the agent of the one God through whom we worship this one God. As God's agent, the Son isn't God any more than my son is me when he acts as my agent. It is through Christ that we can be reconciled to the one God who is the Father. The whole focus of Christ's ministry was to bring us to God the Father which Scriptures show is the one and only God and also the God of Jesus. Let's look at what Paul wrote to Timothy.

1 Timothy 2:5: For there is one God and one mediator between God and men, the man Christ Jesus.

In this passage, Paul clearly states there is one God and Jesus is the mediator (intermediary: NET bible) between this one God and man. Trinitarianism teaches God is a single Being with no separation of substance. God does not have parts. There is no separation in the Trinitarian God, only distinctions of Father, Son and Spirit. Since Paul consistently identifies God as Father in His writings, Trinitarians believe when Paul writes to Timothy that there is one God, he is referring to the Father distinction in the single Being that is God. Jesus is seen as the Son distinction in the single Godhead. The Son is seen as working as mediator between the Father and man within the Trinitarian union of Father, Son and Spirit.

The Trinitarian position is that when NT authors use the word God and Jesus in the same sentence, they are referring to the Father as a distinction of the one God and to Jesus as another distinction of the one God. The Father and the Son are seen within an indwelling relationship of Father Son and Spirit. This position, however, is not substantiated by the Scriptures.

The Scriptures consistently teach there is one God who is the Father. Nowhere does Jesus or the Apostles teach the one God is the Father plus others.

In 1Timothy 2:5, Paul contrasts the one God with the man Jesus. There is no hint here of Jesus also being the one God. Paul consistently identifies the one God as Father and never as Father and Son or Father, Son and Spirit. Paul consistently identifies the Father as God and God as the Father. Jesus consistently identifies God as the Father and only as the Father. The Scriptures consistently speak of the Son of God and the Spirit of God. The Scriptures never speak of the Father of God. As already discussed, if God is a single Being in three distinctions of Father, Son and Spirit, you would expect to see references to the Father of God as you commonly see references to the Son and Spirit of God. Since no such references exist, it gives evidence to the Father and only the Father being God with everything else being of and from the Father including the Son and the Spirit.

Let's take a closer look at the Acts 17 passage cited above. Paul addresses the Athenians and identifies to them the one and only true God who is maker of heaven and earth and the one responsible for their being alive. Paul concludes his remarks by saying the following:

Acts 17:31: For he (God) has set a day when he will judge the world with justice by the man he has appointed. He has given proof of this to all men by raising him from the dead.

God, as creator and sustainer (17:24), is contrasted with the one He raised from the dead. God is seen as appointing Jesus as the man through whom He will judge the world. As you proceed through this material, you will see that God the Father is Supreme Judge and Savior and Jesus is given these designations only as the appointed facilitator of God's judgement and salvation. In leading up to his statement in 1 Timothy 2:6 about there being one God and Jesus being the one mediator between God and man, Paul speaks of God as Savior who wants all men to be saved (1 Timothy 2:3-4). The context of this passage shows the Savior Paul is referring to is the Father. We know it is the Father who sent Christ to save the world (John 3:16-17). Jesus is the facilitator of the Father's will to provide salvation for mankind. This doesn't make Jesus, as facilitator of the Father's will, any more equal with the Father than my son carrying out my will makes my son equal with me.

In addition to the already quoted Scriptures that show the Father to be the God of Jesus, other Scriptures clearly show that God the Father, as the Most High Supreme LORD (*YHWH*) of all reality, is our God and Father as well, while Jesus is our lord as *YHWH's* anointed savior to the world.

Galatians 1:3-5: Grace and peace to you from <u>God our Father</u> and the Lord Jesus Christ, who gave himself for our sins to rescue us from the present evil age, according to the will of <u>our God and Father</u>, to whom be glory for ever and ever. Amen.

Philippians 4:19-20: And <u>my God</u> will meet all your needs according to his glorious riches in Christ Jesus. To <u>our God and Father</u> be glory for ever and ever. Amen.

1 Thessalonians 1:3: We continually remember before <u>our God and Father</u> your work produced by faith, your labor prompted by love, and your endurance inspired by hope in our Lord Jesus Christ.

1 Thessalonians 3:11, 13: Now may <u>our God and Father</u> himself <u>and our Lord</u> Jesus clear the way for us to come to you. Verse 13, May he strengthen your hearts so that you will be blameless and holy in the presence of <u>our God</u>

and Father when **our Lord** Jesus comes with all his holy ones.

In these passages, there clearly is separation of Being indicated between God the Father and the Son. Paul writes of "our God and Father." If God is Father, Son and Spirit, Paul is actually saying "our Father, Son and Spirit and Father" which clearly makes no sense.

Trinitarianism teaches God the Father and Christ the Lord are a single entity called God and have no separation of Being in their co-eternal, co-equal and con-substantial state. Any perceived separation in Being is seen to be a consequence of the Son's "incarnation" as the Christ and not a separation in ontological Being with the Father and Spirit. Many Scriptures make this conclusion highly problematical. Here are just a few.

Revelation 1:5b-6: To him who loves us and has freed us from our sins by his blood, and has made us to be a kingdom and priests to serve <u>his</u> <u>God and Father</u>—to him be glory and power for ever and ever! Amen.

Revelation 7:10: And they cried out in a loud voice: "Salvation belongs <u>to our God</u>, who sits on the throne, <u>and</u> to the Lamb."

Revelation 12:10b: Now have come the salvation and the power and the kingdom of our God, and the authority <u>of his</u> Christ.

Revelation 20:6c: but they will be priests of God <u>and</u> of Christ and will reign with him for a thousand years.

Acts 7:55-56: But Stephen, full of the Holy Spirit, looked up to heaven and saw the glory of God, and Jesus standing at the right hand of God. "Look," he said, "I see

heaven open and the Son of Man standing at the right hand of God."

Colossians 3:1: Since, then, you have been raised with Christ, set your hearts on things above, where Christ is seated at the right hand of God.

All these Scriptures show separation between God and Christ after Christ has ascended to the Father and has been granted great, authority and power as the glorified Son of God who facilitated the Father's salvation for the human race.

When NT writers refer to God and Christ in the same sentence, God is seen as a separate entity from Christ. In Revelation 1:5b-6, God is seen as the God of Jesus. In Revelation 7:10b, we find the Lamb (Christ) seen as separate from God who sits on the throne. In Revelation 12:10b the Son is referred to as God's Christ which means the anointed of God. In reference to the thousand year reign, God is shown as distinct from Christ. Stephen sees Jesus standing next to God. Paul writes of Jesus seated at the right hand of God. Jesus speaks of Himself being at the right hand of the Mighty One (Matthew 26:64). There is not a hint in any of this that the Son, in His glorified state, is ontologically one with God. In these passages of Scripture, we see distinction made between God and Jesus. If Jesus is as much God as the Father is God and God is indeed Father, Son and Spirit, it seems mighty peculiar to see Jesus, in His glorified state, consistently identified as a separate entity from God.

We have seen that Jesus and Paul teach the Father is the one and only God. Therefore, when John, Stephen and Paul speak of God in the above passages, they are speaking of the Father. They are seeing the Father and the Son as separate Beings and not distinctions of the single Being God. When John, Stephen and Paul use the term God in these passages, they understand God as a single, undifferentiated Being who is the Father and only the Father. In Revelation 3:21, we read that Jesus and His Father have a separate throne which gives further evidence to their separateness of Being.

Revelation 3:21: To him who overcomes, I will give the right to sit with me on <u>my</u> throne, just as I overcame and sat down with my Father on <u>his</u> throne.

It is instructive that nowhere in Scripture will you find the phrase God the Son. Jesus is consistently seen as the Son of God the Father and clearly identifies himself as such throughout his ministry. While the word God is associated with the Father in most of the New Testament, there are Scriptures where the word God is associated with Jesus. I address these passages later in this book when I discuss how the words for God are used in the Scriptures. During His ministry, Jesus never used the word God, as in Supreme, Most High God, in reference to Himself or to identify Himself. He only used the word God in association with the Father. One of many examples of this is found in Jesus' conversation with a Samaritan woman where God is identified as the Father.

John 4:23-24: Yet a time is coming and has now come when the true worshipers will worship the Father in spirit and truth, for they are the kind of worshipers the Father seeks. God is spirit, and his worshipers must worship in spirit and in truth.

Jesus speaks of worshiping the Father in spirit and truth. He identifies the Father as God. Jesus gives no hint to the Samaritan women that He also is God. Instead, He clearly identifies Himself to her as the Messiah (John 4:25-26) which is to identify Himself as the anointed of the God He was speaking of.

Within the doctrine of the Trinity, Jesus is seen as co-equal with the Father. Trinitarianism sees no subordination between the "Persons" of the Trinity. Yet Apostle Paul clearly writes of Jesus being subject to God and of God being all in all.

1 Corinthians 11:3: Now I want you to realize that the head of every man is Christ, and the head of the woman is man, and the <u>head of Christ is God</u>.

1 Corinthians 15:27-28: For he "has put everything under his feet." Now when it says that "everything" has been put under him, <u>it is clear that this does not include God himself,</u> who put everything under Christ. When he has done this, then <u>the Son himself will be made subject to him who put everything under him, so that God may be all in all.</u>

Paul makes it perfectly clear that when God says He has put everything under Christ it does not include Himself, God. God being all in all is seen in the context of all things being in subjection to God, including Jesus. Paul clearly shows God to be separate and superior to Jesus. This statement about God and Jesus was made after Jesus had ascended to the Father and was now in His glorified state. This statement alone should put to rest the idea that Christ is equal with the Father in every respect short of being the Father. The above two passages from 1 Corinthians clearly show everything is subject to the one and only Supreme God and this everything includes the Son.

God, who is identified throughout Scripture as the Father, is seen as over all things including Jesus. Jesus is seen as subordinant to the Father which is to say He is subordinant to God. The very language of 1 Corinthians 11:3 and 15:27-28 shows God to be supreme, superior and above all things including His Son Jesus. Fourth century Trinitarian theologian Gregory Nazianzen wrote that "to subordinate any of the three Divine Persons is to overthrow the Trinity." I submit that Apostle Paul overthrows the Trinity.

Trinitarians argue that while the Son is God in every respect short of being the Person of the Father, He willingly submits to the Father and in this manner is seen as subordinant to the Father. While it may be possible to be equal to someone and voluntarily be in submission to them, God is seen as the head over Christ and Christ is seen as subject to Him so that God is all in all. This is not language that speaks of the Son voluntarily subjecting Himself to God the Father while remaining in every respect equal to the Father short of being the Father. As will be seen in Chapters Three and Seventeen of this book, the Father and no one but the Father is identified in Scripture as *YHWH*. *YHWH* is identified as the Most High God. *YHWH*, as the Most High God who is the Father, doesn't have any equal.

Psalms 83:18: Let them know that you, whose name is the LORD (*YHWH*), that <u>you alone</u> are the Most High over all the earth.

It should be evident when Scriptural writers speak of the Father and Jesus in the same context; they are not speaking of co-equal persons who are both the one and only Most High God. At one point during His ministry, Jesus was dealing with an evil spirit who cried out in the following manner:

Mark 5:7b: What do you want with me, Jesus, Son of the Most High God? Swear to God that you won't torture me!

The evil spirit understood Jesus to be the Son <u>of</u> the Most High God <u>and not</u> that the Son <u>is</u> the Most High God. The evil spirit even asks Jesus to swear by God showing this spirit understood God is a separate Being from Jesus. Jesus is identified throughout Scripture as the Son of God and not as God. Luke records it was the power of the Most High that would overshadow Mary resulting in her becoming pregnant with Jesus. The result would be that the one to be born would be called the Son of God (Luke 1:35). Jesus is the Son of God because the Most High God facilitated His birth through Mary and not because He pre-existed as a co-eternal, co-equal and con-substantial distinction of the Most High God. There is only one Most High God and that God is the God of Jesus.

Jesus made it clear that a servant and messenger are not greater than the one who sends him. Scripture makes it clear Jesus was sent by God the Father as His servant. When we consider Jesus' status as a servant of God along with what Paul said about God being the head of Christ and Christ being subordinant to God, it should be obvious the Son and the Father are not equally the Most High God. The Scriptures clearly teach that Jesus is the servant of God and not that Jesus is God.

John 13:16: I tell you the truth, no servant is greater than his master, nor is a messenger greater than the one who sent him.

Matthew 12:18: Here is my servant whom I have chosen, the one I love, in whom I delight; I will put my Spirit on him, and he will proclaim justice to the nations.

Acts 3:13a: The God of Abraham, Isaac and Jacob, the God of our fathers, has glorified his servant Jesus.

In these passages, Jesus is identified as a servant of God and by His comments recorded in John 13:16, it can be seen that Jesus recognizes his subservient relationship to God in saying a messenger is not greater than the one who sends him. Other Scriptures show it is God who sent Jesus.

In addition to Paul and Jesus writing of the Son's subordination to God, Apostle John, when speaking of God and the Son in the same context, also sees the Son as subordinant to God and doesn't see the Son as being the God He is subordinant to.

1 John 1:5-7: This is the message we have heard from him and declare to you: God is light; in him there is no

darkness at all. If we claim to have fellowship with him (God) yet walk in the darkness, we lie and do not live by the truth. But if we walk in the light, as he is in the light, we have fellowship with one another, and the blood of Jesus, his Son, purifies us from all sin.

It is clear from the context of this passage that it is God the Father who is light and is in the light. God the Father, who is light, facilitated the conception of His Son Jesus through whom God's light was expressed in bringing salvation to the world. Jesus is not intrinsically this light but the agent of this light through whom this light became manifested. Paul made it very clear in his letter to Timothy that it is God the Father who alone is intrinsically immortal, lives in unapproachable light and is invisible (1 Timothy 6:16). Apostle John clearly identifies God the Father as the true God and Jesus as the Son of this God.

1 John 5:20: We know also that the Son of God has come and has given us understanding, so that we may know him (God) who is true. And we are in him (God) who is true--even in his Son Jesus Christ. He (God the Father) is the true God and eternal life.

By saying "in his Son Jesus Christ," John identifies the Father as the God who is true. This is the same John who quotes Jesus in John 17:3 and 5:44 as saying the Father is the only true God and the one and only God. John is being consistent in identifying who the true God is. Some Trinitarians believe the phrase; "He is the true God and eternal life" refers to the Son. Is this the case? A review of the scholarly research on this passage reveals almost unanimous consensus that John's reference to the true God is a reference to the Father. 1 John 5:20 is a powerful statement about who God is versus who Christ is and has great significance relative to how we understand the first chapter of John's Gospel which will be addressed in a later chapter of this book.

I titled this book *The God OF Jesus* because Jesus plainly taught the one and only true God is the Father and it is the Father who is His God. Apostles Paul and John, along with the other authors of the New Testament, teach the same thing. Trinitarianism teaches God is Father, Son and Spirit and therefore Jesus is God as the Father and the Spirit is God. In the following chapters, we will comprehensively examine the dynamics of this issue and carefully examine what the Scriptures teach as to the nature of the Father, Son and Spirit.

Chapter Two

The Lord Our God Is One

The Biblical Scriptures teach there is a single God who is responsible for the existence and sustenance of all things. This monotheistic approach is the cornerstone of Judaism, Christianity and Islam. Judaism and Islam believe this God to be a single undifferentiated entity. Much of Christianity is Trinitarian and teaches God is a single entity differentiated into Father, Son and Holy Spirit. Trinitarians see plurality in the single entity that is God. To ancient Israel, God was identified as being one.

Deuteronomy 6:4-5: Hear, O Israel: The LORD (Hebrew: *YHWH*) our God (Hebrew: *Elohim*), the LORD (*YHWH*) is one (Hebrew: *echad*). Love the LORD (*YHWH*) your God (*Elohim*) with all your heart and with all your soul and with all your strength.

This proclamation found in Deuteronomy does not define or identify the nature of the oneness that is God. It is simply a statement of monotheism, a statement saying there is one God Being as opposed to polytheism which is a belief in the existence and efficacy of many separate god Beings. In Judaism, this statement is called the *Shema* which is the Hebrew word "to hear." Jesus affirmed monotheism in the first century. He was asked what the most important commandment was and He gave this answer:

Mark 12:29-30, 32, 34: "The most important one," answered Jesus, "is this: `Hear, O Israel, the Lord (Greek: *kurios*) our God (Greek: *Theos*), the Lord (*kurios*) is one. Love the Lord your God with all your heart and with all your soul and with all your mind and with all your strength.'

Verse 32: "Well said, teacher," the man replied. "You are right in saying that God is one and there is no other but him." Verse 34: When Jesus saw that he had answered wisely, he said to him, "You are not far from the kingdom of God."

It is instructive that in his reply, the man identifies the one God as a him, a personal pronoun denoting singularity of Being. Old Testament (OT) Scriptures consistently testify to God being a single Being who is responsible for creation and who is over all things.

Deuteronomy 4:35: ... the LORD (Hebrew *YHWH* throughout) is God (Hebrew *Elohim* throughout); <u>besides him</u> there is no other.

Deuteronomy 4:39: Acknowledge and take to heart this day that the LORD is God in heaven above and on the earth below. There is no other.

Deuteronomy 32:39a: "See now that <u>I myself</u> am He! There is no god besides me.

1 Kings 8:60: So that all the peoples of the earth may know that the LORD is God and that there is no other.

Isaiah 45:5a: I am the LORD, and there is no other; <u>apart from me</u> there is no God.

Isaiah 44:24: This is what the LORD says-- your Redeemer, who formed you in the womb: I am the LORD, who has made all things, <u>who alone</u> stretched out the heavens, who spread out the earth <u>by myself</u>.

Psalm 83:18: Let them know that you, whose name is the LORD-- that <u>you alone</u> are the Most High over all the earth.

Jeremiah 10:10a: But the LORD is the true God; he is the living God, the eternal King.

In quoting the *Shema*, Jesus confirms Israel's monotheistic understanding of God. While the *Shema* does not identify or define the nature of this one God, Jesus and the Apostles clearly identify this God as the Father. In John 5:44 and 17:3, Jesus says the Father is the one and only true God. Paul does the same in 1 Corinthians 8:6 and John does the same in 1 John 5:20. This being the case, why do most Christians believe the nature of the one God to be a tri-unity of Father, Son and Spirit?

Most Christians are monotheistic. They believe there to be one and only one Supreme God. There are, however, different perspectives as to how to define this one and only God. Unitarians (not to be confused with the Unitarian Church) view God as being of undifferentiated composition. Trinitarians see God as a differentiated plurality of composition. Trinitarianism teaches the one true God is Father, Son and Spirit. The Father is God, the Son is God and the Holy Spirit is God. These are not three Gods but three distinctions, dimensions or expressions of the one and only God. Therefore, the question before us is not the oneness of God per se but how that oneness is to be defined.

Some believe the Trinitarian God has its roots in the OT, including the *Shema*. The word translated "one" found in the *Shema* is from the Hebrew *echad*. Because of the manner in which this word is used in various OT Scriptures, it is felt oneness can be seen as being composed of more than a single entity. This word is felt to express "compound unity." It is argued that *echad*, when modifying a collective noun such as "cluster," implies a plurality in *echad*. An example that is used is **Numbers 13:23b, "they cut off a branch bearing a single (*echad*) cluster of grapes."** Since the word "cluster" is a collective noun in so much as it implies more than one entity making up the cluster, it is felt *echad*, in modifying the noun, implies more than one entity. Some other Scriptures used to suggest *echad* implies a "compound unity" are as follows:

Genesis 2:24: For this reason a man will leave his father and mother and be united to his wife, and they will become one (*echad*) flesh. Here we see two individuals being defined as one.

Genesis 34:16: Then we will give you our daughters and take your daughters for ourselves. We'll settle among you and become one (*echad*) people with you. Here we find "one" including several cultures of people.

Ezra 2:64: The whole (*echad*) company numbered 42,360. Here *echad* is translated as "whole" and includes thousands of people.

To argue that *echad* can signify more than a single entity making up oneness is problematical. The Hebrew *echad* is associated with the numerical one and appears hundreds of times in the OT as designating the absolute singleness of something with no hint of such singleness being more than one of that something. In the example of the man and woman becoming one flesh, the man and woman still remain two autonomous individuals. The persons of the Triune God are not seen as autonomous but as indwelling each other. We know a man and women do not literally become one flesh but remain two separate individuals. There becoming one flesh is descriptive of sexual union and not that they literally become a single individual. Therefore, this analogy is without merit.

In the example of two peoples becoming one people, the two peoples still remain autonomous. They don't indwell each other. They become one only in the sense of becoming one people through intermarriage. They remain separated entities within their one group. Trinitarianism sees God as a single entity of single substance differentiated into three persons or distinctions indwelling each other. Therefore, God is seen as one (*echad*) plurality. In examining how *echad* is used in the OT, it appears that when a collective noun such as "people" is modified by *echad*, the plurality is in the collective noun and not in the modifier. When *echad* modifies a noun that suggests plurality, it signifies a single unit of that plurality. In the Shema, there is nothing in *echad* or *YHWH* that suggests plurality of Being.

As discussed below, the Hebrew *Elohim* is generally rendered "God" in the OT and is a plural noun. When this noun is modified *by echad*, some see *echad* as identifying God (*Elohim*) as a single plurality of Father, Son and Spirit. The Scriptures, however, identify God (*Elohim*) as *YHWH*. There is nothing in the noun *YHWH* to suggest plurality. When the *Shema* says *YHWH* is the one God (*echad Elohim*), it is identifying God (*Elohim*) as the single undifferentiated entity called *YHWH*, who, as will be shown as we proceed with our discussion, is the Father and none other but the Father.

The Hebrew Scriptures consistently show *YHWH* as being the one and only true *Elohim*. While *Elohim* is plural in the Hebrew, *YHWH* is not. There is nothing in the meaning of *YHWH* that denotes plurality. Therefore, it is reasonable to conclude when the Hebrew *echad* is used in reference to *YHWH Elohim*, it is identifying God as one singular, unseparated and undifferentiated Being and not a plurality of entities indwelling each other as taught in Trinitarianism, or a plurality of separate God Beings (God being a family of Beings) as is taught by some Christian groups.

For those who believe God is a family of God Beings, the word God is considered a family name. Under this concept there is one God family which is presently made up of the Father and the Son. It is believed this is an "open family" where, through resurrection from the dead, humans can become members of this God family and virtually become God as God is God. The concept of a Trinitarian God is seen as opposed to the concept of humans becoming members of "the God family" because it is believed Trinitarianism teaches God is a closed family of Beings. It must be understood, however, that Trinitarian theology does not teach God is a closed family of Beings. Under Trinitarianism, God is not a family of separate individual Beings. God is a single Being of indwelling entities of Father, Son and Spirit. Some Trinitarians teach that the human race is centered in this indwelling relationship of Father, Son and Spirit, a concept discussed in the last chapter of this book.

The plurality in God seen by Trinitarians is not that of separation but of indwelling distinctions. It's analogous to the sun being attributes of fire, heat and light which act as one but can be distinguished from one another. Trinitarians see God as a single Being of Father, Son and Spirit indwelling each other. These indwelling distinctions are viewed as being of one mind and power and always acting as one. The concept of God as a family of separate Beings is not found in Trinitarianism. Those who see the concept of a Trinitarian God being opposed to the family of God concept need to better understand how the Trinitarian God is defined.

It should be pointed out that while God is not seen <u>as</u> a family of Beings in either Trinitarianism or Unitarianism, both positions allow for God to <u>have</u> a family. Humans becoming Son's of God through Christ, who himself became a Son of God through Divine birth and resurrection from the dead, is clearly indicated in the Scriptures.

It is sometimes argued that if the writer of the *Shema* had wanted to express an absolute oneness of God he would have used *the Hebrew word yachid* in the *Shema* rather than *echad*. The Hebrew word *yachid* is felt to express the idea of absolute oneness in the OT. For example in Genesis 22:2a, God says to Abraham, **"Take your son, your only (*yachid*) son, Isaac."**

Since the author of the *Shema* used *echad* rather than *yachid*, it is believed the *Shema* does not express absolute oneness and allows for plurality in God. However, as already indicated, plurality is not seen in the word *echad*. As discussed above, plurality is sometimes seen in nouns *echad* modifies including the plural *elohim*, a word commonly associated with *YHWH*. Nothing in the word *YHWH* by itself indicates plurality. Does the plurality found in *elohim* indicate plurality in *YHWH*?

God as *Elohim* in the Old Testament:

As already pointed out, some argue that because the Hebrew *elohim*, which is translated God in the OT, is a plural noun, it shows plurality within God. Therefore, when *echad* is used in association with *elohim* the sense is that there is one God in whom there resides plurality. Some believe when *elohim* is translated into the English word God, it should be translated as God's.

Genesis 1:1: In the beginning "God's" (*elohim*) created the heavens and the earth.

The Hebrew word for God in this passage is *elohim*. This word appears 2,570 times in the Hebrew Scriptures and is used most of the time to identify the one true God. As already discussed, *elohim* appears in a plural form and because *elohim* appears in a plural form, some have concluded this word has an implicit connotation of plurality in the one God.

The *Hebrew Soncino Commentary* shows *elohim* to be a plural word in the Hebrew language and is often used in Hebrew to denote "plenitude of might." Some Hebrew linguists believe *Elohim* is derived from the Hebrew *El*, which has the meaning of "the strong one." The *Gesenius Hebrew-Chaldee Lexicon of the Old Testament* defines *elohim* as "plural of majesty." The *Theological Wordbook of the Old Testament* states the plural *elohim* is "usually described as a plural of majesty and not intended as a true plural when used of God as this noun is consistently used with singular verb forms and with adjectives and pronouns in the singular." Examples of this are found in association with the creation account in Genesis chapter one.

Genesis 1:27-31: So God (*elohim* throughout) created man in his (singular pronoun) own image, in the image of God he (singular pronoun) created him; male and female he (singular pronoun) created them. God blessed them and said to them, "Be fruitful and increase in number; fill the earth and subdue it. Rule over the fish of the sea and the birds of the air and over every living creature that moves on the ground." Then God said, "I (singular) give you every seed-bearing plant on the face of the whole earth and every tree that has fruit with seed in it. They will be yours for food. And to all the beasts of the earth and all the birds of the air and all the creatures that move on the ground--everything that has the breath of life in it--I (singular) give every green plant for food." And it was so. God saw all that he (singular) had made, and it was very good. And there was evening, and there was morning--the sixth day.

Further evidence that *elohim* does not imply plurality of Being is found in how this word is used in other Scriptural passages. For example, in **Exodus 7:1** we read, **"Then the LORD said to Moses, "See, I have made you like God (*elohim*) to Pharaoh, and your brother Aaron will be your prophet."** Moses is one single Being and obviously not made up of several persons. Another example is found in 1 Samuel 5:7 where the Philistines had captured the ark of the God of Israel and set it next to their god Dagon in the temple of Dagon at Ashdod. Israel's God began to bring judgment upon the people of Ashdod which led to the following conclusion:

1 Samuel 5:7: When the men of Ashdod saw what was happening, they said, "The ark of the god (*elohim*) of Israel

must not stay here with us, because his hand is heavy upon us and upon Dagon our god (*elohim*)."

Here we find *elohim* freely used to describe both the God of Israel and Dagon the god of the Philistines. There is no reason to believe Dagon was of plural composition. The god of the Amorites, called Chemosh, is called *elohim* in Judges 11:24.

It should be obvious when looking at the manner *elohim* is used throughout the OT Scriptures that it simply means plenitude of might or plural of majesty as the Hebrew Lexicons clearly show. This word is used to define not only the one true God but also angels, pagan gods and at times humans who are granted power and authority. Humans are seen as made a little lower than *elohim*.

Psalm 8:4-5: What is man that you are mindful of him, the son of man that you care for him? You made him a little lower than the heavenly beings (*elohim*) (NIV).

The Septuagint (The Greek translation of the Hebrew Scriptures that began to be made around 250 B.C.) translates *elohim* in this passage as *angelos* which is the Greek word for angel or messenger. The KJV and NKJV apparently follow the Greek and translate *elohim* as angels. The ASV, NASV, and RVSV translate *elohim* as "God" in this passage which indicates these translators are translating directly from the Hebrew text. By translating *elohim* as "heavenly beings" it appears the NIV (and also the NET) translators are taking a somewhat neutral approach. It is the Septuagint that the writer of Hebrews apparently used when he quotes from this Psalm and goes on to describe Jesus being made in the same fashion as man.

Hebrews 2:6-9: But there is a place where someone has testified: "What is man that you are mindful of him, the son of man that you care for him? You made him a

little lower than the angels; you crowned him with glory and honor and put everything under his feet." In putting everything under him, God left nothing that is not subject to him. Yet at present we do not see everything subject to him. But we see Jesus, who was made a little lower than the angels, now crowned with glory and honor because he suffered death, so that by the grace of God he might taste death for everyone.

The writer to the Hebrews teaches that man, including Jesus, was made a little lower than *elohim.* If the Psalmist is using *elohim* in reference to the one true God, this has implications for our understanding of the origin and nature of Jesus. Trinitarianism teaches Jesus has existed eternally as a co-equal and con-substantial distinction of the one true God. The writer to the Hebrews is saying Jesus was made lower than *elohim* like all other humans. The context of this passage shows it is God the Father who has made Jesus lower than *elohim* and able to die like all humans who are made lower than *elohim.* You will see the implications of this as we proceed with our discussion.

It has been argued that when God said, **"Let us make man in our image, in our likeness" (Genesis 1:26a),** this shows a plurality in God because of the use of the plural pronouns "us" and "our." In verse 27, however, there is an immediate return to the use of singular pronouns to modify the word for God (*Elohim*). **"So God created man in his (singular) own image, in the image of God he (singular) created him; male and female he (singular) created them."** These singular pronouns show God as a single entity. Yet the language of Genesis 1:26 indicates this single entity called God is communicating with others having the same image and likeness as that with which God intends to create man.

Trinitarianism teaches God is a single entity (one essence) and, as such, is Father, Son and Spirit. To a Trinitarian, therefore, the singular pronoun identification of God in the above passages is not a problem because God is believed to be of a single essence but plural in composition. Trinitarians believe in the singularity of God but define that singularity as composed of plurality. God saying, **"Let us make man in our image and likeness"** is seen as God communicating within Himself as Father, Son and Spirit.

Is God talking to Himself in Genesis 1:26? Could God be talking to an attendant council of angels and possibly other supernatural beings who themselves may have been created in the image and likeness of the one God and given various levels of authority and power? In **Job 38:1-7** God is speaking to Job about His creation of the earth and refers to it being a time when, **"all the angels shouted for joy."**

As already discussed, *elohim* is a plural word in the Hebrew language which denotes plenitude of might and plural of majesty. As such, this word is not intended as a true plural when used of God or anyone else. This noun is consistently used with singular verb forms and with adjectives and pronouns in the singular and is not only used to identify the one and only true God but also angels, other heavenly Beings and even humans who have been granted power and authority. This word does not denote quantity of Being, but quality of Being. This word denotes attributes of status, not numerical status.

Let's again look at Deuteronomy 6:4-5. **"Hear, O Israel: The LORD (*YHWH*) our God (*Elohim*), the LORD (*YHWH*) is one (*echad*). Love the LORD (*YHWH*) your God (*Elohim*) with all your heart and with all your soul and with all your strength."** If the plural *Elohim* means Gods, you virtually have to read this passage as follows:

"Hear, O Israel: The LORD (*YHWH*) our <u>Gods</u> (*Elohim*), the LORD (*YHWH*) is one (*echad*). Love the LORD (*YHWH*) your <u>Gods</u> (*Elohim*) with all your heart and with all your soul and with all your strength."

As can be seen, reading this passage in this manner is very awkward. This passage only makes sense if you read it with the understanding that *Elohim* is a single Being whose personal name is *YHWH*. Seeing *YHWH* as the name of two or more Beings (the "family of God" concept), who together comprise the one God (*Elohim*), does not square with Scriptures that identify *YHWH* as a single undifferentiated Being. Therefore, the "family of God" concept is very problematical.

While Trinitarians don't see the plural *Elohim* as meaning a family of separate individuals being the one God, they do see a plurality in *Elohim* in the form of indwelling, un-separated distinctions of the one God Being. As we proceed with this discussion, it will become apparent that viewing *Elohim* (when this word is associated with the one true God) as a plurality of entities who indwell each other as a single Being is equally as problematical as the "family of God" concept.

Chapter Three

YHWH, Adonai, Adoni

YHWH, Adonai and *Adoni* in the Hebrew Scriptures:

While *elohim* does not have intrinsic meaning of deity, the word *YHWH* does. This word appears 6,828 times in the OT and is understood to be the actual name of the Creator God. *YHWH* is invariably accompanied by singular personal pronouns and verbs in the singular. *YHWH* is often referred to as the *Tetragrammaton*, which is a Greek word meaning "word of four letters." The Hebrew language does not have vowels but only consonants and semi-consonants. *YHWH* is composed of four semi-consonants. Vowels must be supplied in the speaking and writing of this language. Between the seventh and tenth centuries A.D., a group of Jewish scribes and scholars called Masoretes began to insert "vowel points" in the Hebrew text for better clarity of meaning but left *YHWH* as is. Consequently we can't be sure how to pronounce or write this name in other languages to this very day.

YHWH is an English transliteration of this Hebrew name for God. A transliteration is the taking of letters in one alphabet and matching them to corresponding letters in another alphabet. Since the vowels are missing in *YHWH*, all spellings of *YHWH* are interpretations of what the transliteration *YHWH* may sound like. For example, the American Standard Bible renders *YHWH* as *Jehovah* and the New Jerusalem Bible (NJB) renders *YHWH* as *Yahweh*. Other renderings that are used include *Yahveh*, *Yehweh and Yahvah*.

Most English versions of the OT Scriptures don't use the transliteration *YHWH* but translate *YHWH* as LORD or Lord.

The NIV and ESV render *YHWH* as LORD (all caps) while the KJV, NASV, NET and other English translations render *YHWH* as Lord (capitol L followed by lower case letters). The Septuagint and Latin Vulgate translation of the Hebrew Scriptures use their equivalent of the Hebrew *YHWH*.

The precise meaning of *YHWH* is much debated. It appears to be taken from the Hebrew root word *hayah* which has the meaning of "be" or "become." *YHWH* came to signify self existent one or eternal one. The OT Scriptures clearly identify the name of God as being *YHWH*.

Exodus 3:15: God (*Elohim*) also said to Moses, "Say to the Israelites, `The LORD, (*YHWH*) the God of your fathers--the God of Abraham, the God of Isaac and the God of Jacob--has sent me to you.' <u>This is my name forever, the name by which I am to be remembered from generation to generation.</u>

Isaiah 42:8: I am the LORD; (*YHWH*) <u>that is my name!</u> I will not give my glory to another or my praise to idols.

As already mentioned, when the Masoretes began to add vowel points to the Hebrew text they left *YHWH* as *YHWH*. However, in 134 passages where *YHWH* appears in the OT text, they substituted the Hebrew word *Adonai* (sometimes spelled *Adonay*) which is taken from the Hebrew root *adon*. This Hebrew word, when substituted for *YHWH*, is translated as Lord with a capitol L to designate the one true God. Since our English translations of the Hebrew Scriptures are often taken from Masoretic Hebrew texts, the use of LORD for *YHWH* and Lord for *Adonai* is an easy way to distinguish between *YHWH* and *Adonai* in English Bibles that use this method of rendering these words into English. *Adonai* is also found in pre-Masoretic Hebrew manuscripts as a replacement for *YHWH* in the text and translated as Lord in the English.

The Hebrew word *adon* is used multiple hundreds of times in the OT in association with *Elohim*, *YHWH*, and man. *Adon* is translated as Lord or lord depending on the suffix attached to this word. Its basic meaning is lord or master. It is used to describe the owner of someone or something. When found as descriptive of *YHWH* this word appears in the Hebrew with the suffix "ai" as *Adonai*. When *adon* appears with the suffix "i" it becomes *adoni* and in this form is never used to describe *YHWH* but is applied to man and angels. *Adoni* is often translated into the English word master. For example, the servants of Abraham consistently refer to him as *adoni* which is translated master. The Pharaoh of Egypt is called *adoni*. So are Joseph and the kings of Israel.

Adonai is mostly seen as a reference to deity and is often found in a plural form but modified by a singular pronoun. In such cases it takes on the same meaning as the plural *elohim* and signifies plural of majesty. Since the root word *adon* can reference both God and man, the word does not have intrinsic meaning of deity as does *YHWH*. In its form as *adonai*, as is true of *elohim*, it is sometimes applied to an angel or a human who has attained a high status. However, *adonai* is used the majority of the time in association with *YHWH*. *Adonai* is found 449 times in the OT in association with *YHWH* or *Elohim* in reference to the one true God.

As mentioned above, the NIV and ESV translate *YHWH* as LORD with all capitol letters and *adonai* as Lord with a capital L followed by lower case letters instead of all caps. *Adoni*, on the other hand, is translated as lord with all lower case letters which is how it is rendered in most English translations with one major exception. In Psalm 110:1, the Hebrew *adoni* is rendered Lord with a capitol L in many English translations. This has led many to assume the Hebrew in this passage is *adonai* rather than *adoni*. This assumption has led to Psalm 110:1 being used as major Scriptural support for the Trinitarian concept of Jesus being God as the Father is God. It is believed David references both the Father and Son as God in this passage.

Psalm 110:1: The LORD (*YHWH*) says to my Lord (*adoni*): "Sit at my right hand until I make your enemies a footstool for your feet" (NIV and many other English translations).

The word translated LORD in Psalm 110:1 is *YHWH*. Therefore, the one true God is identified by His name. The second word Lord in this passage is *adoni*. This form of the Hebrew *adon* is not used in the Hebrew Scriptures to identify deity but always references man in some position of authority and power and a few times references angels. Here are several examples where *adoni* is used to refer to man in contrast to references to God as *YHWH* and *Elohim*.

1 Kings 1:36-37: Benewah son of Jehoiada answered the king, "Amen! May the LORD (*YHWH*), the God (*Elohim*) of my lord (*adoni*) the king, so declare it. As the LORD (*YHWH*) was with my lord (*adoni*) the king, so may he be with Solomon to make his throne even greater than the throne of my lord (*adoni*) King David!"

1 Samuel 24:6: He said to his men, "The LORD (*YHWH*) forbid that I should do such a thing to my master (*adoni*), the LORD's (*YHWH's*) anointed, or lift my hand against him; for he is the anointed of the LORD" (*YHWH*).

Numbers 36:2: They said, "When the LORD (*YHWH*) commanded my lord (*adoni*) to give the land as an inheritance to the Israelites by lot, he ordered you to give the inheritance of our brother Zelophehad to his daughters."

Adoni is used in reference to man and a few times to angels in every one of the 198 passages in which it occurs in the Hebrew Scriptures. In the passages where *adoni* references an angel, even where *YHWH* is seen as speaking through the angel, there is a clear distinction between the angel as *adoni* and references to *YHWH* who speaks through the angel. In the

Septuagint translation of Psalm 110:1, *adoni* is translated as "*ho kurios mou*" which in English means "my lord."

In older English translations of the Hebrew Scriptures, *adoni* is sometimes rendered as Lord (lord with a capitol L) when designating an angel interacting with *YHWH*. Such renderings have been changed to "lord" or some other designation in updates of these translations. For example, in Judges 6:13, *adoni* is rendered "Lord" in the KJV but "lord" in the NKJV. Here *adoni* clearly references an angel in contrast to *YHWH*.

Only in Psalm 110:1 do we still see *adoni* translated with a capitol L in many English translations (KJV, NKJV, ASV, NASV, NIV and ESV). Even though translators of these versions see *adoni* and not A*donai* in the Hebrew, they render it as "Lord" rather than "lord." The *adoni* in Psalm 110:1 appears to be a reference to Christ as will be seen below. Those who translate *adoni* as "Lord" rather than "lord" apparently do so because they assumed Christ is *YHWH*. Therefore, *adoni* is translated as though it was *Adonai* even though *adoni* is not seen as meaning *YHWH* in all other passages where this word is used. *Adoni* is consistently used in reference to a non-deity such as a man or angel in the Hebrew Scriptures in contrast to *Adonai* and *YHWH* which refers to the one true God.

It is instructive that some English versions of the Scriptures, such as the RSV, NRSV, the New American Bible (NAB), the New English Translation (NET) and the Moffatt translation, do not use the capitol L for "lord" in Psalm 110:1, but use the lower case L. Translators of these versions apparently realized the Hebrew *adoni* does not mean deity and therefore should not be made to look as though it does. In view of all this, let's consider what Apostle Peter wrote in reference to Jesus in his quote of Psalm 110:1.

Acts 2:34-36: For David did not ascend to heaven, and yet he said, "`The Lord said to my Lord: "Sit at my right

**hand until I make your enemies a footstool for your feet."
"Therefore let all Israel be assured of this: God has made
this Jesus, whom you crucified, both Lord and Christ."**

Apostle Peter shows the prophetic nature of David's
statement and records that the lord who David referred to is
none other than Christ Jesus who God <u>has made</u> lord and
Christ. Christ (Greek: *Christos*, which means anointed one)
is seen as being made lord and Christ by *YHWH* God. When
Peter quotes Psalm 110:1, it must be understood that to be
consistent, Peter is using Lord in the same sense as David did
and David used the word *adoni* which is not used of deity but
of man throughout the OT. Peter is saying God has elevated
the man Jesus to a position of lordship (having power and
authority) as the promised Christ (the anointed one). Notice
also that in the quote from Psalm 110:1, *YHWH* says to *adoni*,
"sit at my right hand" which implies a separation of Beings as
opposed to the non-separation Trinitarianism requires.

In Matthew's Gospel Jesus refers to the passage from
Psalm 110:1 to show the Pharisees that the *adoni* (lord) David
calls his lord is actually Christ (the anointed one). He is telling
the Pharisees that Christ was more than the Son of David
insomuch as David calls Him his lord. Jesus is not telling the
Pharisees the Christ is LORD (*YHWH Elohim*).

**Matthew 22:42-45: "What do you think about the Christ?
Whose son is he?" "The son of David," they replied. He
said to them, "How is it then that David, speaking by the
Spirit, calls him `Lord'? For he says, "`The Lord said to my
Lord: "Sit at my right hand until I put your enemies under
your feet." If then David calls him `Lord,' how can he be
his son?"**

We know from our analysis of David's statement in Psalm
110:1 and Peter's interpretation of this statement in Acts 2:34-
36, that *YHWH*, the Most High God, is speaking to His servant

42

whom He has made Lord and Christ. Jesus is the *adoni* (lord) of Psalm 110:1. The fact Jesus points to the *adoni* (lord) of this Psalm as referring to the Christ while implying He is this *adoni* (lord), speaks volumes as to who Jesus believed Himself to be as compared to *YHWH* (LORD). Furthermore, if the *adoni* lord of Psalm 110:1 is actually *Adonai* Lord (*YHWH*), you have *YHWH* addressing *YHWH* in this passage. While Trinitarians will see this as *YHWH* the Father speaking to *YHWH* the Son in a triune relationship of Father, Son and Spirit who are collectively *YHWH*, Peter clearly says God (*YHWH*) <u>has make Jesus Lord</u>. If Jesus was *YHWH*, He would have always been Lord.

In Psalm 110:1, David is relating to two different Lord's. David relates to *YHWH* as the Supreme *Adonai* God over all reality. He relates to *adoni* as the lord anointed by *Adonai* God (*YHWH*) to receive from *Adonai* God (*YHWH*) great power and authority as symbolized by seeing *adoni* at *YHWH's* right hand.

It is also noteworthy that Peter, in stating God fulfilled what had been foretold by the prophets, sees Jesus as the Christ <u>of</u> God which clearly identifies Christ as a servant of God the Father. This makes the Trinitarian concept of the Father and the Son being co-equal extremely problematical. Jesus is identified as a prophet in the mold of Moses which shows Him to be an agent of God the Father and no more actual God than Moses was God.

Acts 3:18-22: But this is how God fulfilled what he had foretold through all the prophets, saying that <u>his Christ</u> would suffer. Repent, then, and turn to God, so that your sins may be wiped out, that times of refreshing may come from the Lord, and that he may send the Christ, who has been appointed for you--even Jesus. He must remain in heaven until the time comes for God to restore everything, as he promised long ago through his holy prophets. For Moses said, `The Lord your God will raise up for you a

prophet like me from among your own people; you must listen to everything he tells you (See Deuteronomy 18:15).

Peter's statement in Acts 3:18-22, clearly portrays Jesus as the Christ (anointed one) of God the Father and a prophet like Moses who was raised up from among the people of Israel. While Trinitarians will argue that Jesus the Son is seen as the anointed of the Father within the Trinitarian relationship that is Father, Son and Spirit, the language of both Acts 2:34-36 and 3:18-22 in conjunction with what we see in Psalm 110:1, makes the Trinitarian position highly improbable. The language of these passages portrays God the Father as the source of all Jesus is and all Jesus does. Jesus is seen as the servant of the Father. The Father is seen as the head of Jesus in all things just as Apostle Paul stated in 1 Corinthians 11:3 and 15:27-28 as discussed in Chapter One.

Some point to Psalm 110:5 as support for the proposition the *adoni* of psalm 110:1 is *YHWH* and therefore Jesus is *YHWH*.

Psalm 110:5-7: The Lord (*Adonai*) is at your right hand; he will crush kings on the day of his wrath. He will judge the nations, heaping up the dead and crushing the rulers of the whole earth. He will drink from a brook beside the way; therefore he will lift up his head.

In this verse the English "Lord" is a translation of the Hebrew *Adonai*. It is believed *Adonai* in this passage is a reference to Jesus who is at the right hand of *YHWH* (Psalm 110:1). Therefore, it is concluded that the *adoni* of Psalm 110:1 is in reality *Adonai* which is to say *YHWH*. A number of Hebrew manuscripts from the medieval period actually render *Adonai* as *YHWH* in Psalm 110:5. It is further pointed out that it is the glorified Christ who is seen in Scripture as exercising wrath, crushing kings, judging the nations and so forth, (Revelation 6:12-17). Therefore, the *Adonai* of verse five is believed to be Christ.

Is the *Adonai* (*YHWH*) of Psalm 110:5 the *adoni* of Psalm 110:1? A careful study of Psalm 110 shows it is *YHWH* who addresses *adoni* and invites *adoni* to sit at His right hand until He, *YHWH*, makes *adoni'* enemies a footstool. *YHWH* continues to address *adoni* throughout this Psalm. In verse two, *YHWH* tells *adoni* He will extend his rulership. In verse three, *YHWH* tells *adoni* his troops will prevail. In verse four, *YHWH* designates *adoni* a priest after the order of Melchizedek. Everything that *adoni* is seen as doing is seen as facilitated by *YHWH*. Therefore, there is every reason to believe the *Adonai* (*YHWH*) of verse five continues to address *adoni*. The NET Bible translators appear to have understood this and translate verse five as follows:

O sovereign Lord (Adonai), at your right hand he (adoni) strikes down kings in the day he unleashes his anger.

Here we see the Sovereign *YHWH* continuing to address His servant *adoni*. Even though it appears the translators of the NET are Trinitarians, they have considered the context of Psalm 110 and rendered verse five accordingly. They are to be also commended for translating *adoni* as "lord" rather than "Lord" in verse one. We will conclude this chapter by looking at Isaiah 61:1-2.

Isaiah 61:1-2 is believed to be a prophecy pertaining to Christ. During his ministry, Jesus quoted this passage and said it was being fulfilled as He spoke. A review of this passage will clearly show Christ is the anointed of *YHWH* and not that Christ is *YHWH*.

Isaiah 61:1-2: The Spirit of the Sovereign LORD (*YHWH*) is on me, because the LORD has anointed me to preach good news to the poor. He has sent me to bind up the brokenhearted, to proclaim freedom for the captives and release from darkness for the prisoners, to proclaim the year of the LORD's favor...

Luke 4:18-21: "The Spirit of the Lord is on me, because he has anointed me to preach good news to the poor. He has sent me to proclaim freedom for the prisoners and recovery of sight for the blind, to release the oppressed, to proclaim the year of the Lord's favor." Then he rolled up the scroll, gave it back to the attendant and sat down. The eyes of everyone in the synagogue were fastened on him, and he began by saying to them, "Today this scripture is fulfilled in your hearing."

The Scriptures show God is *YHWH* and *YHWH* is God. Trinitarianism teaches *YHWH* is Father, Son and Spirit which is to say the Father is *YHWH*, the Son is *YHWH* and the Spirit is *YHWH*. In both the Isaiah passage and in Christ's quotation of this passage, *YHWH* is seen as the one who has anointed Jesus (the Son) to proclaim the year of *YHWH's* favor.

Trinitarians explain these passages by postulating that when Isaiah speaks of the Sovereign LORD (*YHWH*), he is speaking of the Father distinction in *YHWH*. *YHWH* the Father is seen addressing *YHWH* the Son. *YHWH* the Father is seen anointing *YHWH* the Son to proclaim the year of *YHWH* (Father, Son and Spirit).

This explanation, however, is very problematic. First of all, it assumes *YHWH* is Father, Son and Spirit which this book will show is highly problematical. Second, this explanation flies in the face of Psalm 110:1 which shows *YHWH* and *adoni* (Christ) are not one and the same, as already discussed. Thirdly, if Isaiah is speaking of *YHWH* as Father, then, when he speaks of the Spirit of *YHWH*, he is speaking of the Spirit of the Father and not of the Spirit as a distinction of a Trinitarian *YHWH*.

Trinitarianism teaches the Spirit is a distinction within an indwelling "Godhead" of Father, Son and Spirit. The Scriptures, however, consistently identify the Spirit as a dynamic of the Father and proceeding from the Father. If the Spirit is a dynamic of the Father and proceeds from the Father, how can the Spirit be distinct from the Father in a "Godhead" of Father, Son and Spirit? If God is indwelling distinctions of Father, Son and Spirit, you would expect to see references to the Father and Son proceeding from the Spirit or the Father proceeding from the Son. You see nothing of the kind in Scripture. Everything is seen as proceeding from the Father. This should tell us something as to who God is. When the whole of Scripture is taken into account, the evidence speaks loudly in favor of God (*YHWH*) being the Father and only the Father. Therefore, the Father is the one and only God over all reality. The Spirit of the Father is the power of the Father by which the Father establishes and upholds all things. The nature of the Spirit of God will be discussed in detail in Chapter Twenty-Three.

Chapter Four

Theos & *Kurios* – God & Lord

Theos:

The Greek word translated "God" in the NT is *theos*. It occurs 1,343 times. *Theos* means to have power, authority and majesty. It is equivalent to *elohim* in meaning but it is not in a plural form as is *elohim*. The Septuagint translates *elohim* as *theos*. As is true of *elohim* in the OT, *theos* can apply to the one true God, pagan gods, and even to humans who have been granted power and authority. *Theos* is used to apply to Greek gods in Greek literature. Therefore, *theos*, like *elohim*, does not have intrinsic meaning of deity but can define one considered deity or having the powers of deity. In the NT *theos* is translated into the English word God and by context can be seen to almost exclusively designate the Father. We also see *theos* referencing Jesus in several NT passages. As we move through this material, we will examine each one of the passages where *theos* references Jesus to determine if such references establish Jesus is God equally with the Father.

Kurios:

The Greek word translated "Lord" in the NT is *kurios*. This word appears 749 times in the NT. In Greek its basic meaning is to have power and authority and characterizes a person to whom another person or thing belongs. The word implies someone having power over others. It also denotes a respect and reverence with which servants greet their master. In NT Scripture, *kurios* is applied to God the Father, to Christ Jesus and occasionally to others. The great majority of the time it is applied to Christ.

The various occurrences of the word lord in the NT are all translations of the Greek word k*urios*. Since this word is used in association with the Father, the Son and others, context must be considered in determining who is being identified. *Kurios*, by itself, does not establish or connote deity. Other information must be known to establish deity where *kurios* is used to identify someone that may be considered deity.

Because the Septuagint uses *kurios* to translate the Hebrew *YHWH* and *Elohim* into Greek, some believe this word, when applied to Christ in the NT Greek Scriptures identifies Christ as God (Greek: *Theos*). It is believed when applied to Christ; the Greek *kurios* is equivalent to *YHWH* and *Adonai* and identifies Jesus as the God of the OT. Therefore, Jesus is seen as the God of Israel. Since Trinitarianism sees the one God (*YHWH*) as distinctions of Father, Son and Spirit, it is believed God manifested Himself to Israel through God (*YHWH*) the Son. The Hebrew Scriptures, however, consistently identify *YHWH* as the Father. *YHWH* as Father is identified in the OT narrative as the one and only Creator God of Israel. *YHWH* is never identified in the OT as God the Son. As pointed out previously, the phrase "God the Son" does not appear in Scripture.

Deuteronomy 32:6: Is this the way you repay the LORD, (*YHWH*) O foolish and unwise people? Is he not <u>your Father</u>, your Creator, who made you and formed you?

1 Chronicles 29:10: Therefore David blessed the Lord (*YHWH*) before all the congregation; and David said: "Blessed are You, Lord (*YHWH*) God of Israel, <u>our Father</u>, forever and ever (NKJV).

Isaiah 63:16b: <u>You, O LORD, (*YHWH*) are our Father</u>; our Redeemer from of old is your name.

Isaiah 64:8: Yet, O LORD, (*YHWH*) you <u>are our Father</u>. We are the clay, you are the potter; we are all the work of your hand.

Psalm 89:26: He will call out to me, You are my Father, my God, the Rock my Savior (The He, refers to David calling out to God).

Malachi 2:10a: Have we not all one Father? Did not one God (*Elohim*) create us?

Trinitarian theologians argue the Father cannot be the Father without the Son and the Son cannot be the Son without the Father. Since Scripture shows the Father has existed eternally, it is concluded the Son has also existed eternally and the Father and Son, along with the Spirit, indwell each other as the single Being called *YHWH*. As seen in the above Scriptural passages, however, it is the Father who is seen as God with no mention of anyone else. This is true throughout the OT narrative.

In the NT Scriptures, God is consistently identified as Father. Jesus constantly spoke of God as our Father. The Father is seen not only as the Father of Jesus but the Father of us all and of all creation. As will be seen as we proceed with this discussion, God became the Father of Jesus and Jesus became the Son of God the Father at the time of His begettal some 2000 years ago. The idea the Father can only be the Father if the Son has eternally existed with the Father is not upheld by the Scriptures.

In Isaiah appears a prophecy of the coming of Jesus. In this prophecy the child to be born is described as Mighty God and Everlasting Father. Since *YHWH* is identified in the Hebrew Scriptures as Father and Mighty God, it is believed this passage about the coming of the Son identifies the Son as *YHWH* since the Son is identified as Mighty God and Everlasting Father.

Isaiah 9:6-7: For to us a child is born, to us a son is given, and the government will be on his shoulders. And he will be called Wonderful Counselor, Mighty (Hebrew: *gibbor*) God (Hebrew: *el*), Everlasting Father, Prince of Peace. Of the increase of his government and peace there will be no end. He will reign on David's throne and over his kingdom, establishing and upholding it with justice and righteousness from that time on and forever. The zeal of the LORD (*YHWH*) Almighty (*gibbor*) will accomplish this.

The Hebrew for mighty is *gibbor* and means to be powerful and strong. In the Hebrew Scripture this word is used around 150 times and refers to men about 95% of the time with only a few references to God. The Hebrew word for God in this passage is *el*. This word means strong, mighty and mighty hero. This word appears around 200 times in the Hebrew Scriptures and is largely used in reference to *YHWH* but is also used of men and angels.

Exodus 3:15 and Isaiah 42:8 identify the name of God as *YHWH*. *YHWH* is identified in the Hebrew Scriptures as Father. Is *YHWH* also the Son in addition to being the Father? Is *YHWH* a tri-unity of Father, Son and Spirit? When Isaiah writes about the zeal of the LORD (*YHWH*) bringing about the birth of the Son, is he saying *YHWH*, in His internal union of Father, Son and Spirit is bringing about the incarnation of the distinction in the "Godhead" called the Son? Are the Son and Father, along with the Spirit, the one and only true God in every respect except that of being each other? In Micah is a prophecy that expositors generally agree pertains to the coming of Christ.

Micah 5:4: He will stand and shepherd his flock in the strength of the LORD (*YHWH*), in the majesty of the name of the LORD (*YHWH*) his God (*Elohim*). And they will live securely, for then his greatness will reach to the ends of the earth.

Here *YHWH* is seen as the God of the promised Messiah. Trinitarians conclude *YHWH* here refers to the Father and when Micah writes of the Son accomplishing things in the name of *YHWH* his God, he is using the word *YHWH* to designate the person of the Father in the Trinitarian relationship that is Father, Son and Spirit who together are God (*Elohim*). To make this work, however, you would virtually have to read this passage in the following manner:

Micah 5:4: He (The Son, Jesus) will stand and shepherd his flock in the strength of the Father (*YHWH*), in the majesty of the name of the Father (*YHWH*) his God (*Elohim*). And they will live securely, for then his greatness will reach to the ends of the earth.

As can be seen, believing *YHWH* is a reference to the Father still makes the Father the God of Jesus. If the Father is the God of Jesus, how can Jesus be that same God?

In another prophecy believed to be about the coming of Christ and uttered many years after the reign and death of King David, Ezekiel writes that *YHWH* will establish David as a Prince over Israel. We know that Scripture shows the Messiah to be a descendant of David and in Scripture is identified with David in Messianic prophecies.

Ezekiel 34:23-24: I will place over them one shepherd, my servant David, and he will tend them; he will tend them and be their shepherd. I the LORD (*YHWH*) will be their God, and my servant David will be prince among them. I the LORD (*YHWH*) have spoken.

This passage of Scripture shows *YHWH* as the God of Israel in contrast to a servant of *YHWH* spoken of as the prince David who will be their shepherd. If the prince is a prophetic reference to Christ, which most expositors believe, then Christ is shown to be a servant of *YHWH*. This would preclude Christ being a co-equal, non-subordinant distinction of a Trinitarian God called *YHWH*. This coordinates well with 1 Corinthians 15:28 where Apostle Paul writes of Jesus being subservient to the Father and Psalm 110:1 where David shows the Son not as *YHWH* or *Adonai* but as *adoni*, the glorified agent of *YHWH* seated at His right hand.

In the Ezekiel passage, *YHWH* is quoted as saying He will be their God and His servant David (Christ) will be prince among them. *YHWH* is their God and David (Christ) is their prince. If Jesus is also *YHWH*, this prophecy makes no sense at all.

All this being considered, it should be apparent when Jesus is referred to as "Mighty God" and "Everlasting Father," He is not being identified as *YHWH*. These are titles of honor given to Jesus Christ as *YHWH*'s agent in facilitating *YHWH*'s will as the promised Messiah. These titles do not mean the Messiah is *YHWH* as it is plain from the passage in Micah that the Messiah relates to *YHWH* as His God and in Ezekiel as the servant of *YHWH*. The Septuagint translates "Everlasting Father" as "Father of the age to come" and the Brown, Driver and Briggs, *Hebrew and English Lexicon of the Old Testament*, translates "Mighty God" as "divine hero."

Jesus is seen as the Father and divine hero of the age to come. The age to come is the New Covenant age which is inaugurated by *YHWH* by facilitating the Christ event. Jesus is pictured here as *YHWH*'s agent in bringing to fruition *YHWH*'s redemption of mankind. The very language of these passages precludes Jesus being *YHWH*. Let's look at Isaiah 42:1 and again at 61:1.

Isaiah 42:1: Here is my servant, whom I uphold, my chosen one in whom I delight; I will put my Spirit on him and he will bring justice to the nations.

Isaiah 61:1: The Spirit of the Sovereign LORD is on me, because the LORD has anointed me to preach good news

to the poor. He has sent me to bind up the brokenhearted, to proclaim freedom for the captives and release from darkness for the prisoners,

Most scholars see these two passages as prophecies about the coming of the Messiah. Isaiah records *YHWH* as speaking of the Messiah as *YHWH's* servant in whom *YHWH* delights and upon whom *YHWH* will put his Spirit. In Isaiah 61:1 the Messiah is pictured as the one speaking and saying the Spirit of the Sovereign *YHWH* is on Him and *YHWH* has anointed Him. In Luke 4:18, we see Jesus seeing Himself as fulfilling this passage. Once again, the very language of Scripture shows the Son as the anointed servant of the Sovereign LORD (*YHWH*) and not that the Son is the Sovereign LORD (*YHWH*). To conclude all this rhetoric is between two co-equal and con-substantial indwelling distinctions of a single Being called *YHWH* runs contrary to the very language of Scripture. Scripture consistently shows *YHWH* as the one and only Sovereign God who has a Son who is subservient to Him as His anointed servant.

In the NT it is plainly revealed God is called Father because He is of all, over all, through all and in all. God is not Father only because He begat the Son. God being eternal Father is not predicated on His having an eternal Son as is argued by Trinitarians. The word Father is applied to the one and only Supreme Creator God because He is at the genesis of all reality, not just the reality that is His directly begotten Son.

Ephesians 4:4-6: There is one body and one Spirit-- just as you were called to one hope when you were called-- one Lord, one faith, one baptism; <u>one God and Father of all, who is over all and through all and in all.</u>

Chapter Five

Rock, Savior and Redeemer

Rock, Savior and Redeemer:

Both *Elohim* and *YHWH* are referred to as Rock, Savior and Redeemer in the OT. Typical of such statements are the following:

Deuteronomy 32: 3-4a: I will proclaim the name of the LORD (*YHWH*). Oh, praise the greatness of our God (Elohim)! He is the <u>Rock</u>, his works are perfect, and all his ways are just.

2 Samuel 22:1-3: David sang to the LORD (*YHWH*) the words of this song when the LORD delivered him from the hand of all his enemies and from the hand of Saul. He said: "The <u>LORD (*YHWH*)</u> is <u>my rock</u>, my fortress and my deliverer; my <u>God (*Elohim*) is my rock</u>, in whom I take refuge, my shield and the horn of my salvation. He is my stronghold, my refuge and <u>my savior</u>-- from violent men you save me.

Psalm 18:46: The LORD (*YHWH*) lives! Praise be to my <u>Rock</u>! Exalted be God (*Elohim*) <u>my Savior</u>!

Psalm 89:26: He will call out to me, `You are my Father, my God (*Elohim*), the <u>Rock my Savior</u>.'

Isaiah 43:11: I, even I, am the LORD (*YHWH*), and <u>apart from me there is no savior.</u>

Isaiah 49:26b: ...Then all mankind will know that I, the LORD (*YHWH*), am your <u>Savior</u>, your <u>Redeemer</u>, the Mighty One of Jacob.

Because Jesus is referred to as Rock, Savior and Redeemer in the NT, some believe Him to be *YHWH Elohim* of the OT. Since the Son is believed to be one of three distinctions of a Trinitarian Godhead named *YHWH*, it is believed it is the Son distinction of *YHWH* who is the God revealed throughout the OT. It is believed Paul's statement that the rock that accompanied Israel was Christ provides strong evidence for this position.

1 Corinthians 10:3-4: They all ate the same spiritual food and drank the same spiritual drink; for they drank from the spiritual rock that accompanied them, and that rock was Christ.

Did Christ, as an eternally existing Son distinction of a single God Being called *YHWH*, literally accompany Israel in the wilderness? Did an eternally existing Being called the Son in a family of two separate God Beings (Father and Son) accompany Israel as some believe? Did the Son as one of three separate God Beings (Father, Son and Spirit) accompany Israel as one Christian group believes? Is Jesus *YHWH* and *Adonai* and, therefore, the God identified throughout the Hebrew Scriptures?

In Luke chapter one, Mary, in response to learning about her and Elizabeth's pregnancy, glorifies the Lord as God her Savior. In this same chapter, Zechariah, the father of John the Baptist, speaks of the Lord, the God of Israel raising up a descendant of the house of David as His agent of salvation to mankind. In chapter two, Luke writes about the man Simeon to whom it was revealed he would not die until he saw the Lord's Christ which he defines as the Lord's salvation. In all three of the following passages, it can be seen by looking at the entire narrative of Luke chapters one and two that it is God the Father who is being addressed by Mary, Zechariah and Simeon.·

Luke 1:46-47: And Mary said: "My soul glorifies the Lord and my spirit rejoices in God my Savior,

Luke 1:68-69: Praise be to the Lord, the God of Israel, because he has come and has redeemed his people. He has raised up a horn of salvation for us in the house of his servant David.

Luke 2:25-30: Now there was a man in Jerusalem called Simeon, who was righteous and devout. He was waiting for the consolation of Israel, and the Holy Spirit was upon him. It had been revealed to him by the Holy Spirit that he would not die before he had seen <u>the Lord's Christ</u>. Moved by the Spirit, he went into the temple courts. When the parents brought in the child Jesus to do for him what the custom of the Law required, Simeon took him in his arms and praised God, saying: "Sovereign Lord, as you have promised, you now dismiss your servant in peace. For my eyes have seen your salvation.

It should be apparent that when Mary, Zechariah and Simeon use the word "Lord" they are relating to the Father as the God of the OT. By context the Greek *kurios* (Lord) is referring to *YHWH* and is equivalent to the OT rendering of *Adonai* (Lord). Jesus is spoken of as "the Lord's Christ (*YHWH's* anointed). Jesus is seen as the anointed of *YHWH* and represents the salvation of *YHWH*. Zechariah sees *YHWH* as the God of Israel who has provided an agent of salvation from the house of David. *YHWH* is seen as the God of Israel in contrast to Christ who is seen as a descendant of David. The very language of this passage and the other two under consideration precludes Jesus being *YHWH*.

How can the Son be the *YHWH* of the OT when the Son is seen as the anointed of the *YHWH* of the OT? As seen in Psalm 110:1, as previously discussed, the Son is not LORD (*YHWH*) but the appointed lord (*adoni*) <u>of</u> *YHWH*. *YHWH* is not the Son but the God <u>of</u> the Son.

Mary, Zechariah and Simeon see Jesus as the agent of the Father through whom salvation is accomplished. While Jesus is seen as savior in Scripture, in realty He is the agent of God the Father's salvation. God the Father (*YHWH*) is seen throughout Scripture as the source of salvation.

John 3:17: For God did not send his Son into the world to condemn the world, but to save the world through him.

1 John 4:13-14: We know that we live in him and he in us, because he has given us of his Spirit. And we have seen and testify that the Father has sent his Son to be the Savior of the world.

In the OT, *YHWH* is seen as Israel's salvation in bringing them out of Egypt and in delivering them from their enemies on an ongoing basis. In the NT, *YHWH* is seen as fulfilling His promise to provide a savior not only to Israel but to all of mankind. Jesus is called the Lord's Christ because He is the anointed agent of *YHWH* in bringing salvation to the world. Jesus is the human descendant of David who fulfilled God's promise to bring a savior to Israel.

Acts 13:22-23: After removing Saul, he made David their king. He testified concerning him: `I have found David son of Jesse a man after my own heart; he will do everything I want him to do.' "From this man's descendants God has brought to Israel the Savior Jesus, as he promised.

Paul writes that Israel ate spiritual food and drank from a spiritual rock that accompanied them and that rock was Christ. Scripture tells us Christ is the fulfillment of God's intention to bring into existence a descendant of David who will be a savior of Israel. David had not yet been born at the time Israel was in the wilderness. The birth and rulership of David occurred many years after the exodus. The birth of Christ occurred centuries later. Whatever Paul meant by his statement in 1 Corinthians 10:4, he could not have meant Christ accompanied Israel in a literal way. Christ first arrived on the scene many centuries after Israel's trek in the wilderness.

Paul appears to be thinking in spiritual terms in the passage of Scripture under consideration and as such is seeing Christ as representative of the salvation that was provided to Israel during their journey in the wilderness. His reference to eating spiritual food and drink from the spiritual rock Christ shows the non-literalness of his thoughts as Israel did not literally eat spiritual food and drink and Christ is not a literal rock.

Jesus is not a person of a tri-unity of Father, Son and Spirit. Jesus is a prophet that was prophesied to appear at an appointed time in history and became the savior of mankind in fulfilling all His Father God's will. Moses, many thousands of years ago, spoke of *YHWH*, the God of Israel, rising up a prophet like himself (Moses). Moses was not God but an agent of God. Jesus was not God made flesh but, just like Moses, was the human agent of the one and only God who is the Father. Upon completion of His mission, He was awarded great power, authority and glory but remains subservient to the One God, his Father. It is the one and only God who is the ultimate Savior. This God facilitated His salvation through the man Jesus. While Jesus is also called Savior in the NT, He is seen as such within the context of being the facilitator of salvation on behalf of God.

Titus 3:4-6: But when the kindness and love of <u>God our Savior</u> appeared, he saved us, not because of righteous things we had done, but because of his mercy. He saved us through the washing of rebirth and renewal by the Holy Spirit, whom he poured out on us generously <u>through Jesus Christ our Savior</u>.

Jude 1:24-25: To him who is able to keep you from falling and to present you before his glorious presence without fault and with great joy--to <u>the only God our Savior</u>

be glory, majesty, power and authority, <u>through Jesus Christ our Lord</u>, before all ages, now and forevermore! Amen.

When NT authors write about God as Savior they are writing about the Father as Savior. Trinitarians acknowledge this and believe God the Father is Savior through the Son in a Trinitarian relationship of Father, Son and Spirit. Jesus, however, clearly said the Father is the one and only true God. Paul and John said the same thing (John 5:43-44, 17:3, 1 John 5:20, I Corinthians 8:6, 1Timothy 2:6). If the Father is the one and only true God, then the Father is ultimately the one and only true Savior. The passages cited above clearly identify God (The Father) as Savior in distinction from Jesus who is seen as the facilitator of salvation on behalf of the Father.

Chapter Six

The Word of God

The phrase "Son of God" and "Spirit of God" are seen repeatedly in the NT narrative. Nowhere will you find the phrase "Father of God." Trinitarians believe God is a single entity of Father, Son and Spirit indwelling each other. If this is the case, all three should be seen as of God if God is Father, Son and Spirit. Yet, only the Son and Spirit are seen as of God while the Father is repeatedly seen as being God.

Another phrase seen throughout the NT is "word of God." Most Christians believe "word of God" is synonymous with "Son of God" and Son of God is synonymous with being God. The Son of God is believed to be the word of God and vice versa. Most Christians believe Apostle John, in chapter one of his Gospel, identifies the word of God as being God in the person of the Son. Is the Son of God the literal word of God? Is the word of God the Son and the Son of God the word? In this Chapter we will carefully examine this issue and proceed, in Chapter Seven, to study the first chapter of John's Gospel.

The phrase "word of God" occurs dozens of times in the NT narrative. In most cases, the context wherein this phrase is found shows "word (Greek: *logos*) of God" to mean the expressed thoughts, will and purpose of God and does not in any way convey the idea the word of God is a person called the Son. The Greek word *logos* appears 330 times in the NT and is translated into English primarily as "word" or "saying." Its basic meaning is "to speak." This word is derived from the verb *legein* which means "to say or speak." It can also mean "reason or mind." Nothing in its definition denotes personhood.

Just before His crucifixion, Jesus was praying to His Father and said, **"I have given them (His disciples) your word (*logos*) and "your word (*logos*) is truth" (John 17:14-17).** There is nothing here to indicate Jesus was referring to Himself as the word (*logos*) that was given to His disciples. It should be plain the *logos* Jesus speaks of is the *logos* of the Father and in keeping with the meaning of *logos*, Jesus is saying He has given to His disciples what is in the mind of the Father. Over and over again, the phrase "word of God" (*logos* of God) is seen as pertaining to the actual thoughts of God delivered through others.

Acts 6:7: So the <u>word (*logos*) of God</u> spread. The number of disciples in Jerusalem increased rapidly, and a large number of priests became obedient to the faith.

Acts 12:24: But the <u>word (*logos*) of God</u> continued to increase and spread.

Acts 13:7b: The proconsul, an intelligent man, sent for Barnabas and Saul because he wanted to hear the <u>word (*logos*) of God.</u>

1 Thessalonians 2:13: And we also thank God continually because, when you received the <u>word (*logos*) of God,</u> which you heard from us, you accepted it not as the <u>word (*logos*) of men,</u> but as it actually is, the <u>word (*logos*) of God</u>, which is at work in you who believe.

In all these passages it should be obvious that "word of God" is not a synonym for "Son of God." It should be clear the phrase "word of God" is being used to convey the understanding that it is the mind of God that is being expressed in the teaching of the Apostles. In the case of Christ, the mind of God was perfectly expressed and, therefore, Christ was seen as the personification of the mind of God. This does not equate with Christ literally being the mind of God as a distinction in a Trinitarian Godhead.

In Deuteronomy 18:18, God speaks of sending a prophet like Moses. Most Christians see this as a prophecy of the coming of Christ. God is recorded as saying, **"I will put my words in his mouth, and he will tell them everything I command him."** This clearly shows Jesus is not the literal word of God but the vehicle through whom the word of God is disseminated. We see Christ fulfilling this prophecy when just before His crucifixion he said, **"I have given them your word (*logos*)" (John 17:14).**

Paul likens the word (*logos*) of God to being the sword of the Spirit. The writer to the Hebrews says something similar.

Ephesians 6:17: Take the helmet of salvation and the sword of the Spirit, which is the word (*logos*) of God.

Hebrews 4:12: For the word (*logos*) of God is living and active. Sharper than any double-edged sword, it penetrates even to dividing soul and spirit, joints and marrow; it judges the thoughts and attitudes of the heart.

Is the writer talking about a person called the Son when discussing the *logos* of God? When Paul says the sword of the Spirit is the *logos* of God, is Paul saying the Son is the sword of the Spirit? Is it the Son, as the *logos* of God, who is living and active and sharper than a two edged sword? Some believe that because John, in the Revelation, writes that a doubled edged sword comes out of the month of Jesus and the name of Christ is the Word of God, Jesus is the actual literal word of God in the person of the Son. Is this the case?

Revelation 1:16: In his right hand he held seven stars, and out of his mouth came a sharp double-edged sword. His face was like the sun shining in all its brilliance.

Revelation 19:13-15a: He is dressed in a robe dipped in blood, and his name is the Word (*logos*) of God. The

armies of heaven were following him, riding on white horses and dressed in fine linen, white and clean. Out of his mouth comes a sharp sword with which to strike down the nations.

It should be apparent that the passage in Ephesians, the passage in Hebrews and the passages in the Revelation are all using symbolic language to describe the word of God. The word is seen as coming out of the month of Christ. If Christ is literally the word of God, how can it be seen as coming out of His own month? When John writes of the name of Christ being the word of God, it should be apparent he is speaking of Jesus coming in the authority of God the Father whose *logos* is manifested in Jesus. In Revelation 1:2 John writes of testifying to the "word (*logos*) of God, and the testimony of Jesus Christ." Here we see Jesus as distinct from the *logos* of God.

Revelation 1:1-2: The revelation of Jesus Christ, which God gave him to show his servants what must soon take place. He made it known by sending his angel to his servant John, who testifies to everything he saw--that is, the word (*logos*) of God <u>and the</u> testimony of Jesus Christ.

Logos is consistently seen as the expression of the thought, will, reason and purpose of God. As such, the *logos* of God is not a person called the Son. The *logos* of God is the expressed and manifested mind of God. Jesus fully expressed and manifested the *logos* of God His Father and as such can be called the *logos* of God (Revelation 19:13). This doesn't mean Jesus is the literal, actual *logos* of the Father. Some believe Jesus is identified as the *logos* of God in Luke 1:2.

Luke 1:1-3: Many have undertaken to draw up an account of the things that have been fulfilled among us, just as they were handed down to us by those who from the first were eyewitnesses and servants of the word (logos). Therefore, since I myself have carefully investigated everything from

the beginning, it seemed good also to me to write an orderly account for you, most excellent Theophilus,

It is often assumed that Luke, in speaking of the "eyewitnesses and servants of the word," is referring to Jesus as the word. If Luke was doing this, it would not be evidence for Jesus being the literal word of God for the reasons already delineated. It should be noted, however, that it is unlikely Luke is directly referring to Jesus in this passage. The context here is Luke revealing how he came to write his own account of events associated with Christ. He is revealing the methodology He used to write his account. That methodology was to review the thoughts, observations and accounts (the *logos*) of those who had been eyewitnesses and followers of these events. The NET Bible provides the following commentary regarding this passage:

The phrase "eyewitnesses and servants of the word" refers to a single group of people who faithfully passed on the accounts about Jesus. The language about delivery (passed on) points to accounts faithfully passed on to the early church.

The thought expressed here is that Luke is not speaking of eyewitnesses and servants of a person called the word but of eyewitnesses and servants of the events and the perceived significance of such events in the life of the person Jesus.

In the OT, the Hebrew word *dabar* is the equivalent to the Greek *logos* and appears hundreds of times in association with God and by context is seen to express the thought and will of God. *Debar* is translated as *logos* in the Septuagint (the Hebrew to Greek translation of the OT). Here is just one of hundreds of examples of how this word is used in the OT Scripture.

Exodus 19:7-8: And Moses came and called for the elders of the people, and laid before their faces all these words (Hebrew *debar*, Greek *logos* in Septuagint) which

the Lord commanded him. And all the people answered together, and said, All that the Lord hath spoken we will do. And Moses returned the words (*debar/logos*) of the people unto the Lord.

It should be evident from this passage, and many passages like it, that the *debar/logos* of God proceeds from Him as His speech, thoughts and will. This is how the Hebrew *debar* is used throughout the OT. It is a word that defines God's expressed thoughts to man and man's expressed thoughts to God. Both *debar* and *logos* have the basic meaning of communication and are so defined in the Concordance of the *Hebrew to Greek Apostolic Bible Polyglot*. These words have absolutely nothing to do with being a literal person of a Trinitarian Godhead or a literal person called the Son.

The word of God is the manifestation and expression of the wisdom, knowledge, understanding, purpose and overall will of God. Jesus Christ, as the begotten Son of the One God, was the human agent through whom the Father's word was perfectly expressed. In this respect, Jesus was seen as personifying the *logos* of God. This doesn't mean Jesus was the literal *logos* of God in an indwelling relationship of three distinctions of a Triune Godhead. Jesus, as the Son of the Father, was the vehicle through whom the *logos* of the Father was and is fully expressed. Jesus is the manifestation of the Father's *logos*.

Jesus perfectly represented the word of God the Father. The Scriptures symbolically picture the word of God as a sword. The Scriptures picture the word of God as a sword coming out of the month of Jesus because Jesus represents the word (*logos*) of God. Representing something, however, does not make you that something.

When the American Secretary of State travels abroad, she represents the President of the United States. She expresses his will in her dealings with other heads of state. She becomes the virtual mouth piece of the President. She virtually becomes the President's *logos*. She speaks as though she was the president. She represents his name, his thoughts and his will. No one would conclude from this that she is the American President or that because she speaks for Him she is somehow an intrinsic part of him, that she is literally his speech.

As will be seen in the next chapter, it is through and by the word of God that all things were created, including the Son. The Son is the materialization of the will and purpose of God and in this sense can be considered God's *logos*. The Father's *logos*, however, is not a literal person called the Son. The word of the Father is the expression of the Father's attributes of wisdom, knowledge, understanding, will, purpose, light, truth, love and life. Jesus expresses these attributes. Jesus is not intrinsically these attributes. Only the one God, the Father, is intrinsically these attributes. These attributes define the very nature of the Father. Christ was a reflection of these attributes. Jesus mirrored these attributes of His Father. Jesus was the image of these attributes as Scripture teaches. This is why Jesus could say, "If your have seen me you have seen the Father."

Being the image of the Father, who is God, does not equate with being God. The Father is the one and only God, as Jesus, Paul and John clearly reveal. Jesus is not co-equal with God the Father as Trinitarians teach. Jesus said His Father was greater than He. Jesus also made a very telltale statement which is recorded in three of the Gospels. I will quote it from Luke:

Luke 18:18-19: A certain ruler asked him, "Good teacher, what must I do to inherit eternal life?" "Why do you call me good?" Jesus answered. "No one is good--except God alone."

Jesus did not consider Himself good in the sense and to the extent that God is good. Jesus plainly said God alone is good. If

Jesus was God in the flesh and knew He was God in the flesh, He could not have made such a statement. Even though Jesus never sinned, He did not consider Himself good compared to God. The goodness He had was a reflection of the goodness of God shinning through Him. Jesus' statement to the ruler clearly shows Jesus did not consider Himself God.

Luke records, **"Jesus grew in wisdom and stature, and in favor with God and men" (Luke 2:52).**

If Jesus was the actual word of God in human form, why do we see Him growing in wisdom? He would already have complete wisdom as God. It should be obvious Jesus grew in wisdom and knowledge like we all do. Jesus was not God in the flesh but a totally human person who had been given an abundance of God's Spirit from birth to facilitate growth in wisdom and stature as Luke points out. This being the case, Jesus was able to represent the nature of God in expressing God's wisdom, knowledge and understanding from early on in His life. Because of the presence of God's Spirit from birth, Jesus was also able to avoid sin as covered in more detail in Chapter Nine and Ten.

Jesus said He was the light of the world. Was He this light because He is God or because God's Spirit was in Him and He expressed the light that is His Father God. Let's look again at 1 John, chapter one. Here John writes that God is light. He goes on to distinguish between the God who is light and His Son whom He sent.

1 John 1:5-7: This is the message we have heard from him and declare to you: <u>God is light;</u> in him there is no darkness at all. If we claim to have fellowship with him (God) yet walk in the darkness, we lie and do not live by the truth. But if we walk in the light, as he is in the light, we have fellowship with one another, and the blood of Jesus, <u>his Son,</u> purifies us from all sin.

John is saying God is light and he distinguishes between God who is light and His Son Jesus. This same John, in the Gospel of John chapter one, writes of the true light coming into the world. He associates this light with Christ. He is not saying Christ is intrinsically this light and therefore God. He shows in his epistle God is light in distinction from the Son He sent. John is seeing Christ as the manifestation of the light that is God. When Jesus said He was the truth and the life, He was expressing the truth and life that is from the Father. Jesus did not have intrinsic life. Jesus plainly said His life was given to Him by the Father.

John 5:26: For as the Father has life in himself, so he has granted the Son to have life in himself.

Jesus was the light of the world in that He manifested the Spirit of God in all He said and did. Jesus taught that we too can be the light of the world if we manifest the Spirit of God and allow it to shine forth in and through us. We receive the light of God through the Son who receives it from the Father. As seen in the foregoing passage from 1 John 1:5-7, light comes from God. We being the light of the world, however, does not equate with us being God and neither does it equate with Jesus being God

Matthew 5:14-16: You are the light of the world. A city on a hill cannot be hidden. Neither do people light a lamp and put it under a bowl. Instead they put it on its stand, and it gives light to everyone in the house. In the same way, let your light shine before men, that they may see your good deeds and praise your Father in heaven.

In 1 Timothy 6:13-16, Paul shows a contrast between Jesus and God. Paul shows it is the one God who is the only Supreme Ruler, King of Kings and Lord of Lords. It is God, in contrast to Jesus, who alone is shown to have innate immortality. Paul describes this God as the one who gives life to everything and lives in unapproachable light whom no one has seen or can see. This can't be referring to Jesus as Jesus was clearly seen while on this earth. During His ministry, Jesus stated that no one has seen God at any time. It's apparent that all life, both temporal and eternal, comes from the one God. All rulership, kingship, lordship and sovereignty are derived from this one God who Paul identifies as the Father throughout his writings.

1 Timothy 6:13-16: In the sight of God, who gives life to everything, and of Christ Jesus, who while testifying before Pontius Pilate made the good confession, I charge you to keep this command without spot or blame until the appearing of our Lord Jesus Christ, which God will bring about in his own time--God, the blessed and only Ruler, the King of kings and Lord of lords, who alone is immortal and who lives in unapproachable light, whom no one has seen or can see. To him be honor and might forever. Amen (NIV).

In OT Scripture the designation king of kings is a title given to those having power and authority to rule. Kings Artaxerxes of Persia and Nebuchadnezzar of Babylon are given this title (Ezra 7:12 & Ezekiel 26:7). This certainly doesn't mean these men were God. Jesus is given the title King of Kings and Lord of Lords (Revelation 17:14 &19:16). Is Jesus given this title because He is God as the Father is God and is therefore King of Kings and Lord of Lords equal with the Father? Daniel, chapter seven, gives us the answer to this question.

Daniel 7:13-14: In my vision at night I looked, and there before me was one like a son of man, coming with the clouds of heaven. He approached the Ancient of Days and was led into his presence. He was given authority, glory and sovereign power; all peoples, nations and men of every language worshiped him. His dominion is an everlasting dominion that will not pass away, and his kingdom is one that will never be destroyed.

Here we have a picture of the risen and ascended Christ being led into the presence of the Father (Ancient of Days) and being granted authority, glory, sovereign power and dominion. If Jesus is co-eternal, co-equal and con-substantial with the Father, He would already have had all these attributes. Jesus is given the title King of Kings and Lord of Lords because the Father, His God, who intrinsically is Ruler, King of Kings and Lord of Lords, gave Him the authority, glory, sovereign power and dominion to warrant this title. It should also be noted that Jesus approaches the Father and is led into His presence. This is certainly odd language if Jesus is one with the Father in a Trinitarian relationship of Father, Son and Spirit. Peter clearly shows it was the God of the patriarchs who raised Jesus from the dead and glorified Him. Scripture shows it is God the Father who is the God of the patriarchs.

Acts 5:30-31: The God of our fathers raised Jesus from the dead--whom you had killed by hanging him on a tree. God exalted him to his own right hand as Prince and Savior that he might give repentance and forgiveness of sins to Israel.

Peter's statement about God raising Jesus from the dead and exalting Him to his right hand as Prince and Savior harmonizes well with the passage in Daniel as it reveals Jesus to be the agent of God through whom salvation is granted. If God had not raised Jesus from the dead, not only would we not have a savior, the Father would not have a living Son. Jesus plainly said to John in the Revelation that He was dead and is now alive.

Revelation 1:18: I am the Living One; <u>I was dead</u>, and behold <u>I am alive</u> for ever and ever! And I hold the keys of death and Hades.

Jesus is alive because His God and Father resurrected Him. He is a powerful glorified Being at the right hand of God

David A Kroll

His Father because God has exalted Him to such position and status. Jesus is not the literal word of God. Jesus is the manifestation of the word of God and is seen as such in chapter one of John's Gospel to which we now turn.

Chapter Seven

John, Chapter One

John 1:1-2: In the beginning was the Word (Greek: *logos* throughout), and the Word was with God, and the Word was God. The same was in the beginning with God (KJV).

The NKJV and RSV renders verse two as, **"He was in the beginning with God."** The NIV renders it, **"He was with God in the beginning."**

As covered in Chapter Six, The Greek word *logos* appears 330 times in the NT and is translated into English primarily as "word" or "saying." Its basic meaning is "to speak." This word is derived from the verb *legein* which means to "say or speak." It can also mean "reason or mind." Nothing in its definition denotes personhood. The capitalization of "word" (*logos*) in John 1:1-2 does not indicate personhood for *logos*. All words were written in capital letters called uncials in Greek manuscripts of the NT until around the eleventh century A.D. Some English translations prior to the 1611 KJV did not capitalize "word." For example, the Tyndale translation of the NT printed in 1526 in the English of that day reads as follows:

John 1: 1-3: In the beginnynge was the worde and the worde was with God: and the worde was God. The same was in the beginnynge with God. All thinges were made by it and with out it was made nothinge that was made.

In this translation the non-capitalization of "word" better reflects the Greek meaning of *logos* being the spoken word rather than giving the false impression *logos* is a person. It should also be noted that "it" is used instead of "Him" to refer to "word." In eight English versions of the NT prior to the 1611 KJV translation, the word "it" is used instead of "Him" to identify *logos* and express what *logos* does. The Geneva Bible translation of 1599 renders verse three as **"All things were made by it, and without it was made nothing that was made."**

It is apparent these translators did not see the *logos* as a person. Even though the Greek *logos* is in the masculine gender and in Greek requires a masculine pronoun such as "he" or "His," they used "it" which is perfectly permissible in translation when context suggests a different pronoun is more applicable.

There is nothing in the word *logos* to indicate personhood. As already stated, this word means "to speak" and is also defined as "reason or mind." A Greek speaking person would understand and use *logos* in a manner equivalent to our use of English words that convey the expression of reason and thought. John's use of *logos* should not be seen as a reference to a person called the Son. *Logos* should be understood in terms of its Greek usage which is expressed will, purpose and thought.

The phrase "and the word was with God" is not a person being with God but is purpose, knowledge and wisdom being with God. In Job 12:13 the writer speaks of God by saying, **"With him is wisdom and strength, he hath counsel and understanding."** In Proverbs 8, wisdom is seen as existing from the beginning and being the instrument whereby God creates. The Hebrew word translated wisdom in this chapter is *qanah* and is very similar in meaning to *logos*. Here is a portion of what is written about wisdom in this chapter.

Proverbs 8:1: Does not wisdom call out? Does not understanding raise her voice?

Proverbs 8:22: The Lord (*YHWH*) possessed me in the beginning of his way, before his works of old (KJV).

74

Proverbs 8:27-31: I (wisdom) was there when he set the heavens in place, when he marked out the horizon on the face of the deep, when he established the clouds above and fixed securely the fountains of the deep, when he gave the sea its boundary so the waters would not overstep his command, and when he marked out the foundations of the earth. Then I (wisdom) was the craftsman at his side. I (wisdom) was filled with delight day after day, rejoicing always in his presence, rejoicing in his whole world and delighting in mankind.

Many Scriptures speak of *YHWH Elohim*, through knowledge, wisdom and purpose of thought, creating heaven and earth.

Proverbs 3:19-20: By wisdom the LORD (*YHWH*) laid the earth's foundations, by understanding he set the heavens in place; by his knowledge the deeps were divided, and the clouds let drop the dew.

Psalm 104:24: How many are your works, O LORD (*YHWH*)! In wisdom you made them all; the earth is full of your creatures.

Jeremiah 10:12: But God (*Elohim*) made the earth by his power; he founded the world by his wisdom and stretched out the heavens by his understanding.

In the Apocrypha book of Wisdom is found a prayer of Solomon that speaks of God creating through His word.

Wisdom 9:1-4: God of my fathers, LORD (*YHWH*) of mercy. you who have <u>made all things by your word</u> and in your wisdom have established man to rule the creatures produced by you, To govern the world in holiness and justice, and to render judgment in integrity of heart: Give me Wisdom, the attendant at your throne.

Here the author speaks of God by His word making all things and in His wisdom establishing man to rule. The author writes that wisdom is attendant at the very throne of God. Is the word of God and the wisdom attendant at his throne a person of a Triune indwelling of Father, Son and Spirit or is the word of God His cognitive function whereby He creates and sustains all things?

There are Biblical Scriptures that make it clear *YHWH* created all things through His word which is seen as the breath of His month. The Psalmist writes of God speaking His creation into existence.

Psalm 33:6-9: <u>By the word (Hebrew *debar*, Septuagint Greek: *logos*) of the LORD (*YHWH*) were the heavens made</u>, their starry host by the <u>breath of his mouth</u>. He gathers the waters of the sea into jars; he puts the deep into storehouses. Let all the earth fear the LORD (*YHWH*); let all the people of the world revere him. <u>For he spoke</u>, and it came to be; he commanded, and it stood firm.

Trinitarianism teaches God is Father, Son and Spirit. OT Scripture identifies *YHWH* as Father. Nowhere is *YHWH* identified as Father, Son and Spirit. The Psalmist writes that *YHWH* by His word (the breath of His month) spoke the creation into existence. *YHWH* is identified as creator. Trinitarianism teaches God (*YHWH*) created everything through the person of the Son who is seen as the word John writes about in John, chapter one. Yet we see nothing in OT creation passages that suggest *YHWH* created through a person called the Son. There is nothing in OT creation passages to suggest the word of God is actually a person of a tri-unity of Father, Son and Spirit and it is this person who did the creating.

Trinitarianism teaches God is a single Being of indwelling distinctions of Father, Son and Spirit. The Father is not the Son or Spirit, the Son is not the Father or Spirit and the Spirit is not the Father or the Son. Yet all three are seen as indwelling each other to form the single entity that is God (*YHWH Elohim*). Because John's use of *logos* in John chapter one is seen to be a reference to the Son, John 1:1-2 is seen to show an indwelling relationship of Father and Son in the entity called God. This concept of mutual indwelling of Father, Son and Spirit is also derived from several other Scriptural passages. Let's review these passages to see if they support the concept of mutual indwelling of Father, Son and Spirit.

Colossians 1:19: For God was pleased to have all his fullness dwell in him (Christ).

Colossians 2:9: For in Christ all the fullness of the Deity lives in bodily form.

John 10:30: I and the Father are one.

John 14:9b-11a: Anyone who has seen me has seen the Father....Don't you believe that I am in the Father, and that the Father is in me? The words I say to you are not just my own. Rather, it is the Father, living in me, who is doing his work. Believe me when I say that I am in the Father and the Father is in me.

While it is true the Scriptures speak of Jesus and the Father being one and the Father being in Christ and Christ in the Father, the Scriptures also speak of the Father being in us and we in the Father and we being one as Christ and the Father are one.

John 17:20-23: "My prayer is not for them alone. I pray also for those who will believe in me through their message, that all of them may be one, Father, just as you are in me and I am in you. May they also be in us so that the world may believe that you have sent me. I have given them the glory that you gave me, that they may be one as we are one: I in them and you in me. May they be brought

to complete unity to let the world know that you sent me and have loved them even as you have loved me.

John 14:20: "On that day you will realize that I am in my Father, and you are in me, and I am in you."

Colossians 2:10: and you have been given fullness in Christ, who is the head over every power and authority.

Ephesians 3:19b: that you may be filled to the measure of all the fullness of God.

1 John 4:12,15: No one has ever seen God; but if we love one another, <u>God lives in us</u> and his love is made complete in us. Verse 15, If anyone acknowledges that Jesus is the Son of God, <u>God lives in him and he in God</u>.

These oneness and fullness passages do not show that we indwell God in a literal sense so that we are God as God is God. Neither do they show Jesus and the Father literally indwelling each other making them of one essence. These are statements pertaining to being one in spirit and purpose. The oneness statements are all about being unified in spirit as the passage from John 17 clearly reveals. The Scriptures clearly show God indwells both us and Christ in a spiritual manner, not in essence of Being. See Chapter Nine for further discussion of this issue.

Because Trinitarians believe the Father and Son dwell in each other in a literal sense, they understand John 1:1-2 to read in the following ways:

John 1:1-2: In the beginning was the Word (the Son), and the Word (the Son) was with God (Father, Son and Spirit) and the Word (the Son) was God (Father, Son and Spirit). The same (the Son) was in the beginning with God (Father, Son and Spirit).

John 1:1-2: In the beginning was the Word (the Son), and the Word (the Son) was with God (A dimension of God) and the Word (the Son) was God (a dimension of God). The same (the Son) was in the beginning with God (A dimension of God).

Some Trinitarians see the first mention of God in John 1:1 and the reference to God in verse two as referring to the Father and understand John 1:1-2 to read as follows:

John 1:1-2: In the beginning was the Word (the Son), and the Word (the Son) was with God (The Father) and the Word (the Son) was God (Father, Son and Spirit or a dimension of God). The same (Son) was in the beginning with God (The Father).

There is a branch of Christianity called "Oneness theology" which rejects Trinitarianism and understands the Father is the one and only God. This theological system also believes the "Word" of John chapter one is God the Son. To avoid apparent polytheism, they see John 1:1 teaching the Son (the Word) and God (the Father) are one and the same single person. When John says the Word became flesh (verse 14), it is believed John is actually saying the one God, who is the Father, became flesh. It is pointed out that since God is Father, when John says the Word was God, it is the same as saying the Word is the Father. Therefore, the Word is seen as the manifestation of the one God who is the Father. This one God, the Father, is seen as becoming incarnate in the Son as to the Son's Divinity and becoming Father to the Son as to the Son's humanity. This teaching is similar to a theology that arose in the second century called Patripassianism. Oneness theologians read John 1:1 as:

John 1:1-2: "In the beginning was the Word (the Son), and the Word (the Son) was with God (The Father) and the Word (the Son) was God (The Father). The same (the Son) was in the beginning with God (The Father).

Believing Jesus and the Father are one and the same person does not square with the many Scriptures we have discussed which clearly show the Father and the Son to be different and separate entities. Jesus is shown as being a separate entity from the Father while He was a human and also after his ascension and glorification. Daniel 7:13-14, as quoted in Chapter Six, is sufficient evidence to establish the separation between Father and Son.

In view of what we have discussed in this Chapter and throughout this book to this point, can it be rightly concluded John is writing about the word of God being a person of a Triune God who became the man Jesus? Would it not be more consistent with the whole of Scripture to conclude John is seeing the word of God the Father (His expressed will and purpose) bringing about the birth of Jesus the Son and not that the word of God is actually God the Son? Remember, this is the same John who records Jesus as saying the Father is the only true God and the Father is the one and only God (John 17:3 and 5:44). This is the same John who quotes Jesus as saying His very life was given to Him by His Father and His Father is greater than He (John 5:26, and 14:28). This is also the same John who distinguishes Jesus from God the Father and writes of the Father being the true God and eternal life (1John 5:20).

Apostle John was a monotheist, as was Jesus. There is every reason to believe John, as did Jesus, embraced the Hebrew *Shema* which defines God as one. Nothing in the *Shema* indicates the oneness that is God is of a pluralistic nature. Is John identifying a new way of understanding the nature of God? Are we seeing progressive revelation at work here? Is John reveling God's oneness to be a pluralistic entity of Father and Son? I submit John is doing none of these things.

In view of what John writes about the Father being the one and only true God, it appears inconceivable John would be writing of Jesus also being this God in the introduction to His

Gospel. I submit John is writing of Jesus being the manifestation of the word of God and not the literal word of God. The literal word of God is the speech of God expressed as His knowledge, wisdom, power and will. Scriptures reveal it is through God's word that all things are created and all things exist through His word. Understanding John's use of the Greek *logos* in John 1:1-2 as relating to the speech of God is consistent with the actual meaning of this word and consistent with how this word is used throughout the NT to reflect the cognitive activity of God.

Understanding John's use of the Greek *logos* as God's spoken word allows for understanding John 1:14 to show that the will and purpose of God the Father to bring salvation to mankind was expressed in the birth of Jesus, the promised Messiah to Israel. Upon completing his Father's will on earth this Messiah was elevated to a position of great glory, power and authority where He remains to this very day.

John 1:14: The Word became flesh and made his dwelling among us. We have seen his glory, the glory of the One and Only, who came from the Father, full of grace and truth.

Trinitarians question how the *logos* could become flesh (Christ) if the *logos* is to be understood as only the spoken word of God the Father. It is asked how a spoken word can become the man Jesus. The Greek word translated "became" is *ginomai*. This word occurs 677 times in the NT and by context can be seen to have a wide range of application both literal and figurative. As seen above, Psalm 33 tells us the creation was made through Gods spoken word which means it came to be as a result of God speaking it into existence. In John 1:3, the writer says all things were made (*ginomai*) by the Word which means all things came to be by the *logos* of God. Therefore, is it really so difficult to see the Son coming to be as a result of the Father's *logos* facilitating the Son's existence as opposed to the Son being the actual *logos* of the Father?

The word of the Father became flesh in that the Father's purpose, as expressed by His *logos*, was made manifest in the birth of Jesus. Jesus became the Son of the Father through the Father's begettal of Jesus in the womb of Mary and through resurrecting Him from the dead. The Son did not pre-exist as the *logos* of the Father. The *logos* is not a person called the Son. Jesus is not an incarnation of an eternally existing person identified as the *logos* of God. Jesus is the human manifestation of the Father's *logos* which is to say He is the manifestation of the will and purpose of God the Father as expressed through His *logos*. Jesus is God's anointed envoy to facilitate God's purpose to have man become adoptive sons of God in an eternal relationship with Him. Jesus fulfilled this purpose of God and was subsequently elevated by God to the highest position in the universe next to God Himself.

In John 1:1-2, the *logos* is revealed to have been from the beginning and was with God and virtually is God. Scripture reveals the *logos* is the expressed wisdom, understanding, knowledge and purpose of God and thus identifies and defines who God is. We are all identified by our speech which is a reflection of our thoughts which defines the essence of who we are. The same is true of God, as the Scriptures reveal. Verse three of John one reveals it was through God's *logos* all things were created. Using the pronoun "He" in association with *logos* is misleading as it suggests personhood for the *logos* which is not supported by the Scriptures we have already discussed.

Trinitarians sometimes point out that *logos* is a masculine noun in the Greek preceded by the masculine pronoun "he" which indicates personhood for *logos*. However, the masculine gender in Greek has nothing to do with such identification. Masculine and feminine genders randomly apply to persons, places and things and are not at all indicative of gender. Though *logos* is masculine, and according to Greek rules of grammar requires a masculine pronoun such as "he" or "him," this has nothing to do with the noun signifying a person. Masculine nouns often relate to places and things in the Greek language. Therefore, masculine nouns can be legitimately translated into another language with a pronoun such as "it." The overall dynamics associated with a word must be considered in order to properly determine how any individual word is used in Scripture. When *logos* is understood to be the speech of God and not a person of a Triune Godhead, it becomes more appropriate to refer to *logos* as "it" which is what translators of the Greek into the English did prior to the KJV of 1611.

In John 1:4-5, the Apostle writes of the *logos* being life and light. In 1 John 1:1-2, the Apostle writes of Jesus being the *logos* of eternal life which was with the Father and appeared in the first century. Since it is the Son who appeared in the first century, it is believed the *logos* is the literal Son of God. Scripture shows the Son originates from the Father. Jesus clearly said His Father is the source of His life (John 5:26). Scripture shows eternal life comes from the Father through the Son. Trinitarians see this as the *logos* literally being the Son.

1 John 1:1-2: That which was from the beginning, which we have heard, which we have seen with our eyes, which we have looked at and our hands have touched-- this we proclaim concerning the Word (*logos*) of life. The life appeared; we have seen it and testify to it, and we proclaim to you the eternal life, which was with the Father and has appeared to us.

Just as all reality is the expression of the logos of God, so was the *logos* of God expressed in the person of Jesus. Jesus is the manifestation of the life and light that is God. This doesn't mean Jesus has intrinsic life and light as God has. This doesn't mean Jesus is the literal *logos* of God. Jesus is the human vehicle through whom God's *logos* is articulated. As previously discussed, God is identified as light and Jesus is identified as the Son of this God who is light. In John's first epistle, light is contrasted with darkness and appears to be a way of expressing righteousness versus unrighteousness, truth versus falsehood, life versus death. Jesus is seen in Scripture as reflecting the righteousness and truth that is of God. Jesus said God's word is truth and Jesus, as the manifestation of the word of God, is seen as light. The use of the word light in association with Jesus in the NT Scripture can be seen by context to refer to Jesus reflecting His Father's will, purpose and righteousness and manifesting the very life of God. Jesus is the light of the world because He is a reflection of God His Father who is identified by John as one in whom there is no darkness at all and who is perfect light.

In the Sermon on the Mount, Jesus instructed His listeners to be a light to the world. The implication is that we also can express the light of God. This does not make us ontologically one with God. Jesus being a light doesn't equate with Him being ontologically one with God.

1 John 1:5-7: This is the message we have heard from him and declare to you: <u>God is light</u>; in him there is no darkness at all. If we claim to have fellowship with him yet walk in the darkness, we lie and do not live by the truth. But if we walk in the light, as he is in the light, we have fellowship with one another, and the blood of Jesus, <u>his Son,</u> purifies us from all sin.

As discussed in Chapter six, John is saying God is light and he distinguishes between God who is light and His Son Jesus. John defines God as light. When Apostle John writes of John the Baptist being a witness to the true light coming into the world, the true light is the Father who is being manifested in the Son. The Father is the true light coming into the world through the agency of Jesus. John is not saying Christ is intrinsically this light and therefore God as God is God. John shows in his epistle God is light in distinction from the Son He sent. In his Gospel, John is seeing Christ as the manifestation of the very light that is God. When Jesus said He was the truth and the life, He was expressing the truth and life that is from the Father. Jesus did not possess intrinsic light or life. Jesus plainly said His life was given to Him by the Father

John 5:26: For as the Father has life in himself, so he has granted the Son to have life in himself.

Paul wrote that all life comes from God and it is God who alone is immortal and who lives in unapproachable light (1 Timothy 6:13,16). The context of 1 Timothy 6 clearly shows when Paul speaks of God he is speaking of the Father. If the life of the Son and the Son being light originates with the Father, the Father is the source and origination of the Son's life and the Son being light. Within the doctrine of the Trinity, there cannot be any origination. In Trinitarian doctrine the three distinctions that are the one God do not derive life or light from each other. They eternally indwell each other and life and light is intrinsic to that eternal indwelling. Yet, oddly enough, Trinitarians teach the Son originates from the Father and see this as an eternal origination or begettal, a concept that will be discussed in Chapter Twelve.

Apostle John plainly teaches the Father is light. It is in the context of God the Father being light that we must read John 1:6-10. Here it is recorded that John the Baptist was a witness to light coming into the world and that the world was made by this light. Jesus was the manifestation of the light that is God. John bemoans the fact that the world did not recognize in Jesus the light that is God the Father.

John 1:6-10: There came a man who was sent from God; his name was John. He came as a witness to testify concerning that light, so that through him all men might believe. He himself was not the light; he came only as a witness to the light. The true light that gives light to every man was coming into the world. He was in the world, and though the world was made through him, the world did not recognize him.

The Greek noun translated "light" is of neuter gender in Greek and requires a neuter pronoun such as "it." By using the masculine pronoun "He" in place of "it," the impression is given that Jesus, in and of Himself, is the true light. But as seen above and below, God the Father is the source of true light and this light came into the world through Jesus.

John the Baptist was a witness to light (God) coming into the world through the man Jesus. It is God the Father who is the light who created the world and all reality. Jesus was/is the representation and manifestation of the light that is God. The light that made the world and all reality was in the world through Jesus. Jesus was to be called Immanuel which was interpreted as "God with us" (Matthew 1:23). The Supreme, Most High, Creator God was not literally walking the streets of Judea. He was present in the world through the human person Jesus, His directly begotten Son. See Chapter Nineteen for an in-depth examination of Matthew 1:23.

Apostle Peter shows Jesus is not the literal *logos* of God but is the expression of God's *logos* in fulfilling the promises made to the fathers.

Acts 13:32-34: "We tell you the good news: What God promised our fathers he has fulfilled for us, their children, by raising up Jesus. As it is written in the second Psalm: "'You are my Son; today I have become your Father' (Thou art my Son, this day have I begotten thee, KJV). The fact that God raised him from the dead, never to decay, is stated in these words: "'I will give you the holy and sure blessings promised to David.'

What God promised to the fathers He fulfilled by raising Jesus from the dead. As mentioned earlier, Jesus was dead. He would have remained dead but for the resurrection facilitated by the source of all life, God the Father. The message delivered to Mary by the angel Gabriel, shows how the Son of God came to be.

Luke 1:31-35: You will be with child and give birth to a son, and you are to give him the name Jesus. He will be great and will be called the Son of the Most High. The Lord God will give him the throne of his father David, and he will reign over the house of Jacob forever; his kingdom will never end." "How will this be," Mary asked the angel, "since I am a virgin?" The angel answered, "The Holy Spirit will come upon you, and the power of the Most High will overshadow you. So the holy one to be born will be called the Son of God.

The one and only Eternal Creator God, here pictured as "the Most High," would by His power (Holy Spirit) beget Jesus who through the Virgin Mary is a human descendant of David. This totally human descendant of David would be given David's throne and because of being conceived by the power of God and later resurrected by God's power to eternal life, He was confirmed as the Son of God. Gabriel said Jesus would be called the Son of the Most High. Scripture reveals there is only one Most High and that is God the Father. Trinitarianism teaches the Son is equal with the Father and Spirit. That would make all three the Most High God. How could Jesus be the Son of the Most High God and also be the Most High God? Jesus is not the Most High. He is the Son of the Most High as Gabriel clearly revealed.

The clear distinction between the Son and the Most High God precludes Jesus being God as God is God which would mean the Son was also the Most High God. Jesus was a descendant of David and was declared to be the Son of God by his resurrection from the dead. The Son began His existence as the child born to Mary some 2000 years ago and through resurrection from the dead became the first to be born from the dead to eternal life.

Romans 1:3-4: regarding his Son, who as to his human nature was a descendant of David, and who through the

Spirit of holiness was declared with power to be the Son of God <u>by his resurrection from the dead</u>: Jesus Christ our Lord.

Some Christian groups, who reject Trinitarianism, nevertheless see the *logos* in John chapter one as a pre-existent Being who became Jesus but is not God as God is God. These taking this position point out that the first mention of God in John 1:1 is the Greek "*tov Theos*" with "*tov*" (the) being the grammatically definite article identifying God as "the God." This part of the passage literally translated can read "was with the God." The second mention of God is without the definite article and can be translated "was a god." or "the word a god was." It is believed that being "a god" does not equate with being "the God." Therefore, Jesus is seen as god (with a small g) and not *YHWH Elohim.*

The conclusion that John 1:1-2 is speaking of the one and only true God the Father and a lesser Being also called God is based on seeing this passage according to a particular perspective as to how the Greek should be read. This perspective includes seeing the definite article or the lack thereof as a significant dynamic in determining how the word God is to be understood. My examination of this issue has led me to conclude the presence or absence of the definite article in association with the word God is not a significant dynamic as to how the word God is to be understood. Various Greek scholars have come to the same conclusion.

While the presence or absence of the definite article doesn't appear to be a significant dynamic relative to determining how the word God is to be understood in John 1:1-2, there are several proposed rules of Greek grammar that are used by Trinitarians to support their position that the Son is a co-eternal, co-equal and con-substantial distinction of the one God. Let us now turn to an examination of these proposed rules.

Chapter Eight

Rules of Greek Grammar

As is true of all languages, Greek has rules of grammar that identify and define the manner in which sentences are constructed and words are used. Various Greek scholars and grammarians have identified certain dynamics in the writing of Greek that some believe provide evidence for Jesus being co-eternal, co-equal and con-substantial with the Father. In this chapter we will deal with two of these dynamics beginning with what is known as Colwell's Rule.

Colwell's Rule:

In the early 1930's the Greek scholar E.C. Colwell, proposed a rule of Greek grammar which states that a predicate nominative (a noun in the nominative case which is more or less the same as the subject) which precedes the verb cannot be translated as an indefinite or a qualitative noun solely because of the absence of the article. If the context suggests that the predicate is definite, it should be translated as a definite noun in spite of the absence of the article. This "rule" is often applied to John 1:1 to "prove" Jesus is God in every respect that the Father and Spirit is God.

John 1:1: In the beginning was the Word (Greek *logos*), and the Word was with God (*tov Theos*), and the Word was God (*Theos*).

The first mention of God in this passage is *tov Theos* where *Theos* is of an articular construction meaning that *Theos* is preceded by the definite article *tov* (the) and literally means "the God." The phrase "*tov Theos*" is called a predicate noun. The second mention of God is *Theos* without the definite article and so it is called an anarthrous noun. Anarthrous simply means non-articulated or without the article. Without the article, *Theos* is a singular predicate noun and occurs before the verb *logos* in the sentence and is literally translated "God was the word." In Greek an articular noun points to an identity whereas a singular predicate noun points to a quality.

Trinitarians see the application of Colwell's rule as confirmation of their position that both occurrences of God in John 1:1 refer to the one God and since it is believed the *logos* is Christ, it is believed Christ is the one God. It is believed that since the first mention of God in this passage has the definite article, thus pointing to an identity, the second occurrence of God, even though it lacks the definite article (the), should be defined in the same manner as the first mention of the word God in this passage where God is preceded by the definite article.

It should be noted, however, that Colwell's rule doesn't always apply as there are numerous exceptions to this rule that have been found in the NT Scriptures. It has been pointed out that Colwell's rule applies well when the anarthrous *theos* is in the genitive and dative case but is not generally true when in the nominative case which is the form used in John 1:1.

More importantly, this "rule" does not require a predicate nominative which precedes the verb to be definite when a predicate in the same passage is definite. Nothing in this rule says anything about what must be definite. All the rule is saying is that if the context indicates it, a predicate nominative should be defined as definite (as though it had the definite article). Some research has shown that anarthrous predicate nominatives preceding the verb are qualitative around 94% of the time. Some feel this could indicate a high probability of the anarthrous being qualitative in John 1:1 rather than pointing to identity. By being qualitative, the phrase "and the Word was God" could be seen as the Word expressing a quality of God rather than identifying "the God."

Jehovah's Witnesses have capitalized on this possibility by rendering "and the Word was God" as "the Word was <u>a</u> God." Jehovah's Witnesses believe the archangel Michael became Jesus and therefore Christ was a created Being who had Divine qualities which made him <u>a</u> God but not <u>the</u> God. Therefore, in an effort to support their doctrine of Christ, they have added "a" to the text, an addition not found in any extant Greek manuscript.

Some have used two late eight century Greek renderings of John 1:1 as evidence Jesus is the one God. These renderings show the second occurrence of *Theos* in this passage to be preceded by the definite article and thus read "the God" in the same way the first occurrence of *Theos* is read. This rendering, however, is not found in any other extant Greek manuscript of the NT.

A Sahidic Coptic (Egyptian) manuscript of early date shows that early Greek manuscripts which are no longer extant, did not have a definite article associated with the second *Theos*. Unlike Koine Greek (the Greek of the Scriptures), which does not have an indefinite article, Sahidic has both the definite and indefinite article. In translating John 1:1 from Greek to Coptic, the translator inserted an indefinite article before the second occurrence of *Theos*. This tells us that the Greek manuscript being used did not have a definite article preceding the word *Theos*. Jehovah Witnesses have pointed to this Coptic rendering of John 1:1 as evidence that early Christians saw the Word as <u>a</u> God and not <u>the</u> God referred to in the first part of John 1:1. As already discussed, however, the Greek of the Scriptures does not have an indefinite article and therefore the Coptic translator, as do translators of Jehovah Witness's New World Bible, are interpreting rather than translating this passage of Scripture.

One has to question the significance of the present or absence of the definite article in establishing how *Theos* is being used. If *Theos* is used as the equivalent of the Hebrew *elohim*, it can be applied to the Supreme God or it can be applied to a lesser being than the Supreme God as is seen in different applications of *elohim* in the OT. The presence or absence of the definite article does not appear to be the determining factor. For example, it can be seen by context in John chapter one, verses 6, 12, 13 and 18, that *Theos* is referring to God the Father. Yet these occurrences are not preceded or followed by the definite article.

The fact that in John 1:1, the author uses the definite article in the first use of *Theos* and doesn't use the article in the second use of *Theos* doesn't, of itself, tell us what is intended. If John's second use of *Theos* in verse one was in John's mind equivalent to his first use of *Theos* and if John is using the Greek *logos* to signify a pre-existent Son of God, his writing presents somewhat of a dilemma.

John writes that the word was with God and was God. How can the Son be <u>with</u> the one God and <u>be</u> the one God at the same time. The word is seen as being with "the God." If Colwell's rule applies to John 1:1, both appearances of *Theos* would have to refer to the one God. Trinitarians believe the one God is Father, Son and Spirit. If the Son is the word, John is virtually saying the Son <u>was with</u> the Father, Son and Spirit and the Son <u>was </u>the Father Son and Spirit. This is tantamount to saying the Son was with Himself and the Son is Himself.

Trinitarians try to get around this problem by saying the first mention of God refers to the Father as God and the second mention of God refers to God as God's essence. Because of the problems seen in applying Colwell's rule to John 1:1, some scholars, such as Daniel B Wallace in his *Greek Grammar, Beyond the Basics*, has concluded the first use of *Theos* in John 1:1 refers to the Father and the second use of *Theos* in John 1:1 is qualitative in that it is describing the Son as having the qualities of the Father. To say, however, that the first mention of God in John 1:1 means Father and the second mention of God means God essence or God qualities is not based on any evidence that this is in fact the case. Rather, such conclusions are quite arbitrary and appear to be an attempt to make this passage support an assumed Jesus is God position.

As previously discussed, some Christian groups take the position God is a family presently consisting of two eternal God Beings, the Father and the Son. It is believed we can be born into this God family through resurrection from the dead at a yet future return of Christ. Proponents of this position understand John 1:1 to identify the Father as one God Being and the Word (the Son) as a separate God Being. The Word of John 1:1 is seen as the Son who became Jesus. The God who the Word is seen as being with in John 1:1 is the Father who is seen as separate and superior to the Son. This position defines Father and Son as separate God Beings and the Spirit as power proceeding from the Father through the Son.

While this position is non-Trinitarian, it still sees the *logos* of John 1:1 as an eternally existing Being called the Son and as the *YHWH* of the OT. As discussed throughout this book, *YHWH* is the one and only Supreme, Most High, eternally existing God and is identified as the Father and only as the Father. Jesus is the supernaturally born Son of *YHWH* who upon completion of His ministry was granted eternal life and great glory, power and authority over *YHWH's* creation.

All of this discussion of Colwell's rule and how it relates to John 1:1 becomes superfluous when *logos* is used in the manner found throughout The NT Scriptures and other Greek literature. *Logos* is the expression in speech of the thoughts and will of an individual. God's *logos* is His speech whereby He expresses His will. It is through His *logos* all creation has occurred including the creation of Jesus. When John writes that the word became flesh (John 1:14), John is informing us God expressed His word (speech, mind and thought) and made it manifest through the power of His Spirit in the birth of Jesus via the supernatural impregnation of Mary.

Sharp's Rule:

Granville Sharp published "six rules" on the use of Greek grammar in 1798. We will discuss the one rule that has become known as Sharp's rule in association with certain Scriptural passages believed to identify Jesus being God as the Father is God. In the Greek language, when two nouns are connected by the Greek *kai* (and), and the article precedes only the first noun, there is a close relationship between the two nouns. When this type of construction involves personal, singular and non-proper names, it is believed the two nouns refer to the same person. Sharp believed this rule applies to Titus 2:13 and 2 Peter 1:1 and therefore these passages prove Jesus is God as God is God. While I will repeat some of the following discussion of Titus 2:13 and 2 Peter 1:1 in greater depth in Chapter Nineteen, I need to address this passage here in relation to Sharp's rule.

Titus 2:11-14: For the grace of God that brings salvation has appeared to all men. It teaches us to say "No" to ungodliness and worldly passions, and to live self-controlled, upright and godly lives in this present age, while we wait for the blessed hope--the glorious appearing <u>of our great God and Savior, Jesus Christ</u>, who gave himself for us to redeem us from all wickedness and to purify for himself a people that are his very own, eager to do what is good (NIV).

The expression "great God" found in Titus 2:13 is the only occurrence of this phrase in the NT narrative. This phrase appears five times in the OT and by context can be seen to always refer to the one and only true God. The NIV translates this passage in such manner as to show one subject (God) and that subject to be Jesus Christ, the great God and Savior who's appearing is anticipated. Other translations suggest this passage may have two subjects referenced and could be read with God being one referent and Jesus being another.

Looking for that blessed hope, and the glorious appearing of <u>the great God</u> <u>and our</u> Saviour Jesus Christ (KJV).

Looking for the blessed hope and appearing of the glory of <u>the great God</u> <u>and our</u> Saviour Jesus Christ (ASV).

Scholars are divided as to how best to render this passage. Some see it referring only to Christ and some see it referring separately to God the Father and to Jesus Christ. The translators of the NET Bible see this passage as "one of the clearest statements in the NT concerning the deity of Christ." Is this the case?

The presence of the Greek *kai* (and) between the first noun (God) which is proceeded by the definite article *tou* (the) and the second noun (Jesus) preceded by no article has led some scholars to conclude that God and Jesus are being identified as the same person in this passage. It is believed that if Jesus is to be identified as separate from God a definite article would precede His name. Other scholars cite Scriptural passages with similar Greek grammar construction where a definite article precedes the first noun but not the second noun and where context clearly shows two different individuals being referenced.

Trinitarians believe the context of this passage calls for Jesus being identified not only as Savior but also the great God. Verse 14 speaks of how Christ gave Himself to redeem us and purify a people for His very own. Since the OT speaks of God (*YHWH*) as Savior and redeemed people are spoken of as being God's possession, it is felt that similar language in the NT testifies of Jesus being the *YHWH* of the OT. It is believed that Jesus is literally identified as the *YHWH* of the OT in being called the great God and Savior in this passage.

It should be pointed out, however, that Jesus plainly said those given to Him were given to Him by God His Father which shows subordination of the Son to the Father rather than the Son being equal with the Father. In praying to the Father Jesus said:

John 17:6-7: I have revealed you to those whom you gave me out of the world. They were yours; you gave them to me and they have obeyed your word. Now they know that everything you have given me comes from you.

Jesus said when He comes He would appear in his Father's glory (Matthew 16:27). Some scholars believe Paul is reflecting on this pronouncement by Christ in His letter to Titus. It is believed God the Father is being referenced as the great God and Savior and Jesus is being referenced as the bringer of salvation. In Verse 10 of Titus 2, Paul speaks of "God our Savior." In verse 11 Paul writes of the "grace of God that brings salvation." In verse 13 God is spoken of as "the great God and Savior." It is believed when Paul addresses God as Savior, he is referring to God the Father as distinguished from Jesus who is seen as God's agent for bringing salvation. This approach by Paul is seen in the following passages:

1 Timothy 1:1: Paul, an apostle of Christ Jesus by the command of God our Savior and of Christ Jesus our hope,

1 Timothy 2:1-5: I urge, then, first of all, that requests, prayers, intercession and thanksgiving be made for everyone-- for kings and all those in authority, that we may live peaceful and quiet lives in all godliness and holiness. This is good, and pleases God our Savior, who wants all men to be saved and to come to a knowledge of the truth.

For there is <u>one God</u> and one mediator <u>between God and men</u>, <u>the man Christ Jesus.</u>

Jude 1:25: to <u>the only God our Savior</u> be glory, majesty, power and authority, <u>through</u> Jesus Christ our Lord, before all ages, now and forevermore! Amen.

Apostle Paul refers to God the Father as savior in his writings and Jesus as the facilitator of that salvation. Jesus is savior as the agent of the one God who is the Father. This being the case, there is every Scriptural reason to believe Paul is referencing the Father as the great God in Titus chapter 2. It is the Father who facilitates salvation through the blessed hope which is Christ. Christ is the Father's agent of salvation and in this manner is designated savior. This is clearly expressed by Paul in Titus 3:3-6.

Titus 3:3-6: At one time we too were foolish, disobedient, deceived and enslaved by all kinds of passions and pleasures. We lived in malice and envy, being hated and hating one another. But when the kindness and love <u>of God our Savior</u> appeared, <u>he saved us</u>, not because of righteous things we had done, but because of his mercy. <u>He saved us</u> through the washing of rebirth and renewal by the Holy Spirit, whom he poured out on us generously <u>through Jesus Christ our Savior,</u>

Trinitarians believe God is Father, Son and Spirit. Therefore, it is Father, Son and Spirit who is our savior and salvation is facilitated through the Son distinction of this Triune God. It must be noted, however, that Paul consistently uses the word God to refer to the Father in his writings. Nowhere does Paul even hint of seeing God as Father, Son and Spirit. Paul uses the word God (Greek *Theos*) over 500 times in the NT documents and by context can be seen to be referring to the Father. All the Scriptural evidence points to Paul referring to the Father as the Great God in Titus 2:13. Here again we see the great importance of looking at the whole of Scripture in determining what is being said in a particular context. Now let's look at 2 Peter 1:1-2.

2 Peter 1:1-2: Simon Peter, a servant and apostle of Jesus Christ, To those who through the righteousness of our God and Savior Jesus Christ have received a faith as precious as ours: Grace and peace be yours in abundance through the knowledge of God and of Jesus our Lord.

Trinitarians point out that the Greek grammatical construction of "our God and Savior Jesus Christ" is the same as in Titus 2:13 except here the writer does not refer to God as the "great God." Furthermore, the same grammatical construction is repeated in verse 11 where Peter writes, **"and you will receive a rich welcome into the eternal kingdom of our Lord and Savior Jesus Christ."** Here the one person Jesus Christ is clearly in view. Therefore, grammatically, verse one can speak of Jesus as God.

However, it is also grammatically correct to view God and Jesus as separate entities in 2 Peter 1:1 as is the case with Titus 2:13. A number of translations of 2 Peter 1:1 show this. Here are a few examples:

"to them that have obtained like precious faith with us through the righteousness of God <u>and our</u> Saviour Jesus Christ" (KJV).

"to them that have obtained a like precious faith with us in the righteousness of our God <u>and the</u> Saviour Jesus Christ:" (ASV).

"to those who are chancing upon an equally precious faith with us, in righteousness of our God, <u>and the</u> Savior, Jesus Christ" (Concordant Literal New Testament).

In 2 Peter 1:2 is found the exact same grammatical construction where Peter says, **"through the knowledge of God <u>and of</u> Jesus our Lord."** Here there is a definite distinction between God and Jesus thus showing that the grammatical construction involving definite articles and their absence does not necessarily dictate that only one person can be referenced. Peter clearly distinguishes between Jesus and God the Father in all his other writing. He refers to Jesus twelve times as Lord and forty-five times to God as Father. There is no other possible reference to Jesus as God found in Peter's writings other than the possible reference in 1 Peter chapter one. The weight of Peter's references to God as Father and the one single possible reference to Jesus as God (God as defined by Trinitarians), makes it highly improbable that Peter is calling Jesus God in this passage.

Both Apostles Paul and Peter, refer to God as Father over 99% of the time and only on a few occasions is there a possible reference to Jesus as God. Such tremendous disparity in the way the word God is used in reference to the Father versus possible reference to the Son is instructive to say the least and creates suspicion as to whether the word God, as in the Eternal, Supreme, Most High God, can be validly applied to Jesus on those few occasions where the Greek grammar allows it.

While Sharp's rule may apply in exegesis of the two passages discussed above, it may be more prudent to determine the intent of Paul and Peter's statements in these two passages based on their consistent emphasis on seeing the one and only God as the Father in contrast to Jesus as God's agent through whom salvation is facilitated. Various scholars, including the renowned NT grammarian G.B. Winer, believe Sharp's rule does not apply to Titus 2:13 because Paul laid such heavy emphasis on God the Father as the one and only God.

While certain grammatical tendencies have been identified in the Greek leading to proposed rules of Greek grammar, context still needs to be the primary determinant of what is being said. When the identity of God versus Jesus is studied in the over all context of the entire Scriptural record, it becomes extremely difficult to maintain the orthodox position of Jesus being co-eternal, co-equal and con-substantial with the Father and thus designated the Most High God as is the Father.

Chapter Nine

Did God Die?

Trinitarian Christians believe Jesus was God incarnate. It is believed God, as the Son distinction in the Trinitarian Godhead, became fully human while remaining fully God. The Scriptures reveal God is intrinsically immortal. God has always existed. God has no beginning and no end. God is innately immortal and eternal. Therefore, God cannot die. Jesus died. Did only the human Jesus die while the "Divine" Jesus did not die? If only the human Jesus died, then God didn't die. Yet most Christians believe God did die and that God had to die in order for our sins to be forgiven. This issue has plagued Christian theologians for centuries.

In the early second century A.D. there existed a form of Christianity known as Gnosticism. Gnostic's held to the belief Jesus was only human but an eternal "Divine Spark" (the Christ) entered Jesus at His baptism. Before the crucifixion, this "Divine Spark" (the Christ) departed from the physical Jesus and returned to God, leaving the purely physical and mortal Jesus to die. Gnostic's believed Christ and Jesus were separate entities. The early fifth century archbishop of Constantinople, a theologian named Nestorius, proposed that the Son was actually two persons, one temporal and the other eternal, and it was the temporal Son who died. This teaching gained a respectable following resulting in a number of Nestorian churches being formed. Nestorius was condemned as a heretic at the Council of Ephesus in 431 A.D. However, his teachings survive to this very day as Nestorian churches still exist in the Orient.

In Trinitarian theology, God is seen as having been present on earth in the person of the Son who was Christ Jesus, the anointed savior. It is believed the distinction of the one God known as the Son became the human Jesus to facilitate reconciliation with the distinction of the one God known as the Father. In doing so, the Son never became disassociated from the "Triune God" but simply became an embodied (incarnated) manifestation of the distinction in the Trinity known as the Son. The Son is seen as adding full humanity to His Deity while also maintaining full Deity. This position is summed up in a statement about Christ made by Gregory Naziansen, Bishop of Constantinople, in the late fourth century. In speaking of the Son, Gregory said the following: *"Remaining what he was, he assumed what he was not."*

This perspective became the basis for the doctrine of incarnation where it came to be believed God entered human flesh with its attributes of suffering and mortality while all the while retaining Divine attributes of immortality and impassibility (inability to suffer). Although God, as to His Divine attributes, is seen as being unable to suffer, He is seen as suffering on the cross in the person of Christ. In an apparent effort to maintain the view that God is impassible, fifth century Bishop Cyril of Alexandria said the Word (Christ) suffers impassibly. He is said to suffer impassibly because as God He remained what He was, which included being impassible, while at the same time assuming what He was not, which included the human ability to suffer.

This, however, is virtually embracing the Nestorian notion that Jesus was two individuals in a single body. The one individual could not suffer while the other individual could suffer. If God is impassible (unable to suffer) and Jesus is God, then Jesus as God did not suffer. In a further effort to maintain the impassibility of God, Trinitarian theology teaches that only the Son became incarnate and was able to suffer. Since the Father and the Spirit did not become incarnate, they could not suffer. However, if Jesus is God in the flesh, He still is God and as God could not suffer anymore than the Father and the Spirit. Furthermore, Trinitarianism teaches the Father, Son, and Spirit indwell each other and equally experience all things. How then can it be said that only the Son experienced suffering? If it is to be maintained that God cannot suffer, then Jesus could only have suffered and died as a human and not as God.

Trinitarians see the human experience of the Son as one of functionality. While Jesus is seen as a human manifestation of the Son distinction in God and therefore fully God, He is seen as functionally subordinant to God the Father during His human sojourn while remaining ontologically one with the Father as the eternal Son. All Scriptural passages that show Jesus to be subordinant to the Father are believed to reflect His functional role as the human Jesus.

This perspective is problematical because most of the Scriptural statements that show Jesus as subordinate to the Father are statements made after Jesus was resurrected and ascended to the Father to receive great authority, power and glory (1 Corinthians 11:3, 15:27-28 and many more). It is in this glorified state that Jesus continues to be identified as subject to the Father who is consistently seen in Scripture as the God of Jesus.

The Scriptures clearly teach Jesus died. Trinitarian theology teaches Jesus is God incarnate. He is seen as totally God and totally human. As totally God, Jesus would be totally immortal as the Scriptures show God to be intrinsically immortal having neither beginning nor end. As totally human, Jesus would have had to have been totally mortal and subject to death as that is the human condition. The recorded death of Jesus is witness to His mortality. For Jesus to have been totally God and totally human he would have had to be totally immortal and totally mortal. Since immortality is exclusive of mortality and mortality is exclusive of immortality, incarnational theology presents an obvious oxymoron.

Furthermore, the Scriptures clearly teach Jesus was made like us humans in every way. We humans are totally mortal. If Jesus was made like us in every way, He could not be totally mortal and totally immortal. We humans can only become immortal by being granted immortality by God the Father. God the Father granted immortality to Jesus by resurrecting Him from the dead. Jesus became the first human to be granted immortality and thus allow for our transition to immortality as well. The Scriptures clearly show Jesus died and is alive because He was raised from the dead, not because He was eternally alive as God.

Hebrews 2:17-18: For this reason he had to be <u>made like his brothers in every way,</u> in order that he might become a merciful and faithful high priest in service to God, and that he might make atonement for the sins of the people. Because he himself suffered when he was tempted, he is able to help those who are being tempted.

Colossians 1:18: And he is the head of the body, the church; he is the beginning and the <u>firstborn from among the dead</u>, so that in everything he might have the supremacy.

1 Corinthians 15:20: But Christ has indeed been raised from the dead, <u>the firstfruits of those who have fallen asleep.</u>

Revelation 1:18: I am the Living One; <u>I was dead</u>, and behold I am alive for ever and ever! And I hold the keys of death and Hades.

Was Jesus God in the flesh? Did God die? Did a distinction of God called the Son die? If God is a single immortal entity of single essence, then God would have had to die if the Son is a dimension of the immortal God. Postulating, however, that a self-existent Being can die is an oxymoron. Nowhere do the Scriptures teach God died. The death of God is a human construct based on the belief Jesus is God. It is widely believed Jesus had to be God to be the sinless sacrifice for the salvation of mankind. It is argued that if Jesus was only human, He would be tinged by the sin of Adam. If Jesus was only human, it is believed He would have been born a sinner and unable to be the sinless sacrifice for the sins of mankind. I will address this issue in detail later in this Chapter.

The Scriptures do not teach God had to die in order for the penalty for sin to be paid. The Scriptures teach that a sinless human sacrifice was required to atone for sin. The Old Covenant required unblemished sacrificial animals be presented before God as a sin offering. Scripture reveals that animal sacrifices could not permanently do away with human sin. God ordained this be accomplished by an unblemished (sinless) human sacrifice. Jesus was this sinless human sacrifice. Jesus had a human ancestry through His mother Mary whose pregnancy was facilitated by the Spirit of God. Jesus was empowered by God to live a sinless life as prefigured by the unblemished sacrificial lambs under the Old Covenant. It is **"with the precious blood of Christ, a lamb without blemish or defect" (1 Peter 1:19)** that our sin is forgiven. The immortal God didn't die. The totally mortal human Son of God died. God resurrected His dead Son to eternal life, making it possible for all humans to be resurrected to eternal life.

Acts 13:22-23: After removing Saul, he made David their king. He testified concerning him: `I have found David son of Jesse a man after my own heart; he will do everything I want him to do.' "From this man's descendants God has brought to Israel the Savior Jesus, as he promised.

Romans 1:1-3: Paul, a servant of Christ Jesus, called to be an apostle and set apart for the gospel of God-- the gospel he promised beforehand through his prophets in the Holy Scriptures regarding his Son, who as to his human nature was a descendant of David (seed of David according to the flesh: KJV).

2 Timothy 2:8: Remember Jesus Christ, raised from the dead, descended from David (seed of David, KJV). This is my gospel.

Paul writes of Jesus having a human ancestry in being a descendant of David. The word "human" and "descendant" in the NIV rendering of the above passages is from the Greek *sperma* which, when used in relation to humans, pertains to human reproduction. The Greek word translated "nature" in the NIV is *sarx* which means flesh and is so rendered in most English translations.

It is clear Jesus was born a human which equates with having human attributes. Such attributes include being able to suffer, being able to be tempted, being able to sin and being able to die. Such attributes include the passions and desires common to all humans. As will be shown, Jesus was tempted but never surrendered to temptation. Therefore, Jesus never sinned and the death He died was for our sins, not His. As Apostle Paul writes:

2 Corinthians 5:21: God made him who had no sin to be sin for us, so that in him we might become the righteousness of God.

Even though you will not find the phrase "God the Son" anywhere in Scripture, it is widely believed God the Father facilitated the begettal of "God the Son" in the womb of Mary. As "God the Son," Jesus is seen as having the perceived Divine attributes of immortality, omnipotence (being all powerful), omnipresence (being everywhere present) and omniscience (being all knowing). It is believed the Son did not exercise the fullness of these attributes as the human Jesus but simply submitted Himself to His Father's will and demonstrated His Godly power to the extent the Father allowed.

Did Jesus demonstrate Godly power because He was God in the flesh or because the one and only true God provided Him with the power to do what He did? Jesus plainly said He could do nothing of himself (John 5:19, 30, 8:28). Jesus attributed what He did to the Father being in Him. Does the Father being in Jesus equate with Jesus being God? Paul wrote that all the fullness of the Deity resided in Jesus. Does this mean Jesus is God?

Colossians 2:9-10: For in Christ all the fullness of the Deity (Greek *theotees*: State of being God) lives in bodily form, and you have been given fullness in Christ, who is the head over every power and authority.

Some see this passage as proof Jesus is God as it is argued the fullness of Deity can't live in someone and that someone not be Deity. However, Paul tells the Colossian Christians that they have been given fullness in Christ and he tells the Ephesian Christians they may be filled to the measure of all the fullness of God.

Ephesians 3:19b: that you may be filled to the measure of all the fullness of God.

If all the fullness of Deity dwelling in the body of Jesus makes Jesus God, then it should follow that the fullness of Christ given to us and dwelling in our bodies makes us God if Christ is God. Furthermore, being filled **"to the measure of all the fullness of God"** should mean we are God if it is true that such fullness of God makes one to be Deity. Since this is obviously not the case, there is no reason to believe Jesus is God when it is said He was given the fullness of the Deity. It is much more Scriptural to conclude that to have the fullness of God equates with having the Spirit of God and having the Spirit of God produces within us attributes of the Divine nature.

Scripture shows humans can participate in the Divine nature (2 Peter 1:4) and express Divine attributes. Does participating in the Divine nature equate with being Divine and therefore being God? The phrase "divine nature" is found twice in the NIV translation of the NT. In Romans 1:20, God the Father is shown to have Divine nature.

Romans 1:20: For since the creation of the world God's invisible qualities--his eternal power and divine nature-- have been clearly seen, being understood from what has been made, so that men are without excuse.

We know Paul is talking about God the Father as this is what the context of this chapter clearly shows. The Greek word translated "divine nature" in this passage is *Thiotees*. It appears just this once in the NT and it is taken from the Greek *Theos* and simply means God nature. Paul is simply saying God (*Theos*) has God nature. The KJV translates *Thiotees* as "Godhead." Of six English translations I reviewed, only the KJV and NKJV version translate *Thiotees* as "Godhead." Other translations render *Thiotees* as "divine nature" or "deity" which appears to be the natural meaning found in Greek usage. The other occurrence of the phrase "divine nature" is found in 2 Peter 1:4 where Peter writes that we can participate in the divine nature.

2 Peter 1:4: Through these he has given us his very great and precious promises, so that through them you may participate (partake in KJV) in the divine nature and escape the corruption in the world caused by evil desires.

In this passage, two separate Greek words are used to say "divine nature." The Greek *Thios* is translated "divine" and *phusis* is translated "nature." *Phusis*, as used in relation to the divine, means "natural characteristics or disposition" (See *Bauer, Arndt, and Gingrich Greek Lexicon*). The Greek *Thios* has the same meaning as *Thiotees*. It means Divine nature. Peter is virtually saying we can participate in the Divine characteristics and disposition of God, the God nature. This, however, does not make us God.

God's Spirit dwelling within us enables us to express the Divine nature and live righteously provided we choose to allow the Divine nature to express itself in our behavior. The frequency with which we make righteous choices is the critical dynamic as to how consistently we express the Divine nature. Paul instructed us to fan into flame the Spirit of God and not quench it (2 Timothy 1:6 and 1 Thessalonians 5:19).

There should be no question Jesus fully and consistently participated in the Divine nature when He walked on this earth as a human Being. Participating in the Divine nature involves having the Spirit of God. Scripture shows Jesus had the Spirit of God His Father in full measure from birth. John 3:34 indicates God gave the Spirit to Jesus without measure. When did Jesus receive the Spirit of God? Luke writes that Jesus, as a child, waxed strong in spirit and was filled with wisdom.

Luke 2:40: And the child grew, and waxed strong in spirit, filled with wisdom: and the grace of God was upon him (KJV).

This is the same language Luke uses in speaking about John the Baptist. In Luke 1:15 the writer states John the Baptist would be filled with the Holy Spirit from birth and he goes on to write that **"the child (John) grew and became strong in spirit" (Luke 1:80).** While there is no direct statement in Scripture about Christ having the Holy Spirit from birth, it appears inconceivable that Jesus, for whom John felt unworthy to untie his shoes (John 1:27), would not have had the Holy Spirit from birth and have it so abundantly that it allowed for Jesus to live a sinless life.

When Mary is told she will give birth to Jesus, she is told that the one to be born through her will be the holy Son of God (Luke 1:35). This newborn is seen as the holy Son of God at the time of His birth. For Jesus to be seen as the holy Son of God at birth provides strong evidence He had the Spirit of His Father from birth. Psalm 22 is believed by most expositors to be about Christ. Look at what is written in Psalm 22.

Psalm 22:9-10: Yet you brought me out of the womb; you made me trust in you even at my mother's breast. From birth I was cast upon you; from my mother's womb you have been my God (the God <u>of</u> Jesus).

The whole of Psalm 22 appears to be about Christ relating to God His Father. Christ is seen as saying God has made Him to trust in God from birth and God has been His God. This statement presupposes the Spirit of God dwelling in Jesus from birth. The very fact Jesus lived a sinless life shows He had power from young on to avoid sin by not surrendering to temptation. This Scripture is also instructive in that it shows Christ as seeing God as His God with no hint of Christ also being God.

Paul wrote that we cannot please God if controlled by the sinful nature. We must be controlled by the Spirit nature.

Romans 8:5-9: Those who live according to the sinful nature have their minds set on what that nature desires; but those who live in accordance with the Spirit have their minds set on what the Spirit desires. The mind of sinful man is death, but the mind controlled by the Spirit is life and peace; the sinful mind is hostile to God. It does not submit to God's law, nor can it do so. Those controlled by the sinful nature cannot please God. You, however, are controlled not by the sinful nature but by the Spirit, if the Spirit of God lives in you. And if anyone does not have the Spirit of Christ, he does not belong to Christ.

Jesus lived His entire life completely controlled by the Spirit of God. Jesus fully participated in the Divine nature from birth. The mind of Jesus was always responsive to what the Spirit of God desires. Jesus never expressed sinful nature. He always expressed divine nature. As will be seen as we proceed with this discussion, humans are born with human nature having a variety of God created human attributes. These attributes are not sinful in and of themselves but can become sinful if expressed contrary to God's will. Jesus never expressed His human attributes contrary to God's will. Therefore, Jesus never developed or expressed sinful nature. All humans, except Jesus, have expressed sinful nature to one degree or another. Only Jesus, out of all humans who have been born, was given the level of power necessary to never express sinful nature but always behave according to the Spirit.

Because Paul speaks of having the Spirit of God and the Spirit of Christ in the same sentence, some conclude this proves Christ is God. It must be understood, however, that Jesus had a full measure of the Spirit of His Father dwelling in Him from birth and continues to have that Spirit in His glorified state. The Spirit proceeds from God the Father into the Son and from the Son into us. Therefore, it is perfectly appropriate to equate having the Spirit of God with having the Spirit of Christ. Having the Spirit of God, however, does not equate with being the one God, either for Christ or for us.

For Jesus, having God's fullness meant fully participating in the Divine nature from birth. This is what enabled Jesus to accomplish what He accomplished. Having Divine nature, however, does not equate with being the eternal God. Jesus had Divine nature in the same manner we can have Divine nature. Jesus had it from birth. We acquire it through conversion and transformation. To the extent we express Divine nature in our lives is the extent to which we live righteously. Jesus always expressed the Divine nature and consequently lived a totally righteous life. Jesus never expressed sinful nature. He never had His mind set on what that nature desires. He always lived in accordance with the Spirit and always had His mind set on what the Spirit desires. Jesus was never controlled by the sinful nature. He was always controlled by the Spirit of God because Jesus had a full measure of the Spirit of God from birth.

Being human, Jesus had the same power of choice all humans have. Jesus always chose righteousness over unrighteousness. Having the fullness of God's Spirit provided Him with the wherewithal to never sin. Jesus completely submitted to the control of the Spirit of God in His life. Therefore, Jesus never sinned. Jesus never sinned not because he couldn't but because He wouldn't. Jesus was not a robot. He had the same free will we all have. He had the ability to choose between right and wrong just as we do. Having free will and the ability to choose presupposes having the ability to make unrighteous choices and sin. Because Jesus allowed His behavior to be fully controlled by the Spirit of God, He always chose righteousness. While Jesus had the human ability to sin, He never exercised that ability because God gave Him the power to resist any temptation to sin.

Chapter Ten

The Doctrine of Original Sin

The Christian doctrine of original sin teaches all humans are born in a state of sin as a result of Adam and Eve committing sin in the Garden of Eden by eating of the forbidden fruit. Humans are seen as having the sin of Adam passed on to them through procreation. It is believed we humans are born with an intrinsically sinful nature which predisposes us to sin. This doctrine is largely based on the teaching of fifth century Catholic theologian Augustine who taught that the whole human race existed in Adam and when Adam sinned we all sinned.

The Scriptural doctrine of salvation teaches Jesus was the sinless sacrifice who atoned for the sins of humanity. Most Protestant and Catholic Christians believe Jesus was sinless because He was God in the flesh. Yet we know from Scripture Jesus was born of a human mother. According to the doctrine of original sin, Jesus should have inherited Adam's sin by virtue of his human birth if indeed the whole human race exists in Adam and inherits Adam's sin by virtue of being born a human. This would make Jesus a sinner by birth and negate His being a sinless sacrifice for human sin.

In centuries past, Catholic theologians were so bothered by this that they created the doctrine of the Immaculate Conception which teaches Mary was born without sin. Catholic theologians believed the humanity of Jesus would have been stained by the sin of Adam if Mary had not been born sinless. This was seen as problematic for Jesus being a sinless sacrifice. Therefore, it was concluded Jesus was sinless from birth not only because He was God in the flesh but also because His mother was sinless from birth. "Problem solved."

Another solution offered as to the perceived problem of Jesus inheriting Adamic sin is based on the belief a newborn inherits Adamic sin only through the human male. This understanding is based on Paul saying we all die in Adam (1 Corinthians 15:22). Since Jesus did not have a human father, it is believed Adamic sin was not passed on to Jesus and He was born sinless even though Mary had Adamic sin.

In another attempt to harmonize the human birth of Christ with the doctrine of original sin, some have conjectured that God facilitated the conception and birth of Jesus to the point where Mary's only involvement was that of being a surrogate mother to the Christ child. No ovum of Mary was involved in the begettal of Jesus. There was no genetic biological connection to Mary. Mary simply provided the environment for the development and subsequent birth of Jesus. It is believed God facilitated the entire birth process of Jesus through supernatural means. This is seen as eliminating the perceived problem of Jesus inheriting Adamic sin.

The problem with these perspectives is that they eliminate any significance to the Scriptural references to Christ being a son of Adam, Abraham and David. As already discussed, Paul clearly states Jesus was a descendant (from the seed of) of David. This strongly indicates a human reproductive involvement in the conception of Jesus (Acts 13:22-23, Romans 1:1-3, 2 Timothy 2:8). The Scriptures show Jesus being of the seed of David and a descendant of Abraham and Adam as the genealogies in Matthew and Luke clearly show.

Most Christians conclude that, because "Jesus is God," He could not have inherited Adamic sin. It's concluded that Jesus' Divine conception negated His being born in Adam. Jesus is seen as the second Adam. As the second Adam, Jesus is seen as being born without sin and not having the capacity to sin while the first Adam is seen as being created without sin yet having the capacity to sin which he proceeded to do and in so doing it is believed the whole human race is condemned to death.

To resolve the issue of Jesus' sinless birth, we must scripturally examine the doctrine of original sin. Are humans born sinners or do humans become sinners? Does human nature equate with sinful nature? Did the whole human race exist in Adam and when Adam sinned we all sinned as taught by Augustine? Or, do we become sinners by choosing to behave contrary to the will of God as did Adam and Eve. Nowhere do the Scriptures teach the human race existed in Adam and when Adam sinned we all sinned. What the Scriptures teach is that we humans have all sinned on our own and are all condemned to death not for Adam's sin but for our own sin.

Romans 3:23a: For all have sinned and fall short of the glory of God.

Romans 5:12: Therefore, just as sin entered the world through one man, and death through sin, and in this way death came to all men, <u>because all sinned</u>.

1 Corinthians 15:22: For as in Adam all die, so in Christ all will be made alive.

Paul clearly shows Adam and Eve introduced sin into the world and with it death. He shows this death has come to all men because all have sinned. There is nothing in what Paul wrote that says we die because we inherit Adam's sin. Paul says we die because, like Adam, we all sin. To die in Adam is to experience the same death consequence for sin that Adam experienced. We don't experience death for Adam's sin; we experience death for our sin.

Adam and Eve were not created sinners. They became sinners when they ate of the tree of the knowledge of good and evil which they were commanded by God not to do. They choose to behave contrary to the will of God. It's apparent they were born with a natural desire to be wise and successful. It wasn't their desire to be wise and successful that was sin. It was their sinful expression of that desire. Their mistake was they choose to express their natural desire in a way contrary to God's expressed will.

Genesis 3:6: When the woman saw that the fruit of the tree was good for food and pleasing to the eye, and also desirable for gaining wisdom (Hebrew: *sakal,* {to be wise, successful, prosper}), she took some and ate it. She also gave some to her husband, who was with her, and he ate it.

Because Paul told the Corinthians that all die in Adam and all are made alive in Christ, it is often concluded the sin of Adam is imputed to us and causes our death and the righteousness of Christ is imputed to us and causes us life. Paul, however, qualified his statement about all dying in Adam when he told the Romans that death came to all men because, like Adam, all men have sinned. While Scripture teaches that God credits righteousness to man through faith in God's resurrection of Jesus (Romans 4:24), Scripture does not teach this crediting of righteousness is to atone for imputed Adamic sin. Scripture shows death has come to all men because all men have sinned. Adam introduced death by sinning. Death has come upon all men because all men sin and fall short of God's glory (Romans 3:23). Therefore, all men need righteousness imputed to them to facilitate reconciliation with God and experience God's glory.

We don't die because Adam and Eve make an unrighteous choice. We die because we make unrighteous choices. Adam and Eve simply started the process. Dying because of ones own sins is clearly established in the Scriptures.

Deuteronomy 24:16: Fathers shall not be put to death for their children, nor children put to death for their fathers; each is to die for his own sin.

Ezekiel 18:4: For every living soul belongs to me, the father as well as the son--both alike belong to me. The soul who sins is the one who will die.

The entire eighteenth chapter of Ezekiel is devoted to pointing out that people die because of their own sins and not because of the sins of others. Ezekiel clearly points out that guilt is not shared. Some may point to what David wrote in Psalm 51 as evidence for humans being born sinners.

Psalm 51:5: Surely I was sinful at birth, sinful from the time my mother conceived me.

It is believed this statement by David shows we humans are sinners at conception. It is believed we inherit Adam's sin through the process of procreation. Having a nature that is capable of sinning is seen as having a nature that is already guilty of having sinned before any sinful behavior is consciously committed. As Augustine taught, the sin of Adam is seen as imputed to us. Is this what David's statement in Psalm 51 is teaching us?

David is expressing his distraught over His sin of adultery with Bathsheba and the murder of her husband Uriah. He is not saying he was already a sinner when he was conceived and this is why he committed these horrendous sins. David is not blaming his sin on being born a sinner. David was bewailing his failure to express control over the human passions he was born with and resist the temptation that was presented to him. He was deeply repentant and horrified at the great sin he had committed against God and man. He was extremely distraught, over his failure to make righteous choices. He was very distressed over not exercising God's Spirit but instead sinfully expressing the desires of the flesh. It is in this context we must read his Psalm.

David uses figurative language in asking for God's mercy and forgiveness for what he had done. In verse 7 David writes,

"Cleanse me with hyssop, and I will be clean; wash me, and I will be whiter than snow." In verse 8 David says **"let the bones you have crushed rejoice."** We would not conclude from these expressions that God literally cleanses us with the herb hyssop or that God literally crushed the bones of David. These are figurative expressions. In like manner, David saying he was sinful from the time he was conceived is a figurative expression of his exasperation over what he had done.

As was the case with David, we sin when we surrender to temptation and allow our human passions to be expressed in ways contrary to God's will. Apostle James explains the process involved in committing sin.

The Birth of Sin:

James 1:13-15: When tempted, no one should say, "God is tempting me." For God cannot be tempted by evil, nor does he tempt anyone. Each one is tempted when, by his own evil desire, he is dragged away and enticed. Then, after desire has conceived, it gives birth to sin; and sin, when it is full-grown, gives birth to death.

James explains that sin occurs when we allow evil desires to tempt us to behave contrary to God's will. All humans are born with a nature made up of a variety of human passions and desires. Those passions and desires are not evil in and of themselves. They become evil passions and desires when expressed in ways contrary to God's will. Adam and Eve had a God created in-born human desire to have knowledge, be successful and become wise. Such created human attributes are certainly not evil in and of themselves. They become evil when they are expressed contrary to the will of God. Adam and Eve choose to gain knowledge and become wise by disobeying God's command to not eat the fruit of the one tree. All humans have expressed human desires in ways contrary to God's will except for the man Christ Jesus.

It is <u>our</u> sinful behavior for which we are condemned to eternal death, not inherited sin over which we have absolutely no control. To be born a sinner is to conclude we are born condemned to eternal death before we have consciously committed sin. We are in essence condemned not for our sin but for somebody else's sin. We are dead on arrival not because of what we do but because of what somebody else did. Adam is seen as changing the human nature God originally created as good into an intrinsically sinful nature predisposed to committing sin. This altered nature is seen as being passed down to all of Adam's progeny.

Scripture shows that by eating of the tree of the knowledge of good and evil, Adam and Eve came to know the difference between good and evil (Genesis 3:22). While it is clear their eating of the tree was an act of disobedience to God and considered sin (Romans 5:14), their coming to know good and evil did not predispose them to choosing evil over good nor does it predispose their progeny to choose evil over good. To conclude we are born with a sinful nature that predisposes us to commit sin is totally incompatible with the many Scriptural admonitions to choose righteousness.

Sin is lawlessness (1 John 3:4). Sin is defined as missing the mark. Sin results from behaving in a manner contrary to the will of God. From the beginning God established parameters of behavior for His human creation and instructed us to choose behavior defined by those parameters. When God gave Israel the law He instructed them to choose obedience and experience life as opposed to choosing disobedience and dying (Deuteronomy 30:19). How could God instruct Israel to choose righteousness over unrighteousness if they were inherently unable to do so because of being born with intrinsically sinful nature which predisposed them to disobedience?

God repeatedly instructed Israel to love Him and obey Him with their whole heart. How could they do this if they were born with an evil heart? In Deuteronomy 5:29, God is recorded as saying, **"O that there were such an heart in them, that they would fear me, and keep all my commandments always, that it might be well with them, and with their children for ever!" (KJV).** God is not here reflecting on having created man with a heart that is predisposed to disobeying Him or a heart that became that way because of what Adam did. God is expressing the desire that Israel have a heart that would be obedient to His will. God is expressing His desire that His chosen people would make righteous choices so all would go well with them. God could not have expressed such a desire if the heart of man is inherently evil making it virtually impossible for man to obey Him in any consistent way.

Prior to the time of Israel, God destroyed His human creation by a great flood when it became apparent they would not choose to live righteously. Were these humans destroyed because they couldn't obey God or because they choose not to obey God? From Genesis to Revelation we are admonished to choose righteousness over unrighteousness. A primary focus of Scripture is to repent and turn from sin. The orthodox teaching is that because of what Adam did we are born with a sinful nature that predisposes us to sin. Theologian John Calvin taught that humans are born utterly depraved. If this is true, there is serious tension between what humans are instructed to do and what we are actually able to do. It is akin to me loaning my car to someone and instructing them not to crash it and then rigging it so that it crashes.

God has not rigged our human nature to crash. The sin of Adam did not rig our human nature to crash. Beginning with Adam and Eve, God has allowed humans to make either righteous or unrighteous choices and live by the consequences.

Why Does Man Sin?

Why does mankind sin? Is it because we are born sinners and have a built in predisposition to sin or is it because God created us with certain attributes and allows us to choose how those attributes are expressed? Adam and Eve sinned by expressing certain of their God given human attributes contrary to God's will. God allowed them to exercise the free will with which they were created. You may ask why they chose to sin. The same could be asked of the angels that sinned. Scripture indicates that a number of angels sinned (2 Peter 2:4). Were these angels predisposed to sin? Were they created with a sinful nature? Why did other angels not sin? I submit that both angels and humans were created with basic passions and desires and the power of choice to express such passions and desires either righteously or unrighteously. God has created within his cognitive Beings the ability to reason and make choices.

What caused Adam and Eve to sin? Scripture says Eve was deceived and became a sinner (1 Timothy 2:14). Sin often results from believing a lie and acting on such belief. To be deceived is to believe a lie. When believing a lie leads to behavior contrary to God's will, we sin. The serpent lied in telling Eve that eating of the tree would not lead to death. Eve chose to believe the serpents lie and eat of the tree. There always are reasons why we believe something. Eve's choice was based on her desire to become wise (Genesis 3:6). She persuaded Adam to eat of the forbidden tree as well. Scripture says Adam was not deceived (1 Timothy 2:14). It's recorded in Genesis 3:17 that because Adam listened to his wife he was being punished. Adam may not have been deceived by the serpent but he apparently was persuaded by Eve that eating of the forbidden fruit was OK.

All indications are that Adam and Eve sinned because they used the reasoning capacity they were created with to choose between obeying God or believing the serpent. They apparently came to believe God was holding something back from them when told by the serpent they could be like God in knowing good and evil if they eat of the tree. They now saw the tree as the pathway to becoming wise like God. They were not predisposed to believe the serpent but simply exercised their

God given attributes of reason and made the choice to believe the serpent.

Some believe it was God's will that all of mankind sin so He could have mercy on all through the Christ event. It is believed Adam and Eve were programmed to sin and the serpent was deliberately placed in the garden by God to facilitate God's will to have Adam and Eve sin. In this respect, the serpent was simply acting as God's servant in carrying out God's will to deceive Eve. Adam and Eve were simply carrying out God's will that they eat of the tree and thus sin. Neither Adam, Eve nor the serpent had the power of free will or choice to behave differently from the way they did. It is believed freewill had no bearing on Eve's eating of the forbidden fruit because her belief in what the serpent told her determined her behavior and she could not have behaved in any other way. Her behavior was determined by her belief in the serpent's lie. She could not have chosen to do something different because her belief was that the serpent was telling the truth and that belief dictated her behavior. There was no freewill because she couldn't choose contrary to her belief. It is supposed that believing the serpent's lie removed Eve's ability to have control over her behavior and, therefore, freewill had no bearing on what she did.

It must be understood, however, that while Eve's belief that the serpent was telling the truth determined her behavior, she still was responsible for the choice of behavior she made and she was held accountable for that choice by God. Eve chose to believe the serpent. She could have chosen to believe God. Eve's choice to believe the serpent resulted in her eating of the forbidden tree. Eve's sin was that she made the wrong choice. Sin results from making the wrong choice.

While it is true that God is sovereign over all things and whatever He wills is carried out, it is evident from the account of Adam and Eve's sin that what God willed is that they not eat of the tree and if they did they would sin and suffer specific consequences. God did not will that they eat of the tree. This should be evident by how God reacted when thy behaved contrary to His instruction. Adam and Eve were both punished for their disobedience and even the serpent was cursed for its lying behavior. God said to the serpent, **"because you have done this, "Cursed are you above all the livestock and all the wild animals! You will crawl on your belly and you will eat dust all the days of your life" (Genesis 3:14).** God said to Adam, "**Because you listened to your wife and ate from the tree about which I commanded you, `You must not eat of it,' "Cursed is the ground because of you; through painful toil you will eat of it all the days of your life" (Genesis 3:17).**

If God willed the sinning behavior of these three participants in what is commonly referred to as the "fall," it appears rather strange that He punishes them for the very behavior He willed upon them. It is clear God held these three participants accountable for their behavior which presupposes their behavior was the result of the exercise of free will. Adam and Eve had the ability to make righteous choices but chose not to. The very language God used in informing the serpent and Adam as to the consequences of their sin tells us their punishment was because of what they chose to do and not because of what God willed that they do. It was not God's will that Adam and Eve sin. It was God's will they have the ability to choose whether or not to sin, the same ability to choose all humans have.

Throughout Scripture it can be seen that God holds humans accountable for their behavior. If God foreordained that we sin, how can He justly hold us accountable for sin? Scripture teaches we are held accountable for sin because we have the God given power of choice to sin or not sin.

Are the descendants of Adam and Eve predisposed to sin because of what Adam and Eve did? Does the whole human race exist in Adam and when Adam sinned we all sinned? Jeremiah wrote that the heart is deceitful above all things, and desperately wicked (Jeremiah 17:9 [KJV]). Jesus said that from within men's hearts, come evil thoughts, sexual immorality, theft, murder, adultery, greed, malice, deceit, lewdness, envy, slander, arrogance and folly (Mark 7:21-22). Paul often spoke of the sinful nature of man (Romans 7:5, 18, 25, Ephesians 2:3). In Galatians chapter 5, Paul provides a list of behaviors that he classifies as acts of the sinful nature.

Are these human evils the result of us being born with a sinful nature that has these evils resident within such nature or do these evils result from expressing inborn human passions and desires in an evil way? Is the heart inherently deceitful and is our nature intrinsically sinful by virtue of being born a human? Or, is a deceitful heart and sinful nature the result of the choices we make? Jesus spoke of man having both good and evil in his heart.

Luke 6:45: The good man brings good things out of the good stored up in his heart, and the evil man brings evil things out of the evil stored up in his heart. For out of the overflow of his heart his mouth speaks.

This teaching from the lips of Christ provides important insight into the human makeup. Humans were created with the ability to express both good and evil. Simple observation will reveal this to be the case. This ability involves the attribute of choice. God created Adam and Eve with the ability to choose good and evil, obedience or disobedience. Their sin was not in desiring wisdom and knowledge. They were created with such desire. There sin was in expressing that desire contrary to God's command. Their eating of the forbidden fruit opened their eyes to the reality of evil in contrast to the reality of good. They came to understand what evil is and that there is a price to be paid for evil behavior.

When Jeremiah said the heart is deceitful and wicked (Jeremiah 17:9), he quotes God in the very next verse as saying: "I

the LORD search the heart and examine the mind, to reward a man according to his conduct, according to what his deeds deserve" (Jeremiah 17:10 [NIV]). For God to search and examine an inherently evil heart and mind would be superfluous. The implication here is that God examines the choices we make and the behavior that derives from those choices and responds to us accordingly. This is the approach found throughout Scripture. Humans are rewarded for righteousness and punished for sin. This presupposes the ability to choose between good and evil and not that we are inherently good or evil.

It should be evident from a review of human history that while much evil behavior has occurred and continues to occur, humans have also produced a great deal of good. As Christ said, **"a good man brings forth good things out of the good stored up in him,"** or as the KJV renders it, **"out of the good treasure of his heart."** Many humans live the Law of Love and express their humanity within the parameters established by God. Only one person has done this perfectly throughout His life, the man Jesus. In a parable, Jesus speaks of how the word of God can fall on good soil characterized by a noble and good heart.

Luke 8:15: The seed on good soil stands for those with a noble and good heart, who hear the word, retain it, and by persevering produce a crop.

The human heart is not inherently good or evil. The heart can develop good or evil proclivities based on how we express our human passions and desires. Adam and Eve introduced sin into the world by behaving contrary to God's will. The descendants of Adam and Eve have continued to make sinful choices to one extent or another. Much of our sinful expression of human nature results from being born into a world where sinful behavior has prevailed since creation. We all have been conditioned by this culture of sin and we all participate in it to one degree or another.

Being conditioned by the culture of sin we are born into does not equate with having an inherited predisposition to sin. It is evident from the Scriptures and simple observation that we have the power of choice over our behavior. We don't sin because we have an inborn proclivity to sin. We are not born defiled as is commonly taught. We become defiled when we make sinful choices. Jesus taught that it is evil thoughts of the heart that generates sin and leads to defilement of the man and not that man is inherently defiled. We become defiled by choosing to express our God created human passions contrary to righteousness.

Mark 7:21-23: For from within, out of the heart of men, proceed evil thoughts, adulteries, fornications, murders, Thefts, covetousness, wickedness, deceit, lasciviousness, an evil eye, blasphemy, pride, foolishness: All these evil things come from within, and defile the man (KJV).

As is apparently true with the angels, we sin because we have God given ability to reason and make decisions as to how we express our God given attributes. Human nature is not sinful in and of itself. If we express our human nature sinfully it becomes a sinful nature. If we express our human nature righteously it becomes a Godly nature. It's how we express human nature that determines whether it is sinful or righteous. Apostle Paul makes this evident.

Romans 8:5-8: Those who live according to the sinful nature have their minds set on what that nature desires; but those who live in accordance with the Spirit have their minds set on what the Spirit desires. The mind of sinful man is death, but the mind controlled by the Spirit is life and peace; the sinful mind is hostile to God. It does not submit to God's law, nor can it do so. Those controlled by the sinful nature cannot please God.

Paul associates sinful nature with what goes on in the mind. It is in the mind where behavioral choices are made.

God wants us to have thoughts that are expressed in righteous behavior and Paul associates such thinking with having the mind of God. Sinful thoughts are hostile (against) to God and can't be subject to God. God wants us to pursue righteous thoughts which result in righteous behavior. Jesus had the mind of God from birth. Therefore, Jesus never expressed a sin nature. As already stated, Jesus was not a robot. He was able to choose between good and evil. Having the ability to choose either to obey or disobey God is foundational to the makeup of humans and even angels. As already discussed, indication is that a third of the angels sinned. There is no indication they sinned because they were created with a sin nature. They apparently sinned because they choose to express the passions they were created with in a manner contrary to God's will. As is true of His human creation, God created angels with free will.

It is apparent we humans were created with certain passions and desires and the power to choose how those passions and desires are expressed. Human passions and desires are not sinful in and of themselves. They become sinful when expressed contrary to what God intends. For example, sexual passion is not sinful in and of itself. It becomes sinful when expressed as fornication, adultery and other forms of prohibited sexual conduct. Anger is not sinful in and of itself. When expressed as rage or when it leads to hatred, it becomes sinful. Desiring to have something someone else has is not sinful but if it leads to envy, greed or theft, it becomes sinful behavior (See Galatians 5:20-21).

When Paul wrote in Galatians 5:24 that **"those who belong to Christ Jesus have crucified the sinful nature with its passions and desires,"** he was not teaching that in Christ we lose our human passions and desires. He was teaching that in Christ our human passions and desires are no longer sinfully expressed. Our human passions and desires are now expressed in righteous behavior pleasing to God.

Jesus had the same human passions and desires we all have but never made choices that resulted in those passions and desires being expressed in behavior contrary to God's will. He was totally orientated to obeying His Father God. No other human has ever been born with the level of power Jesus was given to submit to the will of God. Jesus had the appropriate level of power to consistently resist temptation to sin. This is why Jesus was able to be tempted in every way we are and yet without sin.

We humans are not sinners because we inherit Adamic sin. We humans are sinners because, like Adam, we yield to temptation which leads to sin. Paul wrote to the Roman and Corinthian Christians that sin entered the world through Adam and like Adam we all sin and because we all sin we all die. We die because of <u>our</u> sin, not Adam's sin. Adam was not created a sinner and we are not born sinners. We are born with the ability to make choices. Our choices determine whether our behavior is sinful or righteous. Apostle James wrote, **"Anyone, then, who knows the good he ought to do and doesn't do it, sins" (James 4:17)**. This statement by James is a witness to our ability to choose how we behave. All humans, except for one, have make sinful choices and have consequently been condemned to death since the wages of sin is death (Romans 6:23). Jesus never sinned because of the powerful presence of God's Spirit He had from birth which gave Him the ability to resist sin throughout His life.

Chapter Eleven

Could Jesus Have Sinned?

Apostle James writes that God cannot be tempted by evil (James 1:13). The implication is that God by nature is unable to be tempted by evil. It is impossible for evil to lure or entice God. Because Jesus is believed to be God, it's argued Jesus was unable to be tempted to sin when presented with temptations to do so. Therefore, Jesus was inherently unable to sin. It is believed temptation had no effect on Jesus. It is believed when tempted by Satan, nothing Satan said or did could actually tempt Jesus because Jesus was God and by nature unable to be tempted or sin. It's believed Jesus was immune to temptations presented to Him. Yet we read the following in Hebrews.

Hebrews 4:15: For we do not have a high priest who is unable to sympathize with our weaknesses, but we have one who has been tempted in every way, just as we are-- yet was without sin.

Being confronted with temptations and never sinning presupposes having the potential to yield to temptation and sin. If Jesus was by nature unable to yield to temptation and sin, this statement in Hebrews would be superfluous. It would be meaningless to say Jesus was tempted and yet without sin if Jesus was inherently unable to be tempted or sin. Of what significance would it be to say Jesus was tempted in every way without sinning if Jesus by nature was unable to be tempted and sin? It is apparent Jesus had to ask for help from God to resist temptation to sin like we all do.

Hebrews 5:7-9: During the days of Jesus' life on earth, he offered up prayers and petitions with loud cries and

129

tears to the one who could save him from death, and he was heard because of his reverent submission. Although he was a son, he learned obedience from what he suffered and, once made perfect, he became the source of eternal salvation for all who obey him.

In Hebrews, chapter 5, the writer explains how a priest experiences the same weaknesses as those unto whom he ministers so he can identify with what they go through. The writer goes on to explain that Jesus, our High Priest, offered up prayers and petitions with strong cryings and tears to his Father who was able to save Him from death and was heard because of His reverent submission. While Hebrews 5:7-9 is often seen as alluding to Jesus' petitions to the Father to save Him from the ordeal of the crucifixion (Mark 14:32-42, Matthew 26:36-46, Luke 22:39-46), the overall context of Hebrews implies Jesus had to petition His Father throughout his life for the strength to remain obedient in the face of temptation and thus avoid sin death. In Hebrews 2:17-18, Jesus is seen as suffering when tempted so He can help us who are tempted.

Hebrews 2:17-18: For this reason he had to be made like his brothers in every way, in order that he might become a merciful and faithful high priest in service to God, and that he might make atonement for the sins of the people. Because he himself suffered when he was tempted, he is able to help those who are being tempted.

These three passages in Hebrews portray a Christ who had to resist temptation like we all do in order to avoid sinning. If Jesus had to resist temptation like we do to avoid sin, it should be obvious Jesus had the ability to be tempted and sin. Jesus was tempted in every way we are and yet without sin. To be tempted and not sin presupposes having the ability to yield to temptation and sin. Jesus suffered through a great deal of persecution during His ministry. He suffered the insults of His trial and crucifixion. He could have retaliated and sinned in the process. He did not do this. Peter writes that when He suffered He did not threaten anyone (1 Peter 2:23).

To suffer when being tempted or tried involves practicing restraint and not reacting in an unrighteous manner. While Christ was born with the power to resist all temptation to sin, He still had to exercise that power when confronted with temptation and trial. Jesus had to put forth effort to remain sinless. While the NT narrative only reveals trials and temptations presented to Jesus by His Jewish persecutors and Satan, the fact that the writer to the Hebrews reveals Jesus was tempted in all ways we are tempted suggests Jesus faced many other temptations which He had to successfully resist in order to avoid sin.

These passages in Hebrews plainly indicate Jesus faced temptations like other humans. The Greek word translated "tempted" is *pirazo* and means to be tried, tested, proved or tempted. It is the same word used in the account of Satan tempting Jesus in the wilderness. The testing, trials and proving Jesus experienced were not like passing a math test, overcoming the trial of a health problem or proving an ability to run a mile. Scripture clearly says Jesus was tempted in every way as we are, yet without sin. This clearly shows Jesus' temptations and trials were associated with resisting sin which presupposes an ability to sin.

Scripture shows Jesus struggled against surrendering to trial and temptation just as we do. While we often yield to temptation, Jesus never did. Jesus never allowed temptations He faced to overpower Him because God gave Him sufficient ability to not allow temptations to overpower Him. Scripture clearly teaches Jesus experienced the same struggles we experience. This would be a rather hollow teaching if Jesus was inherently unable to be tempted or inherently unable to sin. Jesus had the human ability to be tempted and sin. However, He never once made a sinful choice. He was so led by the Spirit of God that when confronted with temptation to sin, such temptation had no effect on Him. This is why the Scripture says Jesus was tempted as we are but without sin. Jesus was born with the same ability we all have to yield to temptation and sin. In the case of Jesus, however, temptation to sin had no power over Him because of the mighty presence of God's Spirit in His life. God enabled Jesus to always be successful in not allowing temptation to actually tempt Him. Jesus was able to successfully resist all temptation not because He was God but because God gave Him the wherewithal to successfully resist all temptation.

Age of Accountability:

If humans are not born sinners but become sinners by the choices they make, what about babies and children? Do babies and small children sin? Is there an "age of accountability" below which a person is not held accountable for sin or where behavior is unclassified? Paul taught that all men have sinned (Romans 3:23, 5:12). Does Paul's "all" include babies and young children? Paul taught that all humans die in Adam (1 Corinthians 15:22). Does Paul's "all" include newborns and aborted babies?

When a two year old is told by His mother not to take cookies out of the cookie jar and the child succumbs to his desire for a cookie and chooses to take a cookie, is this two year old held accountable before God as a sinner because he expressed his desire to have a cookie in a way contrary to his mothers orders? Did this two year old child become a sinner in God's sight by disobeying God's command to honor one's parents? Furthermore, did the child take the cookie because of having a sinful nature that predisposes him to disobey his parents or is he simply expressing his natural desire to want a cookie but because his action runs contrary to the instruction of his mother his action becomes a sinful action. Does the child take the cookie because he is a sinner by birth, becomes a sinner by taking the cookie, or is neither the case?

The Scriptural indications are that we become sinners by the choices we make and not that we make sinful choices because we are born with a sinful disposition. Sinful choices are made when we express our human nature in ways contrary to righteousness. That is when sin occurs. All humans express their human nature in sinful ways from time to time. Some sin a great deal during their lives and others sin little, comparatively speaking. But we all sin and therefore are all in need of Christ's atonement. At what point a baby or young child is seen as committing sin and/or is accountable for sin is not spelled out in Scripture unless you believe all humans are born sinners which would make this discussion of an age of accountability superfluous.

Jesus taught that we must receive the Kingdom as little children in order to enter it. Jesus equates being humble as a child with being great in the Kingdom (Matthew 18:3-4, Mark 10:14-15). In Isaiah 7:16, a child is spoken of who was not at an age to know how to choose the evil from the good. In Deuteronomy 1:39, small children are spoken of as not knowing the good from the bad. What any of this means relative to an age of accountability is uncertain.

Does not knowing the good from the bad remove accountability for doing bad? What about disabled adults who cognitively don't know the good from the bad? Does ignorance of the law remove the penalty for breaking the law? No it does not. Breaking of law has natural consequences whether we are aware of such law or not.

If we are to take Paul's statements about all sinning and all dying in Adam as meaning all humans who have every lived, then it would appear that all humans are seen as sinning and being held accountable for sin whether or not they are cognizant of their sin. Having an inability to comprehend certain behavior as sinful does not negate the sinfulness of such behavior or remove its consequences. However, if it

133

should turn out that babies or children under a certain age are not held accountable for sin, it takes nothing away from what Christ did in facilitating salvation for all who are accountable for sin. In either case, eternal life is a gift from God and not dependent on anything we humans do or don't do. Since the Scriptures do not present a clear teaching as to an age of accountability for babies and children, we should not be dogmatic on this matter.

Original Sin and the Nature of Jesus:

Hebrews 2:17, records that Jesus was made like his brothers in every way. Paul told the Philippian Christians that Jesus was made in the likeness of man (Philippians 2:7). Paul told the Roman Christians that God sent Jesus in the likeness of sinful man (Romans 8:3). In the Romans passage the Greek word translated "man" in the NIV is *sarx* which is better translated "flesh" and is rendered as such in most translations. The Greek *sarx* appears 151 times in the NT and by context can be seen to simply mean the fleshly body and/or the fleshly nature which can be expressed sinfully or righteously.

The English rendering of "like" and "likeness" in these three passages is from a basic Greek word which means to be like something. This word can mean being exactly like something, similar to something or an image of something. The Scriptures show Jesus to be flesh. Paul said Jesus was of the seed of David according to the flesh (Romans 1:3). Peter spoke of the flesh of Christ not seeing corruption (Acts 2:31). Paul speaks of being reconciled to God through the fleshly body of Christ (Colossians 1:22). Paul wrote to Timothy that Christ was manifest in the flesh (1 Timothy 3:16). Peter wrote that Christ suffered in the flesh (1 Peter 4:1). In 1 John 4, John speaks of Christ coming in the flesh.

Since Jesus is consistently seen as being flesh in Scripture, it appears reasonable to conclude when Paul writes that Jesus is in the likeness of man, He is truly in the likeness of man and not merely a facsimile of man. Being in the likeness of man means Jesus had the same passions and desires as all other humans. What differentiates Jesus from all other humans is that He never expressed his human passions and desires in a sinful way.

What does Paul mean in Romans 8:3 in saying God sent Jesus in the likeness of sinful flesh? Sinful flesh is often associated in Scripture with behaving sinfully. We know from Scripture Jesus never sinned. So what is Paul saying in Romans 8:3?

Romans 8:3: For what the law could not do, in that it was weak through the flesh, God sending his own Son in the likeness of sinful flesh, and for sin, condemned sin in the flesh (KJV).

Paul wrote to the Corinthian's that Christ took our sins upon Himself on the cross and virtually became sin for us (2 Corinthians 5:21). The context of Romans 8:1-3 is God sending Jesus to condemn sin in the flesh by becoming a sin offering. Paul appears to be saying to the Romans the same thing he said to the Corinthians. Jesus took upon himself the sins of humanity and suffered sin death on our behalf. Jesus had sinful flesh in that He became sin for us at the time of His crucifixion.

Paul makes it clear that to behave righteously or unrighteously is a choice. Humans are not inherently predisposed to do one or the other. What we inherently are predisposed to do is make choices. In Romans 6:15-18, Paul complements the Romans for having turned from being slaves to sin (choosing sin) to being slaves to righteousness (choosing righteousness). Sin and righteousness are manifested through behavioral choices not through inherent predispositions. Jesus showed this to be the case when He said; **"If anyone chooses to do God's will,**

he will find out whether my teaching comes from God or whether I speak on my own" (John 7:17). Let's now consider Romans 8:8-9.

Romans 8:8-9a: So then they that are in the flesh cannot please God. But ye are not in the flesh, but in the Spirit, if so be that the Spirit of God dwell in you (KJV).

When Paul tells the Romans they are not in the flesh but in the Spirit, he is not telling them they are no longer in their fleshly body or no longer have human passions. He is not telling them they have lost their human nature. He is telling them they are no longer exercising their human passions in a sinful way. God didn't design humans to have sinful nature. Adam's sin didn't change God's design of the human heart so that it became inherently sinful. Sinful nature results from expressing our human nature in ways contrary to righteousness. Sinful expression of our natural and normal human passions and desires became ubiquitous after Adam and Eve were tossed out of the garden. We see this in what led God to bring the flood upon the earth. Did God destroy his human creation because they were inherently sinful or because they allowed sinful behavior to dominate their lives?

Genesis 6:5-7: The LORD saw how great man's wickedness on the earth had become, and that every inclination of the thoughts of his heart was only evil all the time. The LORD was grieved (Hebrew: *nakham*) that he had made man on the earth, and his heart was filled with pain (Hebrew: *atsav*). So the LORD said, "I will wipe mankind, whom I have created, from the face of the earth--men and animals, and creatures that move along the ground, and birds of the air--for I am grieved (*nakham*) that I have made them."

The Hebrew word translated grieved in this passage is *nakham* and literally means to be sorry and regretful over something. The NET bible translates *nakham* as "regretted." In the phrase "his heart was filled with pain," the word "pain" is translated from the Hebrew word *atsav* and means to experience emotional pain and depression, embarrassment and to be offended. The NET Bible translates *atsav* as "offended." These Hebrews words are used a number of times in the OT and by context can be seen to reflect these definitions. It is apparent that God became truly sorry He had made man when he saw to what extant man became evil.

Was God surprised by the extent to which man became evil? If God created man with an inclination to sin, why would God be sorry and regret having made man? If, as some believe, God created man to be a sinner, wasn't man simply carrying out God's will? Why then did God become grieved with His creation? Furthermore, if God willed that man be born with an inclination to sin, how could He instruct man to obey Him and then punish man when man didn't obey Him? It is counter-intuitive to require that a person ought to do something and then disallow the freedom of will and choice to do it or create barriers that make it difficult or impossible to do.

It appears much more reasonable to conclude God created man with basic passions and desires with the ability to choose how those passions and desires are expressed. It appears reasonable to believe that from the beginning God intended for man to choose righteousness. When man consistently chose unrighteousness, God became sorry that He had created man. Prior to the flood, man's evil choices became so dominant that a virtual culture of wickedness developed. God destroyed His human creation not because they were born predisposed to sin but because they became predisposed to sin by the choices they made. After the flood God reflected on human behavior and concluded he would not ever again curse the ground because of man's sinning ways as it was apparent that man will always make sinful choices to one extent or another (Genesis 8:21).

God foresaw from the beginning that in creating man with certain human passions and the free will to choose how those passions are expressed, man would express those passions in a sinful way to one degree or another. It is apparent God did not anticipate the extent to which his creation would make sinful choices and He became grieved that He had made man. He decided to destroy man but preserved his creation through Noah and essentially started the human race all over again.

A common Christian teaching is that God is omniscient which means He knows everything that will ever happen before it happens. Nowhere does the Bible teach God is omniscient. The word omniscient doesn't appear in Scripture. God being grieved over His creation would make no sense if God knew in advance how sinful man would become and that He would have to destroy His creation in a flood.

Scriptures reveals God does not know everything in advance. In 1 Samuel 15:11 it is recorded God was grieved that He made Saul to be King over Israel because Saul failed to do His will. If God knew in advance that Saul would not do His will, why did He appoint him King over Israel? In Genesis 22:11-12, we see God testing Abraham and when Abraham passes the test God says; "Now I know that you fear God." It is apparent God did not know this beforehand. God is seen as testing Israel in various ways to see if they will obey Him (see Exodus 16:4, Deuteronomy 8:2, Judges 2:21-22). Such testing would be superfluous if God knew in advance how Israel would respond. The following passage, where God is quoted, speaks for itself as to the issue of God knowing everything in advance.

Jeremiah 32:35: They built high places for Baal in the Valley of Ben Hinnom to sacrifice their sons and daughters to Molech, though I never commanded, nor did it enter my mind, that they should do such a detestable thing and so make Judah sin.

God did not predetermine that man must sin. God created within man a nature that, minus a strong presence of the Holy Spirit of God, <u>would</u> sin. God foresaw that man would sin and in mercy pre-determined to provide a savior to atone for sin and in so doing make us righteous before God despite our sinful behavior. The righteousness of God is not imputed to us in exchange for the supposed imputed sinfulness of Adam. God's righteousness is imputed to us in exchange for Christ's sacrificial death that delivers us from the eternal death we have all earned by failing to live by God's Spiritual standards. A careful reading of the Scriptures reveals that God's Spirit has always been available to those who seek after it. It is man's failure to seek after God's Spirit and the righteousness it brings that has resulted in the massive amount of sin extant in the world.

Some will point to something Paul wrote to the Romans and Galatians as evidence God pre-determined that all humans must sin so He can have mercy on them all.

Romans 11:32: For God has bound (Greek: sugkleio) all men over to disobedience so that he may have mercy on them all (NIV).

Galatians 3:22: But the Scripture declares that the whole world is a prisoner (*sugkleio*) of sin, so that what was promised, being given through faith in Jesus Christ, might be given to those who believe.

The Greek word *sugkleio*, translated "bound" in the NIV rendering of Romans 11:32, is variously translated as "concluded" (KJV), "committed" (NKJV), "shut up" (ASV) and "consigned" (ESV). In the Galatians passage *sugkleio* is variously translated as "concluded" (KJV), "confined" (NKJV), "shut up" (ASV), "imprisoned" (ESV and NET). The Greek Lexicons define *sugkleio* as to "enclose, hem in, confine or imprison." Luke uses this word to describe the enclosure of a large number of fish in a net (Luke 5:6).

Is Paul teaching that God, when creating man, pre-determined that man sin so that God can have mercy on all men and deliver man from the sin He pre-determined man commit? Has God intentionally consigned man to sin and made man a prisoner of sin so He can have mercy on man? Did God specifically create a "sin nature" in man so He could deliver man from the very nature with which He created man? Romans chapter one debunks such an idea. In this chapter, Paul describes in detail how wretched man had become. Paul repeatedly shows that because man has rejected the way of righteousness and has consistently chosen to disobey God, God has given man up to even more wretchedness (Romans 1:18-28). God is essentially saying to man that since man chooses to behave contrary to righteousness, God is going to step back and allow man to have his way and suffer the consequences.

God has bound all men over to disobedience and made the whole world a prisoner of sin not because God intended and pre-determined that man sin. God has done this because man has chosen to live contrary to righteousness and God has allowed such choice. Because man has consistently chosen to live contrary to God's will, God has given man up to even greater sin (Romans 1:18-28) resulting in the whole world becoming a prisoner of sin. God is seen as consistently condemning sin. To conclude that God on the one hand condemns sin and at the same time pre-determined that man sin is an absolute oxymoron. The Scriptures make it clear that it is God's will that man live righteously but if man chooses to be disobedient, God not only allows it but stands aside and gives man great latitude as to how far He allows man to go in his disobedience.

Psalm 81:10-12; I am the LORD your God, who brought you up out of Egypt. Open wide your mouth and I will fill it. "But my people would not listen to me; Israel would not submit to me. So I gave them over to their stubborn hearts to follow their own devices.

140

When God created man He created human attributes which included various passions and desires. God created man with the power of choice as to how the human nature He created could be expressed. There is no indication God created man with a predisposition to express human nature in a sinful way. He pronounced his creation of man to be very good (Genesis 1:31). The doctrine of original sin implies that when Adam sinned, mans nature was changed to a sinful nature and all mankind inherits this sinful nature through procreation. This doctrine virtually gives Adam the power to have changed what God made very good into something very evil. This is not what the Scriptures teach.

The Scriptures associate sinful nature with the deeds done by the body. The sinful nature is something we produce by sinfully expressing the passions, desires and free will God created in us. Paul makes this evident when he defines the sinful nature as the misdeeds of the body which can be displaced by deeds engendered by the Spirit. It is not our human nature that is changed. It is our expression of our nature that is changed.

Romans 8:13-14: For if you live according to the <u>sinful nature</u>, you will die; but if by the Spirit you put to death the <u>misdeeds of the body</u>, you will live, because those who are led by the Spirit of God are sons of God.

Paul speaks of putting to death the misdeeds of the body. He associates misdeeds of the body with the sinful nature. If the fleshly body with its fleshly nature is sinful in and of itself, Paul would be instructing us to kill our bodies. Obviously, this is not what Paul is teaching. Paul is not instructing the Romans to put to death their fleshly nature but to put to death the sinful expression of their fleshly nature.

Jesus never expressed the attributes of His human nature in a sinful way and therefore did not have to put to death sinful nature. Jesus never developed sinful nature. All other humans have. Jesus was led by the Spirit of God from birth. Jesus always expressed His human nature according to the Spirit. He was totally led by God's Spirit throughout His life. Jesus never expressed sinful nature. He lived His whole life according to the Spirit. Jesus was successfully able to resist all temptation to sin because God gave Him the power to do so. God insured Jesus would never sin by equipping Him with the power to never sin. The presence of God was so pronounced in Jesus that His will and the Father's will were the same as Scripture clearly shows. Jesus was a son of God from birth because He was led by the Spirit of God from birth. We become sons of God through spiritual transformation which leads to expressing our human nature in a Godly way as opposed to expressing it in a sinful way. We experience a spiritual rebirth which changes how we think and therefore how we behave. Spiritual rebirth places us in the kingdom (John 3:5-8). Being in the kingdom is all about expressing righteousness, peace and joy in the Holy Spirit (Romans 14:17).

No human other than Jesus has been given the power to express the tenets of the kingdom as perfectly as Jesus did. No other human has been given the level of power Jesus had to consistently express righteous behavior. Jesus was given this level of power so He could remain sinless and be the perfect sacrifice for our sins. All other humans, including those transformed by the Spirit of God, have sinned and need to be reconciled to God through the sacrifice of Christ.

Did God Die In Jesus?

God is eternal and cannot die. Trinitarians acknowledge God cannot die but believe God died as a human incarnation of the Son distinction in the Godhead. Functionally the Son of God is seen as being humanly born, able to suffer and able to die while all the while remaining ontologically one with the Father and Spirit. In His role as a human sacrifice for sin, Jesus is seen as remaining sinless because, while functionally a human, He remained fully God and therefore did not have the ability to sin.

Scripture, however, shows Jesus remained sinless not because He was God in the flesh but because God gave Him the power to be sinless. As already discussed, Apostle Peter wrote that it is through Divine power that we can escape the corruption in the world caused by evil desires. Peter shows this to be equivalent to participating in the Divine nature.

2 Peter 1:3-4: His divine power has given us everything we need for life and godliness through our knowledge of him who called us by his own glory and goodness. Through these he has given us his very great and precious promises, so that through them you may participate in the divine nature and escape the corruption in the world caused by evil desires.

We know Jesus had a full measure of God's Spirit which allowed Him to participate in the Divine nature. It is evident He participated in the Divine nature from birth. That is why Jesus would not sin and did not sin. It was not that Jesus could not sin but that He would not sin. It must be understood, however, that having fullness of the Spirit of God and participating in the Divine nature of God does not equate with being God, either for us or for Jesus.

There is no need for a doctrine of Immaculate Conception to mitigate what is believed to be a sinful birth for Jesus. There is no need to postulate Jesus had to be God in the flesh in order to be the perfect sacrifice for sin. Just the opposite is true. Jesus had to be a total human in the flesh so He could experience what we experience and face temptation like we face temptation. Jesus had to experience what we experience in order to be a merciful and faithful high priest, representing us before His Father God. Jesus even had to experience our sin. He did this when He took our sin upon Himself on the cross.

143

When we see Jesus in this light, it makes what He did truly extraordinary. When we understand that Jesus was totally human and struggled to overcome temptation so He could be the sinless sacrifice for our sins, it should elevate our love for Jesus to new heights.

The Two Adams:

The Scriptures compare Jesus with the first Adam. The first Adam was directly created by God, placed in the Garden of Eden and given authority over the physical creation. This first Adam sinned and all humans have followed in his footsteps except one. As the second Adam, Jesus lived a sinless life and was thus able to be the perfect sacrifice for the sin that began with the first Adam. The Scriptures clearly show that as sin and death came about as a result of the actions of the man Adam, salvation from the consequences of sin came about as the result of the actions of the man Jesus.

Paul speaks of the first Adam being a pattern of the one that was to come (Romans 5:14). The first Adam was born without sin but with the ability to sin. Adam yielded to temptation which led to disobeying God's command. Eve was actually the first to sin as a consequence of being deceived by the serpent into believing she wouldn't die if she ate the fruit of the tree (Genesis 3:3-6, 1 Timothy 2:14). Adam was well aware of God's command not to eat of the tree of the knowledge of good and evil and what the consequences of eating of that tree would be (Genesis 2:16-17). It is very likely it was Adam who instructed Eve regarding this matter. There is nothing recorded as to any noticeable change in Eve when she eat of the fruit of the forbidden tree. In seeing no apparent change in Eve, Adam may have reasoned that the serpent was right and chose to eat of the tree as well and behave contrary to God's command. It appears the change in them took place after they both ate of the tree (Genesis 3:7). Adam and Eve brought death upon themselves because of the sin they committed and humans have continued to bring death upon themselves by committing sin.

Adam was created without sin but became a sinner. He was created with the ability to die but did not become subject to death until he sinned. Jesus, the second Adam, was born without sin and also had the ability to die but never became subject to death because He never sinned. Jesus died not because of sin He committed but because He took our sin upon Himself. As Scripture reveals, death could not hold Jesus because Jesus never sinned. The first Adam succumbed to temptation and sinned. Christ, the second Adam, was able to resist temptation and never sin. Therefore, Jesus became the vehicle through whom death is replaced with life for all of mankind. Because of sin, the first Adam was limited to being a living human Being subject to eternal death. The last Adam, by not sinning, could not be held by death and was resurrected to life and became a life giving spirit.

1 Corinthians 15:45: The first man Adam became a living being; the last Adam, a life-giving spirit.

It was through the disobedience of the man Adam that sin and death came about. It was through the obedience of the man Jesus (the second or last Adam) that sin and death is eliminated and eternal life came about. Since God cannot die, it should be plain that Jesus is not the eternal God. Jesus died. Jesus was made to be like all other humans. The first Adam was directly created by God and was called a son of God. Jesus, as the second Adam, was directly begotten by God in the womb of Mary and became the only directly begotten Son of God. In order for Jesus to be patterned after Adam He had to have had the ability to be tempted like Adam so He could resist temptation and succeed where Adam failed.

Trinitarian theology teaches Jesus was God the Son who added humanity to His Divinity. In reality, just the opposite is true. Jesus was born totally human to which His Father added the necessary attributes of the Divine nature for Jesus to successfully fulfill all of God's will. God gave Jesus supernatural powers to heal the sick, turn water into wine, feed the five thousand and calm the storm. Much of this was done to demonstrate Jesus was indeed the promised Messiah. Above all, God gave Jesus the power to resist all temptation to sin so He could be the perfect sacrifice for the sins of the world.

Jesus was God's servant to facilitate the replacement of death with life. In Acts chapter three, Peter identifies Jesus as God's servant (verse 13 & 26), as God's Christ (verse 18) and as the offspring of Abraham (verse 25). A careful reading of the Scriptures will show that the Messiah was not God but the anointed servant of the Most High God. The OT indicates the promised Messiah would be a ruler in the mold of Moses and David. Moses and David did not exist prior to their human birth. The OT passages that foreshadow events in the life of Christ do not give any indication the Messiah would be a pre-existent Being.

Because of what Jesus accomplished as the human Son of God and because of His elevation to being the most powerful Being in the universe next to God, Jesus is worthy of the highest level of reverence next to God Himself. While Jesus is not the Most High God, He is above all powers extant under the Most High God and is to be worshiped accordingly.

Chapter Twelve

Is Jesus Eternally Begotten?

It is a common tenet of Trinitarian theology that Jesus is eternally begotten. Since Jesus is believed to be co-eternal with the Father, it became necessary to view the Scriptural passages that speak of Christ's begettal in a different manner from the way begettal is normally understood. Belief in the eternal begettal of Jesus is largely tied to the Nicene and Constantinople Creeds of the fourth century. We will begin our discussion of this issue by providing a short historical overview of perspectives that led to the development of these Creeds.

Historically, there have been a variety of positions held as to the nature of God and the relationship between the Father, the Son and the Holy Spirit. Second century theologians such as Irenaeus and Justin appear to have believed in the deity and eternal existence of the Father and the Son while also believing the Father and Son were not equal in authority since the Scriptures show the Son as being subordinant to the Father. There is some indication that Justin may not have believed in the eternal existence of the Son.

In the early second century a teaching appeared called Docetism taken from the Greek word *dokeo*, which means "to seem" or "to appear." This view maintained that Jesus was only divine and was not at all human but only appeared to be human. A leading proponent of this view was the philosopher/theologian Marcion. Marcion taught there were two Gods, the legalistic God of the Old Testament and the forgiving God of the New Testament.

In the late second and early third century, a view of God developed called Monarchianism. One form of Monarchianism called Dynamic or Adoptionist Monarchianism taught God was a one of a kind deity and Jesus was not deity but a created human person filled with the Holy Spirit and thus able to fulfill God's (His Father's) will. Some early Adoptionists even believed Jesus was not born of a virgin but from a normal sexual union of Joseph and Mary. It was believed Jesus was later "adopted" by God the Father at His baptism or at His resurrection at which time He became the Son of God. This view was held by a Jewish Christian group called Ebionites.

A form of Monarchianism called Modalism was taught in the third century by a theologian named Sabellius. Sabellius taught God is only one person who acts as Father in creating the universe, as Son in redeeming sinners and as Holy Spirit in sanctifying believers. While this position may appear Trinitarian on the surface, it is not Trinitarian as it does not view the one God as made up of the three persons of Father, Son and Holy Spirit. It sees no relationship in God. It views the one God playing three different roles at different times in history while retaining single personhood. This view was actually quite popular in the early church as it preserved the oneness of God while allowing for the deity of Jesus.

Early in the third century a Bishop from Rome named Callistus proposed the idea that the Father actually became Jesus the Son. This belief was called Patripassian as it postulated the Father participated in humanity as the man Jesus. This was an attempt to preserve the monotheism of the Scriptures while accounting for the deity of the Son. This view has present day proponents in what is called Oneness Theology which I discussed in an earlier Chapter.

Also in the third century, the respected scholar and theologian Origen maintained the subordination of the Word (Greek *logos*) to God the Father. Origen believed the *logos* of John chapter one is Jesus Christ. Origen emphasized the independence of the *logos* as well as its distinction from the Being and substance of the Father. Origen apparently believed the *logos* was not of the same substance as the Father but merely an image of the Father. Origen believed there could be degrees or grades of divinity, with the Son being slightly less divine than the Father.

Origen pictured God within a framework of the Father being the Supreme Deity over all things while the Son was over creation in a lesser way with the Spirit acting only within the context of the church. The Spirit was seen as leading back to the Son and the Son back to the Father. It appears Origen considered the Father and the Son to be deity and of eternal existence but not con-substantial and co-equal as in later Trinitarian thought.

In the early fourth century a church leader named Marcellus proposed that the word of God existed eternally as the intrinsic reasoning faculty of God. When God decided to make the heavens and the earth, the word became the power and energy through which God created all things. The word later became flesh in the person of Jesus Christ. In this manner Marcellus strove to maintain the oneness of God.

Also in the early fourth century, a presbyter by the name of Arius advanced the position that the Father alone is God with the Son having been created by this one and only God at some point before the universe was created. It appears Arius believed it was through the Son that God created the universe although it isn't certain whether he understood this in a literal or a figurative sense. Arius firmly believed the Son was subordinant to the Father. Arius felt this view maintained monotheism as opposed to the polytheism he saw in seeing the Son as equal deity with the Father. This view was embraced by a number of Church leaders but hotly contested by other Church leaders who believed the Son to be deity on par with the Father. Much controversy ensued over this issue with Arius being excommunicated by the Bishop of Alexandria which created a great deal of conflict within segments of the Christian Community.

It is interesting that Origen, as well as many fourth century Bishops such as Eusebius of Nicomedia and Eusebius of Caesarea; all believed the Son was subordinant to the Father not only as the human Jesus, but also in His glorified state. This position was a major dynamic in generating a showdown with Bishop Alexander of Alexandria, Egypt and his associate Athanasius at the Council of Nicaea in A.D. 325. Both of these men believed the Son was not subordinant to the Father and that the Son was equally God with the Father.

The Council at Nicaea was attended by over 250 Bishops, mainly from the Eastern Roman Empire. Emperor Constantine hosted this event. Very few attended from the Western part of the Empire. The Bishop of Alexandria and Athanasius firmly advocated that Jesus is God as much as the Father is God and the Son is not subordinant to the Father. Church leaders representing the Alexander/Athanasius position went head to head with defenders of the Arian position led by Eusebius, the Bishop of Nicomedia. After all was said and done, the Alexander/Athanasius position prevailed and the belief the Son is con-substantial with the Father ("God of very God") became the accepted position among many of the church hierarchy. This position was articulated in what became known as the Nicene Creed. However, many Christians and Church leaders continued to take the Arian view.

Following Nicaea, dozens of Councils were held at which proponents of both the Arian and Athanasian position were alternately condemned and reinstated. In A.D. 359 a Council at Rimini-Seleucia was attended by more than 500 Bishops from both the Eastern and Western parts of the Empire. This Council adopted an Arian Creed only to have it later rescinded.

A good overview of the dynamics involved in this conflict can be found in the book, *When Jesus Became God,* by Richard E. Rubenstein. The tenet of the Nicene Creed pertaining to our discussion reads as follows:

We believe in one God, the Father Almighty, Maker of all things visible and invisible. And in one Lord Jesus Christ, the Son of God, begotten of the Father [the only-begotten; that is, of the essence of the Father, God of God], Light of Light, very God of very God, begotten, not made, being of one substance with the Father; by whom all things were made [both in heaven and on earth]; who for us men, and for our salvation, came down and was incarnate and was made man; And in the Holy Ghost.

The Nicene Creed states belief in one God the Father Almighty and in one Lord Jesus Christ, the Son of God, who is begotten of the Father. To this point, the Creed is in total harmony with what the Scriptures instruct as to who the one God is and who the one Lord is. The Creed shows the one God to be the Father just as Christ, Paul and John taught. The Creed shows Jesus to be the Son of this one Father God as is seen throughout the NT. The Creed shows Jesus is begotten by God the Father as is taught in the NT Scriptures. After these introductory statements, however, this Creed begins to teach some things not found in the Scriptures.

This Creed goes on to define begotten as being of the same essence as the Father. It states Jesus is of the same essence as the Father. The Creed uses the Greek word *homoousios* to say "of one essence." *Homoousios* means "same in substance or essence." *Homoousios*, however, is not found in the Greek Scriptures. NT writers do not use this word to define the relationship between the Son and the Father. The very use of *homoousios* (substance/essence) in speaking of God may be problematical as the word substance is ordinarily associated with the material world. Scripture teaches God is Spirit. Can we really associate a word like substance with Spirit?

Trinitarianism teaches God is a Being in three distinctions of Father, Son and Spirit and of one *homoousios*. To say the word God is to say Father, Son and Spirit. While the Trinitarian

God is seen as having internal differentiation as characterized by the three distinctions seen in this God, it is believed that when this God acts, He acts as one single Being and never as individual distinctions of his Being. He always acts as Father, Son and Spirit. God is seen as undivided. Trinitarians believe this undivided God became incarnate in Jesus through the distinction in the Godhead called the Son. The distinctions of Father and Spirit did not become incarnate. Only the distinction called the Son became incarnate. Yet if God is a single undivided Being of Father, Son and Spirit, it would appear that if the Son became incarnate in Jesus, the whole of the Godhead became incarnate in Jesus. Trinitarians appear to dance around this issue with statements such as the following taken from page 108 of *The Christian Doctrine of God, One Being Three Persons*, written by prominent twentieth century Trinitarian theologian Thomas F Torrance.

"It was, of course, not the Godhead or the Being of God as such who became incarnate, but the Son of God, not the Father or the Spirit, who came among us, certainly from the Being of the Father and as completely homoousios with him, yet because in him the whole fullness of the Godhead dwells, the whole undivided Trinity must be recognized as participating in the incarnate Life and Work of Christ." On page 118 of his book, Torrance quotes Athanasius as saying, *"Jesus Christ is from the Being of the Father and of one and the same being or homoousios with God."*

Torrance is saying only the Son became incarnate and came <u>from</u> the Being of the Father. Trinitarianism teaches God is a single Being of Father, Son and Spirit. How then can it be said the Son came <u>from</u> the Being of the Father? In Trinitarian thought, the Son is one in Being with the Father and Spirit. The Father doesn't have his own separate Being. God is seen as a single, undivided Being of Father, Son and Spirit. There is only one God Being not three Beings. Therefore, if the Son became incarnate it would follow the Father and Spirit also became incarnate. Yet Torrance says only the Son became incarnate and then virtually contradicts himself by writing that the whole of the undivided Trinity is represented in the incarnate Christ. This is tantamount to saying the whole Being of God became Christ which is the only thing you can say if you believe Christ is one in Being with the Father and the Spirit. If this is the case, however, when Christ died, the whole of God died which, as seen in Chapter Nine of this book, is an absolute absurdity.

Trinitarians teach God is one Being in three persons or distinctions. Yet in their writings there is reference to the Being of the Father and the Being of the Son which on the surface gives the impression the Father and Son are their own separate Beings. The following is typical of such writing as seen on Page 145 of Torrance's book where he appears to largely be quoting Athanasius.

"The whole Being of the Son is proper to the Being of the Father and the Being of the Son is the fullness of the Father's Godhead. Hence Athanasius could say repeatedly that the Son shares perfectly and fully in the one Being of the Godhead. When considered in himself, he is himself very God, and has his divine Life from himself. 'For as the Father has life in himself, so he has given the Son to have life in himself' "

It appears when Torrance writes that the Being of the Son resides in the Being of the Father, what he means is that the Person of the Son resides in the Person of the Father who, along with the Spirit, constitute Divine Being. Therefore, the Son is seen as having divine life from Himself. However, Jesus said it is the Father who has life in Himself and He (Jesus) derives His life from the Father as Athanasius implies by quoting John 5:26. If Jesus derives His life from the Father, He does not have life from Himself and cannot be considered equal to the one He receives His life from. As discussed elsewhere in this book, all life ultimately comes from the Father, including the life of the Son. Jesus, as the begotten Son of God, did not have intrinsic life from Himself. His life was given to Him by the giver of all life, the one and only Supreme God who is the God and Father of Jesus.

Trinitarians acknowledge that the life of the Son comes from the Father. Trinitarianism teaches the Father is the unoriginate God which means the Father has always been. He has no origination. The Son and the Spirit are seen as eternally generated from the Father. They originate from the Father. The Son is said to be eternally begotten and the Spirit is seen as eternally proceeding from the Father. Because the Son and the Spirit are seen as of the Father, they are considered to be of the same essence as the Father and together with the Father constitute the one God. The three are considered ontologically one which means they are one in Being. Therefore, when Trinitarians speak of Father, Son and Spirit being co-eternal, co-equal and con-substantial, they are primarily referring to their ontological oneness.

Functionally, the three are seen as acting in different ways while all the while being in total agreement and unity as to what they do. Therefore, while functionally different, it is believed they always act with singleness of will and purpose. They always act as Father, Son and Spirit. It is believed when Scripture speaks of the Son and the Spirit being of the Father, it is speaking of their eternal generation from the Father. When the Son, as the human man Jesus, calls the Father His God, says the Father is greater than He, says the Father grants Him His life, and says the Father is the one and only true God, it is believed Jesus is relating to the Father within the relational structure of the Trinity wherein the Father is seen as the life source of the Son but not ontologically superior to the Son.

Trinitarians give the example of a human generating a new life through procreation. It is pointed out that a newborn is of the same human essence as its parents. In like manner the Son of God is seen as being generated by the Father and being of the same essence as the Father. C.S. Lewis writes on page 157 of his book *Mere Christianity, "What God begets is God; just as what man begets is man."*

It is true that when humans beget other humans, they pass on human physicality which could be labeled human essence. However, a human newborn is a separate Being from its parents and exhibits many different characteristics from that of its parents as it develops. Within Trinitarianism, being of the essence of the Father is seen as being identical with the Father in every way short of being the Father. This obviously is not true in the transmission of human essence to a newborn. In the transmission of human essence, the basic components of human life are transmitted to the newborn from which the newborn develops many characteristics that are often quite different from the parents. When I procreated my son, he became a different Being from me in multiple ways. We are not the same Being. Jesus is considered ontologically one with the Father which is to say He is one in Being with the Father. While physical procreation produces another Being of the same basic human essence, that human is an entirely separate Being having a number of attributes different from the parent. This does not analogize with the Trinitarian concept of the Father, Son and Spirit indwelling each other and being a single entity called God.

Can God only beget God as C.S Lewis states? Trinitarians make a big issue out of defining beget as passing along ones essence to someone while to create is to make something other than your own kind. C.S. Lewis argues that *"To beget is to become the father of: to create is to make."* He writes, *"When you beget, you beget something of the same kind as yourself"* (page 157 of *Mere Christianity*). This is a very arbitrary limitation placed on the word beget as used in relation to God the Father. While it is true that at the physical level organisms can only beget other organisms of the same kind, there is no evidence to show that God is limited in this manner. While it may be

155

inherent to physical begettal that physical essence is passed on from one organism to another, it is rather presumptuous to conclude God must pass on His Godly essence when begetting a physical life.

As mentioned, C.S. Lewis writes, *"To beget is to become the Father of."* There is nothing limiting how God the Father becomes the father of a human. There is nothing necessitating God pass along to such human newborn His Divine essence. God can generate a life in any way He pleases. The Scriptures show God the Father directly generated a life in a human female through the power of His Spirit. In so doing He became the Father of a Son named Jesus. To beget is to become the Father of. God can beget in any way He chooses. To beget a life is to bring into existence a life that didn't exist before. God isn't limited as to how he begets. God is not under obligation to pass along His Divine essence when He supernaturally begets a physical life. God is the source of all life and can facilitate life in any way He chooses.

Since both Trinitarians and non-Trinitarians agree the Son receives His life from the Father, the question that needs to be answered is when this occurred. Trinitarians believe this occurs as a continuous process of begettal throughout all eternity. Is this concept found in the Scriptures? No it is not. The Scriptures teach the begettal of the Son took place at a particular moment of time when the Most High God through the power of His Spirit brought about the conception of Jesus in the womb of Mary.

We know from Scripture the Son is generated by the Father and plainly reveals the Father is greater than He. The Scriptures reveal the Son receives His life from the Father and relates to the Father as His God. This should be sufficient evidence the Father is both ontologically and functionally at a higher level than the Son. How can the recipient of life be ontologically equal to the giver of life? The whole of Scripture points to the Father as the giver of life. Therefore, it appears quite reasonable to conclude the Father is both ontologically and functionally superior to the Son. It is reasonable to conclude the power that generates life and from whom life originates is greater than the life such power generates.

Since the Father is the source of the Son and Spirit, the Father is seen as the first person of the Trinity with the Son being the second and the Spirit being the third. On page 137 of his book, Mr. Torrance writes, *"The relationship between the Son and the Father is irreversible, for the Son is from the Father, not the Father from the Son. The Father comes first because he is the Father, although the Son is not less divine because he is the Son of the Father for there is no difference in Being or nature between them."* On page 176, Torrance writes, *"while the Father 'naturally' comes first, the Son is nevertheless everything the Father is except being the Father."*

If the Son is everything the Father is except being the Father, the Son must have the same level of power, wisdom, understanding and knowledge as the Father. The Son must be omnipotent, omniscient and omnipresent as the Father is said to be. The Son must be able to speak things into existence as the Father does. In fact, if God is a single essence of Father, Son and Spirit and always acts as Father, Son and Spirit, there really are no distinctions in God. It's superfluous to speak in terms of the Son and the Spirit being distinct from the Father and from each other if all three have the same level of Divinity and indwell each other.

If the Father, Son and Spirit indwell each other, as Trinitarians teach, they are equally Divine. Why then does Jesus, as "God incarnate," relate to the Father as His God when He also is God in every respect short of being the Father? Why does Jesus say the Father is greater than He when He is ontologically one with the Father and of identical mind and will with the Father? How can the word "greater" even be used in describing the relationship between the Father and the Son if they are of equal

Divinity? Why does Jesus say the Father grants Him His life if, as Athanasius writes, He has His divine life from Himself? Why does Jesus, as "God incarnate," say the Father is the one and only true God when He also is the one and only true God? There can be only one, one and only true God.

Trinitarians take the position that when Jesus and the Apostles speak of the Father as the one and only God, they are seeing the Father as the head or first person of the Trinitarian Godhead of Father, Son and Spirit. Therefore, when Jesus says the Father is greater than He and grants Him life, this is seen within the context of the Father being the source of the Son's existence within the Trinitarian Godhead. All the dozens of Scriptural passages that appear to show the Son as lower in status than the Father, are seen within the context of the Father generating the Son and Spirit within the Trinitarian Godhead.

The problem with this approach is that on the one hand the Father is seen as the source of the Son and Spirit while at the same time the Son and Spirit are seen as being equal to the Father in every way short of being the Father. If the Father has always existed and the Son and Spirit have always existed, it would follow that all three are unoriginate and not just the Father. It is superfluous to say the Son and Spirit originate from the Father if in fact they have always existed just as the Father has always existed.

Trinitarians respond by saying origination of the Son and Spirit is not in time but is in the Father and since the Father has always existed so has the Son and Spirit. The Scriptures clearly teach the Father is unoriginate. The Scriptures show that the Spirit proceeds from the Father and always has. As you will see in Chapter Twenty-Three, the Spirit is the power and cognitive activity of the Father. The Scriptures teach the Spirit encompasses all that the Father is in power, glory, purpose and will. Therefore, the Spirit is unoriginate with the Father since the Father would always have Spirit. The Spirit of the Father is intrinsic to what the Father is. It is not something the Father generates but is integral to the very makeup of the Father. It proceeds from the Father as the Father's mind and power. The Spirit is a dynamic of what God is just as the human spirit is a dynamic of what a human is. On the other hand, Scripture clearly shows the Son as being begotten by the Father which would make the Son to have a beginning in time. As will be seen, begettal involves a beginning in time.

Scripture shows the Father to be the one and only God. This one and only God is seen as begetting the Son at a specific moment in time and giving Him a physical, mortal life which ended at the cross. The Father resurrected His dead Son and granted Him immortal life. The Scriptures clearly show Jesus was the first human to be born from the dead to eternal life (Colossians 1:18, Romans 8:29, 1 Corinthians 15:20, Revelation 1:5).

Eternal Begettal:

How did the concept of eternal begettal develop? Before we get to what the Scriptures say about the term begettal, let's briefly review the history that led to the concept of eternal begettal.

In the book I have been quoting from author Thomas Torrance, he writes that the *"Nicene term homoousios is not a Biblical term but it was appropriated by the fathers of Nicaea and recoined through believing commitment to God's self-revelation in Jesus Christ and careful interpretation of the Biblical witness in order to give unequivocal expression to the Deity of Christ, the incarnate Lord and Savior"* (page 94). Mr. Torrance goes on to write, *"As the epitomized expression of this truth, the homoousion is the ontological and epistemological linchpin of Christian theology. It gives expression to the truth with which everything hangs together and without which everything ultimately falls apart"* (page 95).

Mr. Torrance, as do other Trinitarians, sees the non-Biblical term *homoousios* as the basis for understanding who God is. This non-Biblical word is seen as the linchpin (number one dynamic) in understanding the relationship between the Father, Son and Spirit. While I don't see a problem in using non-Biblical words to help us understand Biblical concepts, it should become evident as you move through the material presented in this book that *homoousios* is not the "ontological and epistemological linchpin of Christian theology," much less the means whereby God is identified as a Trinity.

After formulation of the Nicene Creed, controversy over the relationship between the Father and the Son raged on for many years. Both the Arian and the Athanasian views were supported by various Church leaders and Roman government officials during this time. Just before his death, Arius, who had been excommunicated, was reinstated at the request of Emperor Constantine. Because of this and Constantine's baptism just before his death by an Arian Bishop, some believe Constantine died an Arian. Athanasius, who had become Bishop of Alexandria, was alternately condemned by various Church Councils and reinstated by others. At times the Arian view prevailed in the Church and at other times the Athanasian view prevailed. Roman Emperors often participated in this ongoing conflict. With the exception of the Athanasian Egyptian Churches, the Greek speaking Churches of the Eastern Roman Empire were largely Arian while the Latin speaking Churches of the Western Roman Empire largely followed Athanasius.

Upon the death of the Eastern Arian Emperor Valens in A.D. 378, a pro-Nicene Emperor took his place and called together 180 selected Eastern Bishops for a council at Constantinople in A.D. 381. The Nicene Creed was updated at this council to include the Holy Spirit as proceeding from the Father and worthy of worship as is the Father and the Son. Thus was established a Trinitarian concept of God. This concept was affirmed in the Western Empire at the Council of Aqulileia later in 381 although some Western theologians argued that the Creed should be worded to say the Spirit proceeds from both the Father and the Son. This argument became an important dynamic in developments that led to the West separating from the East and the formation of the Greek Orthodox Church.

The Trinitarian concept of God was made the orthodox view of God throughout the Roman Empire and any advocacy of the Arian or any other view became punishable by death. Thus the role of Imperial power continued to play a significant role in establishing and enforcing what was determined to be orthodox doctrine. Many outside the Empire, however, continued to follow the Arian position for hundreds of years. The tenets of the Constantinople Creed pertaining to our discussion are as follows:

We believe in one God, the Father Almighty, Maker of heaven and earth, and of all things visible and invisible. And in one Lord Jesus Christ, the only-begotten Son of God, begotten of the Father before all worlds (aeons), Light of Light, very God of very God, begotten, not made, being of one substance with the Father; by whom all things were made; who for us men, and for our salvation, came down from heaven, and was incarnate by the Holy Ghost of the Virgin Mary, and was made man; And in the Holy Ghost, the Lord and Giver of life, who proceedeth from the Father, who with the Father and the Son together is worshiped and glorified.

It is largely from the Nicene and Constantinople Creeds that the concept of "eternal begettal" developed. It is believed Jesus is eternally begotten by the Father. It is believed that in order for the Father to eternally be the Father, He always had to have the Son. Therefore, since the Father has always existed, so must the Son have always existed. The Son is seen as being eternally begotten from the very essence of the Father. This concept was formulated as a rebuttal to the Arian proposition that *"there was once when he was not,"* thus implying the Son was created. The essence of the Father came to be called the divine essence as it was believed to be the same single essence that is Father, Son and Spirit and not just the essence of the Father. The divine essence was defined as the attributes of eternal existence, omnipotence, omnipresence and omniscience.

As covered above, Trinitarian theology teaches the Son originates from the Father. This is seen as what differentiates the Father from the Son and vice versa. The Father is seen as unoriginated while the Son is seen as originating from the Father but doing so in an eternal way. When asked to explain this construct, the answer is that it is an unexplainable mystery. Is the origination of the Son an unexplainable mystery?

In the English language the word beget means to become the father of a child and is also used in various ways to designate the beginning of something. The word has the intrinsic meaning of beginning. Therefore, the phrase "eternal begettal" is a virtual oxymoron. To postulate an eternal beginning is to postulate a contradiction. Yet, the concept of the eternal begettal of the Son of God is firmly entrenched in Christian theology.

In the NT Scriptures, *gennao* is the Greek word commonly translated as beget, begat, begotten and born. It means to become the Father of and is used in a variety of ways to designate a beginning. *Gennao* appears 97 times in the NT and by context can be seen to most often refer to becoming the father of someone and where it is not used in this manner it can be seen to show the beginning of something.

In Acts 13, Apostle Paul addresses an assembly of Israelites and Gentiles who had gathered together in a synagogue on the Sabbath. He provides a short history of the Nation of Israel and shows how God brought Jesus to Israel through the descendants of David. He then relates how the people and leadership of Israel did not recognize Jesus for who He was and condemned Him to death. Paul then makes the following statement:

Acts 13:32-33: We tell you the good news: What God promised our fathers he has fulfilled for us, their children, by raising up Jesus. As it is written in the second Psalm, "You are my Son; today I have become your Father" (NIV).

The Greek word translated "become" in this passages is *gennao*. In most English translations of this passage this word is translated "begotten." Paul shows Jesus to be a descendant of David and goes on to apply to Him the OT passage that speaks of God becoming a Father of the Son. We know from our review of OT Scripture, the Father is *YHWH* and is without beginning or end. Trinitarians claim the Son is also *YHWH* and without beginning or end. Yet we see the Father becoming the Father of Jesus at a specific point in time indicating a beginning for the Son. We see more of this in the letter to the Hebrews.

Hebrews 1:5: For to which of the angels did God ever say, "You are my Son; today I have become your Father"? Or again, "I will be his Father, and he will be my Son"?

Hebrews 5:5: So Christ also did not take upon himself the glory of becoming a high priest. But God said to him, "You are my Son; today I have become your Father."

As in Acts 13, the Greek word translated "become" in these passages is *gennao*. In most English translations of this passage this word is translated "begotten." When did God the Father become the Father of Jesus? When was Jesus begotten by the Father?

Matthew 1:20: But after he had considered this, an angel of the Lord appeared to him in a dream and said,

"Joseph son of David, do not be afraid to take Mary home as your wife, because what is conceived (*gennao*) in her is from the Holy Spirit."

Luke 1:35: The angel answered, "The Holy Spirit will come upon you, and the power of the Most High will overshadow you. So the holy one to be born (*gennao*) will be called the Son of God."

Jesus came to be called the Son of God as a result of God the Father bringing about the impregnation of Mary through the power of His Spirit. The Most High God, the Father, played a direct role in facilitating the begettal of Jesus and thus became the Father of Jesus. There is no Scriptural reason to believe God eternally begat the Son. The very concept of eternal begettal is a contradiction in terminology. Begettal means a beginning as opposed to a non beginning which the word eternal implies. To say Christ is eternally begotten is to say Christ has an eternal beginning which is an absolute oxymoron. Matthew makes it clear Jesus had an origin and is not without beginning.

Matthew 1:18: This is how the birth of Jesus Christ came about: His mother Mary was pledged to be married to Joseph, but before they came together, she was found to be with child through the Holy Spirit.

Some will argue Matthew is only referring to the human Jesus in this passage who had an obvious beginning as the "incarnate" Son of God. The passages quoted from Acts and Hebrews, however, make it clear God became the Father of His Son at a specific time in history which negates the concept of eternal co-existence of the Son with the Father and certainly cancels out the concept of eternal begettal. In the second Psalm, in what is considered a prophecy of the coming of Christ, it is clearly shown the Messiah is the anointed of YHWH and not that the anointed is YHWH.

Psalm 2:2, 6-9: The kings of the earth take their stand and the rulers gather together against the LORD (*YHWH*) and against <u>his</u> Anointed One. Verse 6-9: "I (*YHWH*) have installed my King on Zion, my holy hill." I will proclaim the decree of the LORD: He said to me, "You are my Son; today I have become your Father. Ask of me, and I will make the nations your inheritance, the ends of the earth your possession. You will rule them with an iron scepter; you will dash them to pieces like pottery."

The decree of *YHWH* was that He, *YHWH*, would beget a Son and anoint Him to be King. As shown in the quote from Acts 13:32-33, Apostle Paul quotes the second Psalm in showing Jesus became the Son of the Father which is to say He became the Son of *YHWH*. These passages speak strongly against the idea of eternal begettal and against the Son being *YHWH*.

In Isaiah 9:6, in a prophecy about the birth of Christ, the prophet says, "**For to us a child is born, to us a son is given.**" Here the arrival of the Son of God is tied to the Son of God being born at a specific moment in the past.

Among the Dead Sea Scrolls discovered at Qumran in 1947 are documents called "Rule Scrolls." Rule Scroll 1QSa says the Messiah will come when God will have begotten him. The writer of this Scroll apparently understood that the coming of the Christ would take place when God begat Him. There is no reason to believe this writer understood begotten in any way other than a beginning at a point in time and not some process that has been going on eternally.

The Greek word translated into the English word birth in Matthew 1:18, is *gennesis* which is a derivative of *gennao* and means to be begotten or born. Like *gennao*, *gennesis* implies a beginning. In the oldest Greek Manuscripts, the Greek word *genesis* is found in this passage instead of *gennesis*. *Genesis* can mean birth but can also mean creation, beginning and origination. It is interesting that Matthew uses the Greek *genesis* at the start of his Gospel to introduce the ancestry of Jesus.

Matthew 1:1: The book of the generation (Greek genesis) of Jesus Christ, the son of David, the son of Abraham.

Some argue that because Mary was impregnated by the power of God, immortal divine essence of the Father was passed on to Jesus the Son much like mortal human essence is passed on to a baby through human begettal. Scripture says nothing about the begettal of Jesus happening in this manner. Scripture simply reveals Mary becoming pregnant through the power of God. This is all Scripture reveals about this event. We don't know how God did this other than knowing it was accomplished through the power of His Spirit.

Unless we are willing to totally disregard the meaning of words in order to uphold a particular doctrinal position, it should be evident that when the Scriptures speak of the begettal of the Son, they are speaking of His origination at a particular time in history. To look at accounts of the Son's begettal and conclude these accounts are speaking of such begettal being an ongoing event throughout all eternity and continuing to this very day is ludicrous to say the least. One Trinitarian theologian actually stated to me that the concept of eternal begettal is an oxymoron. When asked to explain "eternal begettal," Trinitarians say it is an inexplicable, incomprehensible mystery. Yet, with no evidence for the validity of this "mystery," we are asked to accept it as fact.

Chapter Thirteen

The "I Am" Statements

In the NT Scriptures, the Greek phrase *ego eimi* is translated into English 141 times as "I am" or some equivalent. *Ego eimi* is the first person singular present tense of the verb "to be" in the Greek language. Being in the present tense signifies a present happening or circumstance. *Ego eimi* is a common Greek clause often found with a predicate. The predicate in a sentence tells us what the subject of the sentence is doing.

For example we see Jesus making such statements as "I am (*ego eimi* throughout) the bread of life, "I am the good Shepherd," "I am the light of the world." In these statements the phrase "I am" refers back to the subject Jesus and the rest of the sentence forms the predicate which identifies what it is that Jesus is doing. Such a sentence could be read as, "I, Jesus, am presently the bread of life, the good shepherd or the light of the world." If a predicate is not present, the context must be consulted to determine who or what *ego eimi* is referring to.

Trinitarians argue that where *ego eimi* is associated with Jesus, and there is no predicate connected with this phrase, *ego eimi* identifies Jesus as *YHWH Elohim*, the God of Israel. It is believed Jesus is saying he is God. This perspective is based on what God told Moses to tell the Israelites if they questioned who it was that was sending Moses to them.

Exodus 3:14: God said to Moses, "I AM WHO I AM." This is what you are to say to the Israelites: "I AM has sent me to you."

The common English rendering of "I AM WHO I AM," is translated from the Hebrew words *ehyeh asher ehyeh*. When translated into English, many translators fully capitalize this phrase. Therefore, it is often seen as a proper name for God. This phrase, however, is not capitalized in the Hebrew text of the OT. *Ehyeh asher ehyeh* is often found to be in the future tense in Hebrew texts of Exodus 3:14. Some scholars have noted that in some ancient Hebrew texts of the OT, *Ehyeh* is in the first person singular imperfect tense where the imperfect is used to indicate incomplete but ongoing action. In more modern Hebrew texts, *ehyeh* appears in the future tense.

Because of the grammatical way *ehyeh asher ehyeh* is found in the Hebrew texts, some Hebrew scholars believe *ehyeh asher ehyeh* is better translated "I will be what I will be." Some English translations of Exodus 3:14 render *ehyeh asher ehyeh* as "I will be what I will be" and others footnote this phrase with "I will be what I will be." The word *asher,* as seen in Exodus 3:14, is a pronoun which can mean "that," "who," "which" or "where." The word *ehyeh* is used in a total of 43 places in the Hebrew Scriptures and is usually translated as "I will be." Here are a few examples:

Genesis 26:2-3a: The LORD appeared to Isaac and said, "Do not go down to Egypt; live in the land where I tell you to live. Stay in this land for a while, and I will be (*ehyeh*) with you and will bless you."

Exodus 3:12a: And God said, "I will be (*ehyeh*) with you."

Because *ehyeh* is most often used in the Hebrew Scriptures to indicate a future action, some Hebrew scholars believe *ehyeh asher ehyeh* is not intended as a name for God but identifies God as the one who will be with Israel in fulfilling His covenant promises to Abraham, Isaac and Jacob. *Ehyeh asher ehyeh* is seen more as a title for God, describing how God will relate to Israel, than it being a name for God. The name whereby God identifies Himself and whereby He wants Israel to remember Him is found in Exodus 3:15.

Exodus 3:15: God also said to Moses, "Say to the Israelites, `The LORD, (*YHWH*) the God (*Elohim*) of your fathers--the God of Abraham, the God of Isaac and the God of Jacob--has sent me to you.' This is my name forever, the name by which I am to be remembered from generation to generation.

Isaiah 42:8: I am the LORD; (*YHWH*) <u>that is my name</u>! I will not give my glory to another or my praise to idols.

In Exodus 3:13, Moses asks God by what name He is to be identified before Israel. God begins His answer by saying *ehyeh asher ehyeh* and proceeds to tell Moses it is *ehyeh* who is sending him to Israel. God then proceeds to tell Moses it is the name *YHWH* whereby He is to be identified to Israel. *YHWH* is used 6,823 times in the OT to reference God. *YHWH* is the name God wants Moses to use in identifying Himself to Israel.

YHWH is the one and only proper or personal name of God in the Hebrew Scriptures. All others descriptions or designations ascribed to *YHWH* are titles that define certain aspects of who *YHWH* is and what He does.

Both *YHWH* and *ehyeh* are derived from the same verbal root *hayah*. As discussed in Chapter Three, the precise meaning of *hayah* is much debated. It appears to mean "to be" or "become." *YHWH* came to be defined as the ever living or ever becoming one. Because *hayah* is the root word for both *ehyeh* and *YHWH* and appears to mean "to be" or "become," *ehyeh asher ehyeh* and *YHWH* are often seen as meaning the same thing. The Greek (Septuagint) rendering of the Hebrew in Exodus 3:14 is *ego eimi ho on* which in English means "I am the being" or "I am the one being." *Ego eimi* means "I am" and *ho on* means the being. *Ho on* is used to translate the third appearance of *ehyeh* at the end of verse 14 as "the being." Most English translations render the third appearance of *ehyeh* in Exodus 3:14 as "I AM."

It is apparent the translators of the Hebrew into the Greek saw this passage as God telling Moses to tell the Israelites that He as "the one being" is sending Moses to them. Nowhere in the "I am" statements associated with Jesus is the Greek *ho on* attached to *ego eimi* to signify Jesus was identifying Himself as "the being" or the "one being" who spoke to Moses out of the burning bush. As already discussed, *ehyeh asher ehyeh* is better translated as "I will be what I will be" and *ehyeh*, when used by itself, is frequently translated as "I will be with you." *Ego eimi* is nowhere used in the NT to mean "I will be what I will be" or "I will be with you." *Ego eimi* is translated as "I am" and can be seen to be associated with a person who is explicitly or implicitly identified somewhere within the context of where *ego eimi* appears. It is in this manner *ego eimi* is used throughout the NT. When seen in association with Jesus, *ego eimi* identifies Him as the man Jesus or the Christ. Nowhere is *ego eimi* seen to identify Jesus as *YHWH*.

Both *ehyeh* and *ego eimi* are verb forms meaning "to be" which means they point to the existence of something or someone. Context must determine who or what that something or someone is. In the case of Exodus 3:12, the context clearly shows it is *YHWH* who is being referred to. Whether *ehyeh asher ehyeh* is to be understood as God saying He will be with Moses and Israel or as identifying God as the self existent Being, e*hyeh asher ehyeh* and *ehyeh* both point to *YHWH* as the subject of the passage under consideration. In the NT, *ego eimi* is a Greek "to be" verb which points to the subject associated with it as seen by direct reference or by context.

Ego eimi is used in the NT to identify Paul, Peter, John the Baptist and others. It is used to identify Jesus dozens of times. When Jesus walked on the water toward the boat the disciples were in and they expressed great fear at what they were seeing, Jesus said, **"It is I; (ego eimi) don't be afraid" (John 6:20)**. Jesus is not identifying Himself as *YHWH* but simply telling His disciples it was He, Jesus. Shortly before His crucifixion, Jesus told the Jews, **"You will look for me, but you will not find me; and where I am, (*ego eimi*) you cannot come" (John 7:34)**. Here Jesus uses "I am" to identify Himself as being in a place they won't find Him. When Jesus was speaking to the Samaritan women and she spoke of the coming Messiah, Jesus said **"I who speak to you am (*ego eimi*) he" (John 4:26)**. Here Jesus is simply saying He is the Messiah. When Jesus spoke to Paul on the road to Damascus, He said **"I am (*ego eimi*) Jesus, whom you are persecuting," (Acts 9:5)**. *Ego eimi* is used dozens of times to either explicitly or implicitly identify Jesus as being Jesus.

Sometimes translators add "he" to clarify who **ego eimi** is referring to, as seen in John 4:26 above and in John 13:19 below. Some translations, such as the NIV, insert phrases such as "the one I claim to be." Those who believe Jesus claimed to be *YHWH* believe the NIV supports that perspective.

John 13:19: I am telling you now before it happens, so that when it does happen you will believe that I am (*ego eimi*) He.

John 8:24 Jesus says: I told you that you would die in your sins; if you do not believe that I am (*ego eimi*) [the one I claim to be], you will indeed die in your sins.

John 8:28: So Jesus said, "When you have lifted up the Son of Man, then you will know that I am (*ego eimi*) [the one I claim to be] and that I do nothing on my own but speak just what the Father has taught me.

Who is the "He" and the one Jesus claimed to be? Jesus claimed to be the promised Messiah and the Son of God. Nowhere does Jesus claim to be *YHWH* or *Elohim*. As seen above, when the Samaritan women spoke of the Messiah coming, Jesus identified Himself to her as that Messiah. When

Peter was asked by Jesus who he thought Jesus was, Peter answered and Jesus responded in the following manner:

Matthew 16:16-17: "You are the Christ, the Son of the living God." Jesus replied, "Blessed are you, Simon son of Jonah, for this was not revealed to you by man, but by my Father in heaven."

Jesus confirmed that Peter gave the right answer in identifying who Jesus is. Peter identified Jesus as the Christ (Messiah), Son of the living God. Nowhere in Scripture is Jesus identified as the living God. The few Scriptures that speak of Jesus being God are not teaching Jesus is the Supreme Self-Existent Living Creator God identified as *YHWH* in the OT and as the Father in the NT. Jesus revealed the Father as the one and only God as did Paul and other NT writers. The few NT references to Jesus as God will be discussed as we go along. Now let's look at a passage in John eighteen.

John 18:4-8: Jesus, knowing all that was going to happen to him, went out and asked them, "Who is it you want?" "Jesus of Nazareth," they replied. "I am (*ego eimi*) he," Jesus said. (And Judas the traitor was standing there with them.) When Jesus said, "I am (*ego eimi*) he," they drew back and fell to the ground. Again he asked them, "Who is it you want?" And they said, "Jesus of Nazareth." "I told you that I am (*ego eimi*) he," Jesus answered. "If you are looking for me, then let these men go."

Some claim that when those coming to arrest Jesus drew back and fell to the ground, they did so because Jesus was representing Himself as the *ehyeh asher ehyeh* of Exodus 3:14 when He answered "I am" (*ego eimi*). It is believed those arresting Jesus were stunned by the power of His proclamation of being *YHWH*. The overall context of this passage, however, does not support such a conclusion. Jesus asked "Who is it you want?" They said "Jesus of Nazareth." Jesus said "I

172

am." The translators add the word "he" to support the intended meaning of *ego eimi*. Jesus asked them a second time who they were looking for and He responded by saying "I told you that I am (*ego eimi*) he so if you are looking for me let these other men go."

It must be kept in mind that soldiers had come to arrest Jesus and Jesus told them He was the one they were looking for. They probably drew back and fell to the ground simply in response to Jesus offering Himself to them without resistance, something they probably weren't use to. The recorded interaction between Jesus and the crowd after His initial identification of Himself makes it evident *ego eimi* is not being used to identify Jesus as *YHWH*. In response to the second inquiry by the arresters, Jesus is seen as virtually saying "I have already told you I am the one you are looking for so let's get on with it." Furthermore, as already discussed, *ego eimi* does not match the Hebrew *ehyeh asher ehyeh* in meaning or the Greek translation of e*hyeh asher ehyeh* which is *ego eimi ho on* and in English means "I am the being" or "I am the one being." Jesus was not saying "I am the being" or "I am the one being." He said "I am" which can be seen by context to mean Jesus was identifying Himself as the "Jesus of Nazareth" His arresters were looking for.

Some have looked at Mark 13:6 and concluded Jesus is identifying Himself as the e*hyeh asher ehyeh* of Exodus 3:12. When Mark 13:6 is compared with Matthew's account of Jesus' same statement, it is clear He is identifying Himself as the Christ. Identifying Himself as the Christ is to identify Himself as the <u>anointed</u> of God and not that He <u>is</u> God.

Mark 13:6: Many will come in my name, claiming, `I am he,' (*ego eimi*) and will deceive many.

Matthew 24:5: For many will come in my name, claiming, `I am (*ego eimi*) the Christ,' and will deceive many.

Not only is it evident from Matthew 24:5 that Jesus is saying "I am" in reference to Himself as the Christ, it should be apparent that many coming and claiming to be the Christ does not mean many would come and claim to be *YHWH*. Therefore, Jesus' use of "I am" in this passage does not identify Jesus as *YHWH*. Now let's look at a passage that is often touted as proving Jesus is *YHWH*.

John 8:58: "I tell you the truth," Jesus answered, "before Abraham was born, I am!" (*ego eimi*).

After Jesus made this statement, it is recorded the Jews tried to stone Him. It is often concluded this attempted stoning took place because Jesus identified Himself as *YHWH* by using the phrase "I am" (*ego eimi*). Is Jesus identifying Himself as *YHWH* in this passage and is this why the Jews tried to stone Him?

A careful reading of John chapter eight shows the Jews placing great stock in their being descendants of Abraham. Jesus tells them this means nothing in view of the way they were behaving toward Him. Jesus proceeds to make statements that make him out to be greater than Abraham. The Jews recoil at this and actually accuse Jesus of having a demon. When Jesus said, **"Your father Abraham rejoiced at the thought of seeing my day; he saw it and was glad" (John 8:56)**, it incensed the Jews even more. Jesus saying "before Abraham was born I am" was the last straw. The Jews couldn't take any more of Jesus promoting Himself as being superior to Abraham and at that point they try to stone Him. In reading John 8 you can virtually feel the tension building up between Jesus and the Jews leading to the attempted stoning.

As already discussed, *ego eimi* is a verb form meaning "to be." It virtually means to exist in some manner as opposed to not existing. When *ego eimi* is used in a narrative, it attests to the existence of the person, place or thing this phrase points to. Therefore, when Jesus says before Abraham was born "I am," He is saying He existed before Abraham was born. Was Jesus saying He literally existed before Abraham was born and, if so, is He saying He existed as *YHWH* before Abraham was born. Is Jesus identifying Himself as *YHWH*? If Jesus is saying He is *YHWH* in this passage, He is contradicting statements He made about His Father being the one and only true God (*YHWH*) and similar statements made by Paul and John (John 17:3. 5:43-44, Romans 16:25-27, 1 Corinthians 8:6, Ephesians 4:4-6, 1 Timothy 2:5, 1 John 5:20).

Jesus is not contradicting Himself and neither is He saying He literally existed before Abraham was born. Jesus is speaking proleptically. Proleptic language speaks of things as already existing though they have not yet come to actually exist. This kind of language is commonly found in the Biblical Scriptures.

For example, the Scriptures indicate Jesus was slain from the time of the earth's creation even though He wasn't actually crucified until the first century A.D. (Revelation 13:8). Paul speaks of the grace that was given to us in Christ Jesus before the beginning of time (2 Timothy 1:9). This grace was not made effective, however, until the Christ event actually occurred. Jesus speaks of the Kingdom having been prepared for us since the creation of the world (Matthew 25:34). The Kingdom wasn't actually available to enter into until the Christ event. Paul told the Ephesian Christians that God "chose us in him before the creation of the world to be holy and blameless in his sight" (Ephesians 1:4). This didn't come to fruition until the first century.

A review of the NT Scripture shows the sacrifice of Christ, salvation, establishment of the Kingdom and other events were in the purpose of God from early on but first became manifest through Christ who, Himself, was in the purpose of God and became manifest in the first century as the begotten Son of God. Paul, in addressing Christians of His day, says in **Ephesians**

David A Kroll

2:6, "God raised us up with Christ and seated us with him in the heavenly places in Christ Jesus." Christians were proleptically seated in heavenly places. This is anticipatory language which is found throughout Scripture. Christ is using this kind of rhetorical mechanism when saying He pre-existed Abraham. In view of what we have discussed to this point, it is highly problematical to conclude Jesus pre-existed His human birth. To maintain consistency in the Scriptures, it is much more reasonable to conclude Jesus was in the purpose of God from early on and this purpose was revealed to Abraham and in this manner Jesus could say He existed before Abraham.

Anglican Bishop Samuel Parker (1640-1687) wrote in 1667, *"It was a proverbial form of speech among the Jews to express matters of great moment, resolved upon only in the divine decree, as they were really existing. Thus they say that the Messiah is more ancient than the sun and the Mosaic order older than the world, not as if they understood them really as such, but only to express their absolute usefulness and necessity... The glory which Jesus prayed for in John 17:5... was that honor with which God had from eternity designed to dignify the Messiah."*

Grammarians who have studied John 8:58 find that in the Greek construction of this verse the phrase *ego eimi* is in the perfect indicative tense which expresses a past action that is still going on. Therefore, the actual meaning of this passage is that "before Abraham came to be I have been." The grammatical construction of this passage gives the sense that *ego eimi* covers the entire period from some time before Abraham to the time Jesus was speaking to Jews standing before Him. Various translations render this passage with this understanding of the Greek grammar. For example, one Greek scholar, K. L. McKay in his *A New Syntax of the Verb in the New Testament Greek*, renders this passage as "I have been in existence since before Abraham was born." This rendering portrays the sense of continuing existence from before Abraham up to and including the present. Some translations, such as the 1971 edition of the *New American Standard Bible,* footnote "I AM" with (or, "I have been.").

We know Jesus was in the purpose of His Father God from early on and in that respect was in existence before Abraham was born. The key to understanding Jesus' statement in John 8:58 is John 8:56.

John 8:56: Your father Abraham rejoiced at the thought of seeing my day; he saw it and was glad.

This is a proleptic statement. Abraham is portrayed as seeing in advance the day of Christ. Abraham saw the day of Christ in the promises made to him at the time he was told to leave his homeland and travel to the land of Canaan. John writes that Abraham rejoiced <u>at the thought</u> of seeing the day of Jesus. This tells us Abraham didn't literally see Jesus or that Jesus literally existed in Abraham's day. Abraham saw Jesus in thought in being given the Gospel in advance.

Galatians 3:8: The Scripture foresaw that God would justify the Gentiles by faith, and announced the gospel in advance to Abraham: "All nations will be blessed through you."

Galatians 3:16: The promises were spoken to Abraham and to his seed. The Scripture does not say "and to seeds," meaning many people, but "and to your seed," meaning one person, who is Christ.

Abraham saw the day of Christ in advance because God revealed to Abraham that through his seed (Christ) all nations would be blessed. When Abraham was willing to sacrifice his son, he was told that because he was willing to do this, all nations would be blessed through his offspring (Genesis 22:15-18). Jesus is that one seed of Abraham that became the Christ through whom salvation from God the Father was facilitated. It was in the plan of *YHWH* to provide a human sacrifice for sin from the time of the creation of the world (Revelation 13:8) and actually from before the creation of the world (1 Peter 1:18-20). This plan of *YHWH's* wasn't actuated until the appearing of Christ in the first century as Peter makes clear.

1 Peter 1:18-20: For you know that it was not with perishable things such as silver or gold that you were redeemed from the empty way of life handed down to you from your forefathers, but with the precious blood of Christ, a lamb without blemish or defect. He was chosen before the creation of the world, but was revealed in these last times for your sake.

Jesus wasn't actually crucified until the end of His ministry. In the purpose of God, however, Christ was as good as crucified from the time God determined to engender a Son who would become the Savior of the world. Christ was before Abraham in the purpose of God and Abraham was made privy to God's plan and able to see the day of Christ in advance and rejoice over it.

The "I am" statement in John 8:58 is not Jesus announcing to the Jews He is *YHWH*. Jesus is saying "I am He." "I am the one." I am the one who was prophesied to come. I am the promised Messiah who was in the purpose of *YHWH* before Abraham was born and Abraham was allowed to see my day. Israel was not expecting *YHWH* as the prophesied Messiah. There is nothing in the prophetic writings that would lead Israel to believe the prophesied Messiah would be God in the flesh. What they did see in the prophetic writings was that God would raise up a prophet from among their brothers who would be like Moses. In Acts, Peter shows this prophet was Christ Jesus.

Deuteronomy 18:15: The LORD (*YHWH*) your God will raise up for you a prophet like me from among your own brothers. You must listen to him.

Acts 3:22: For Moses said, `The Lord your God will raise up for you a prophet like me from among your own people; you must listen to everything he tells you.

The Jews didn't believe Jesus was the prophet Moses wrote about. They looked upon Jesus as an impostor. When Jesus kept insisting He was the promised Messiah and how this made Him greater than Abraham, they became incensed to the point of wanting to stone Him. To postulate John 8:58 shows Jesus to be *YHWH* contradicts Jesus' own statements about His Father being the one and only true God. It contradicts Paul and John's statements about the Father being the one and only God. It contradicts the dozens of Scriptural statements which show *YHWH* to be the God of Jesus.

In Deuteronomy 32:39, *YHWH* is quoted as saying, "I am He." There are similar statements found in Isaiah 41:4, 43:10, 13; 46:4, 48:12 and 52:6. In these passages, "I am He" is translated from the Hebrew *ani eua* and in the Septuagint, the Greek words *ego eimi* are used to translate the Hebrew *ani eua* into English. Since *the* Greek words *ego eimi* are used to translate the "I am" statements found in these Hebrew passages and are also found in the NT narrative in association with Christ saying "I am," some theologians believe Jesus is identified with the *YHWH* of the Deuteronomy and Isaiah passages.

As covered above, *ego eimi* is a Greek "to be" verb which points to the subject associated with it. In the NT, when associated with Jesus, it simply identifies Jesus as the one being referred to in relation to some activity. The same is true of its usage in the Septuagint version of the OT. In **Deuteronomy 32:39**, *YHWH* says, **"See now that I, even I, am he, and there is no god with me" (KJV).** *YHWH* is simply saying He is the one God and there is no other. This passage goes on to quote *YHWH* as citing His various attributes.

David A Kroll

There simply is no Scriptural reason to believe the "I am" statements associated with Jesus in the NT correlate with the "I am" statements associated with *YHWH* in the OT passages in such manner as to identify Jesus as *YHWH*. "I am" statements associated with *YHWH*, either implicitly or explicitly identify *YHWH* as the one and only God. "I am" statements associated with Jesus, either implicitly or explicitly identify Jesus as the Christ of *YHWH*, the promised Messiah to Israel.

Chapter Fourteen

Did Jesus claim to be God?

John 10:30-36: "I and the Father are one." Again the Jews picked up stones to stone him, but Jesus said to them, "I have shown you many great miracles from the Father. For which of these do you stone me?" "We are not stoning you for any of these," replied the Jews, "but for blasphemy, because you, a mere man, claim to be God." Jesus answered them, "Is it not written in your Law, `I have said you are gods'? If he called them `gods,' to whom the word of God came--and the Scripture cannot be broken-- what about the one whom the Father set apart as his very own and sent into the world? Why then do you accuse me of blasphemy because I said, `I am God's Son'?

Trinitarians see a double proof in this passage that Jesus is God. First Jesus says "I and the Father are one." Then the religious leaders claim Jesus is blaspheming because He claims to be God. It is assumed that for Jesus and the Father to be one it must mean Jesus is in a Trinitarian relationship with God and therefore is God. It is also assumed that because the religious leaders said Jesus claimed to be God He must be God.

When Jesus says "I and the Father are one" He is not talking about being God. In Christ's prayer to the Father shortly before His crucifixion, He said this: **"I have given them (the Apostles) the glory that you gave me, that they may be one as we are one" (John 17:22)**. The Apostles becoming one with each other would not make them one Being. If Christ meant for them to become one with the Father as He was, it certainly didn't mean they became God. Christ's statement about being one with the Father has nothing to do with identifying Himself as God but simply shows how He was in total harmony with the Father in all things. In referring to the Holy Spirit that He would send after His ascension, Christ said: **"On that day you will realize that I am in my Father, and you are in me, and I am in you" (John 14:20)**. This is a statement of relationship which has nothing to do with identification of Being. Christ didn't mean the Apostles would become God by them being in Him and He in them as He is in the Father. Christ was showing that through the Holy Spirit they could be one in purpose just as He and the Father are.

John 14:9c-11a: Anyone who has seen me has seen the Father....Don't you believe that I am in the Father, and that the Father is in me? The words I say to you are not just my own. Rather, it is the Father, living in me, who is doing his work. Believe me when I say that I am in the Father and the Father is in me.

Jesus is not saying that if you see Him you see the Father in the sense that Jesus and the Father are of identical substance of Being. Jesus is not talking about substance of Being but of being in spiritual unity with the Father. The Father lives in Christ through His Spirit and that same Spirit that lives in Christ can live in us as the Scriptures clearly show.

Did Jesus claim to be God as accused by the Jews as seen in the John 10 passage? It should be evident from how Jesus responded to this accusation of claiming to be God that He wasn't claiming to be the one and only Supreme, Creator God but that He was god in the same sense as men of authority and power spoken of in the OT. Jesus appears to refer to a statement found in Psalm 82.

Psalm 82:1-7: God (*Elohim*) presides in the great assembly; he gives judgment among the "gods": (*elohim*) "How long will you defend the unjust and show partiality to the wicked? Selah. Defend the cause of the weak and

fatherless; maintain the rights of the poor and oppressed. Rescue the weak and needy; deliver them from the hand of the wicked. "They know nothing, they understand nothing. They walk about in darkness; all the foundations of the earth are shaken. "<u>I said, `You are "gods</u>"; (*elohim*) you are all sons of the Most High.' But you will die like mere men; you will fall like every other ruler.

Here God (*Elohim*) is speaking to an assembly of gods (*elohim*) who are seen as appointed by Him to administer justice but have failed to do so. The second occurrence of *elohim* is followed by a plural predicate "you" thus signifying a plurality of Beings called "gods" who are being addressed. Jesus, in John 10, identifies these "gods" as those to whom the word (*logos*) of God came. The word or speech of God is seen as given to these Beings called "gods." The context of Psalm 82 shows these "gods" are of the human realm as human conditions such as weakness, being fatherless and needy and needing deliverance from the wicked is what God is discussing with these "gods." This passage is referring to human leaders, in positions of rulership, power and authority, failing to properly fulfill their responsibilities. God tells them that, even though they have been granted powers of rulership, they will die like every other ruler, which shows their humanity. Jesus is virtually comparing Himself to this type of god. He is saying that He too has been granted power and authority and has been sent by God. Thus, Jesus distinguishes Himself as a Son of the Most High God, just as these human leaders whom God was addressing as "gods" were seen as sons of the Most High God.

While it is true that Jesus was a unique Son of the Most High God because of His direct begettal by the Spirit of God, nowhere do the Scriptures show this unique status to mean Jesus is the Most High God in the Person of God the Son. The phrase God the Son is not found in Scripture. It is always the Son of God. When the Jews accused Jesus of claiming to be God, He answers their accusation by quoting from Psalm 82.

He finishes His response to the Jews, not by saying He is God but by asking **"Why then do you accuse me of blasphemy because I said, `I am <u>God's Son</u>'?"** Jesus identifies Himself as God's Son, not as God.

As discussed earlier, *elohim* is used throughout the OT in reference to the creator God as well as to designate human rulers and other appointees of the creator God. By answering His accusers as He did, he is virtually saying He is a god in the same sense as the "gods" referred to in the OT who are also called sons of the Most High. Jesus is saying that just as God sent rulers to represent His interests in OT times, God has now sent Him, the promised Messiah as His directly begotten Son. Jesus is not saying He is God as the Most High God is God. He is saying He is a Son of the Most High God which makes Him an agent of the Most High God just as the gods mentioned in Psalm 82. Jesus' use of Psalm 82 in His defense speaks volumes as to who He believed He was in relationship to the one true God.

In Chapter Twelve we discussed the Greek word *gennao* and saw how it means to become the Father of and is used in a variety of ways to designate a beginning. We saw how this word is used in association with the birth of Jesus and identifies Jesus as the begotten of the Father. There is another Greek word, *monogenes*, which is translated into English as begotten in the KJV version and several other English translations. Scholarship has shown this word is better translated as "only," "one and only," or "unique in kind" and is so translated in the NIV and other more modern translations. There are four passages in the Gospel of John and one in his first letter that give witness to Jesus being the one and only unique Son of God. Here are these passages as seen in the NIV.

John 1:14: The Word became flesh and made his dwelling among us. We have seen his glory, the glory of the One and Only, who came from the Father, full of grace and truth.

John 1:18: No one has ever seen God, but God the One and Only, who is at the Father's side, has made him known. (The implication that Jesus is God in this translation is discussed in Chapter Fourteen)

John 3:16: "For God so loved the world that he gave his one and only Son, that whoever believes in him shall not perish but have eternal life.

John 3:18: Whoever believes in him is not condemned, but whoever does not believe stands condemned already because he has not believed in the name of God's one and only Son.

1 John 4:9: This is how God showed his love among us: He sent his one and only Son into the world that we might live through him.

If you read the above passages from a Trinitarian mindset, you end up with rather peculiar phraseology. If God is Father, Son and Spirit, John 3:16 would have to read "For Father, Son and Spirit gave His only Son." John 3:18 would read: "in the name of Father, Son and Spirit's one and only Son." 1 John 4:9 would read: "This is how Father, Son and Spirit showed His love among us: He sent his one and only Son." Pronouns such as "His" and "He" would have to apply to Father, Son and Spirit as the single Being God. Yet in John 1:14 and 18, John appears to identify God as Father and identity Father as God. John gives no hint of seeing God as Father, Son and Spirit. It should be apparent when John uses the word God in his writings; he means the Father and not Father, Son and Spirit. For John, God is the Father and the Father is God. There is no scriptural reason to believe John ever sees Jesus as being God as God is God. John, as is true with all NT writers, sees Jesus as the anointed of God, God's Christ to fulfill the promises made to Abraham, Isaac and Jacob.

Jesus is the one and only, one of a kind unique Son of God because he is the only son of God directly begotten by God in the womb of a human mother. Jesus is the one and only unique Son of God because He had a full measure of God's Spirit from birth and was ordained to fulfill a special mission. Jesus is the one and only unique Son of God because He took our sins upon Himself and willingly suffered the pain and disgrace of crucifixion so we could have the death penalty for sin removed and be granted eternal life. Jesus is the unique Son of God because He was the first human resurrected to eternal life. Jesus was the first human to experience moving from mortality to immortality. Because of this, we also can experience this same transformation and become sons of God.

Jesus was dead. He went to the grave as a mortal human being. God the Father, who is the source of all life, resurrected Jesus and granted Him eternal life. Death could not hold Jesus because Jesus never sinned. He died as a sacrifice for our sins and was resurrected to eternal life and given great glory and honor because of what He accomplished as God's agent to facilitate our salvation.

Acts 2:24: But God raised him from the dead, freeing him from the agony of death, because it was impossible for death to keep its hold on him.

Romans 6:9-11: For we know that since Christ was raised from the dead, he cannot die again; death no longer has mastery over him. The death he died, he died to sin once for all; but the life he lives, he lives to God. In the same way, count yourselves dead to sin but alive to God in Christ Jesus.

Galatians 1:1: Paul, an apostle--sent not from men nor by man, but by Jesus Christ and God the Father, who raised him from the dead--

Romans 8:11: And if the Spirit of him who raised Jesus from the dead is living in you, he who raised Christ from the dead will also give life to your mortal bodies through his Spirit, who lives in you.

These Scriptures clearly show it is the Spirit of God the Father that facilitated Jesus' resurrection to life and it is this same Spirit that facilitates our resurrection to life. It is instructive that Paul in the Romans 6:9-11 passage writes that Jesus "died to sin once for all; but the life he lives, he lives to God." Paul is seeing Jesus in His glorified state living His life to God. Even if one concludes by God Paul means the Father, we see Jesus, in his resurrected and glorified state continuing to be subservient to God the Father. This is just one more of the dozens of Scriptures I could reference that show Jesus in His glorified state is not ontologically one with the Father and is not God as God is God as the Creeds proclaim.

Some argue that because Jesus, in referring to His resurrection, said **"Destroy this temple, and I will raise it again in three days" (John 2:19)**, He was saying He resurrected Himself and is therefore God as the Father is God. The overwhelming testimony of Scripture, however, makes it clear it was through the power of God the Father Jesus was resurrected. Therefore, it must be concluded that in John 2:19, Jesus was simply saying He would be resurrected in three days and not that He was resurrecting Himself.

The Scriptures speak of Jesus being the first born from the dead. When the Scriptures speak of Jesus being the first born from the dead, they are speaking of Him being the first to be raised from the dead to never die again. Others, such as Lazarus, had been physically resurrected only to die again. Jesus' resurrection was a resurrection to eternal life. Jesus was born to eternal life.

Colossians 1:18: And he (Jesus) is the head of the body, the church; he is the beginning and <u>the firstborn from among the dead</u>, so that in everything he might have the supremacy.

Revelation 1:5: and from Jesus Christ, who is the faithful witness, <u>the firstborn from the dead</u> ...

1 Corinthians 15:20: But Christ has indeed been raised from the dead, <u>the firstfruits of those who have fallen asleep.</u>

Paul shows Christ to be the firstborn among many brothers thus signifying He is the first in a line of many others who will be born to eternal life.

Romans 8:29: For those God foreknew he also predestined to be conformed to the likeness (image) of his Son, that he might be the firstborn among many brothers.

Jesus was the first to be born to eternal life and in so doing facilitated our being born to eternal life. Being born to eternal life involves becoming a new creation. Through resurrection to eternal life, Jesus began the process of facilitating a new creation. The whole purpose of the Christ event was to facilitate reconciliation of humanity with God.

2 Corinthians 5:17-19: Therefore, if anyone is in Christ, he is a new creation; the old has gone, the new has come! All this is from God, who reconciled us to himself through Christ and gave us the ministry of reconciliation: that God was reconciling the world to himself in Christ, not counting men's sins against them. And he has committed to us the message of reconciliation.

Jesus began the process of establishing a new creation by being born to eternal life and thus facilitating our birth to eternal life as well. In Christ we are a new creation in so much that we have passed from death unto life and become sons of God.

It is evident from the Scriptures that Jesus is not God as God is God and never claimed to be God as God is God. Jesus is the unique Son of God because of His direct begettal by God the Father and the unique purpose for which He was born. Jesus died and was resurrected and became the first human to be born to eternal life. As Paul wrote, Jesus is the firstborn of many brothers. Throughout Scripture, Jesus is identified as the Son of God and never as God the Son. The few references to Jesus as God in the NT are references to being god in the same sense as seen in Psalm 82. We will further explore these references as we continue to move through this material.

Is Jesus Divine?

The Greek word *thios* is translated "divine" several times in the NT in association with God the Father. The Greek *thios* implies a supernatural, someone who exceeds the bounds of being human. *Thios* is also use to define those in close association to the Divine as seen in some ancient literature. Peter uses this word in relation to the power and nature of God in 2 Peter 1:3. We know it is God the Father who is referenced by Peter because he speaks of divinity in association with Him who has called us and we know from other Scriptures it is the Father who calls us.

2 Peter 1:3: His divine (*thios*) power has given us everything we need for life and godliness through our knowledge of him who called us by his own glory and goodness.

Paul uses *thios* in Acts 17:29 to show the contrast between man-made gods and the one true God. The context of Acts 17 shows Paul speaking of the Father as Divine Being. In verse 31 Paul speaks of God judging the world through Jesus whom He has raised from the dead, thus identifying the Father as the Divine Being he is talking about.

Acts 17:29: Therefore since we are God's offspring, we should not think that the divine being is like gold or silver or stone--an image made by man's design and skill.

Acts 17:31: For he has set a day when he will judge the world with justice by the man he has appointed. He has given proof of this to all men by raising him from the dead.

To be divine is to exceed the bounds of normal humanity and manifest supernatural qualities. It is clear from the Scriptures God the Father is intrinsically divine and the source of all divine qualities. Scripture shows He shares such qualities with humans commensurate with His will. God gave Jesus an abundance of His divine qualities as His anointed agent. Upon completion of His earthly mission and ascension to His God and Father, His God and Father glorified Him with still greater divine qualities. Therefore, Jesus can certainly be viewed as divine. Jesus can also be viewed as *elohim* (god) in the same sense He compared Himself to the gods (small g) spoken of in the OT. Words such as *elohim, theos, kurios and thios* do not intrinsically mean the One and Only Supreme God as these words are applied to Beings of lesser status to whom power and authority is granted.

Jesus is one unto whom great power and authority has been granted. This does not equate Jesus with the one and only Most High Supreme God who is the source of all power and authority. There is only one God who reflects that identification and who can be called the true God. Jesus confirmed this identification when He said His Father was the one and only true God. Paul and John did the same as previously discussed.

I personally do not hesitate to relate to Jesus as divine and as god as long as I maintain the understanding that He is not the One and Only Supreme Divinity, the Most High Creator God who is the God and Father of all reality including the reality that is Jesus.

Chapter Fifteen

Colossians, Chapter One

Certain comments made by Apostle Paul in chapter one of his letter to the Colossian Church is often seen as evidence Jesus is God as the Father is God.

Apostle Paul begins his letter to the Colossian Church by introducing himself as an Apostle of Christ Jesus by the will of God. Paul identifies God as the God and Father of Jesus (Colossians 1:3). In verses twelve and thirteen, Paul exhorts the Colossians to give thanks to the Father who has qualified them to share in the inheritance of the saints in the kingdom of light by having rescued them from the dominion of darkness and bringing them into the kingdom of the Son he loves. As is true throughout Paul's writings, Paul identifies God the Father as the God of Jesus. Paul goes on to show how Jesus reflects God.

Colossians 1:15: He is the image of the invisible God, the firstborn over all creation.

The Greek word translated image in this passage is *eikon*. It means image, likeness and representation. It is argued that because Jesus is seen as being in the image of God He must be God. Is being in the image of something or someone equal to being that something or someone? In all three gospels is the account of Christ asking whose image (same Greek word) is on the coin that was handed to Him. It was the image of Emperor Caesar. The coin represented Caesar as the imperial ruler of Rome. The coin wasn't Caesar but represented Caesar. Jesus being in the image of God doesn't mean Jesus was God. Scripture reveals Jesus was the perfect representative of the character of the one and only God and not that Jesus is the one and only God.

It should also be noted that Paul tells the Roman Christians to be conformed to the image (*eikon*) of Jesus (Romans 8:29). If Jesus is God, then being conformed to the image of Jesus is to be conformed to the image of God and if being in the image of God is being God then we are as much God as Jesus is God. This, however, is not the case for us or is it the case for Jesus.

The NIV shows Paul writing that Jesus is "the firstborn over all creation." The NET Bible translates this passage in the same manner and notes that the genitive construction of this passage is a genitive of subordination and therefore should be translated as "over all creation." The theology being advanced in these translations is that Jesus is before creation of all things and He has supremacy over all creation and all creation is subordinate to Him. Is this what Paul is saying in this passage?

Most other English versions translate Colossians 1:15 as "first born of all creation." The Greek language does not have a preposition "of." In this passage, the phrase "of all creation" is in a genitive form where the word "of" is implied. Greek scholar Jason Beduhn flatly states that "over" in no way can be derived from the Greek in this phrase and that the NIV translators make their translation on the basis of doctrine rather than language (Beduhn: *Truth In Translation,* page 81).

Paul writes Jesus is the firstborn of all creation. Scholarship shows that the Greek word translated "firstborn" can refer to a first born child, or it can refer to one who is preeminent in rank. What creation is Jesus the first born of and preeminent in rank over? Is it the physical universe or is it the new creation of spiritual transformation that Jesus began by God raising Him from the dead?

Colossians 1:18: And he is the head of the body, the church; he is the beginning and the firstborn from among the dead, so that in everything he might have the supremacy.

We have seen that because Jesus is the firstborn from the dead, we can also be born from the dead and made a new creation in Christ. It should be evident that the creation Jesus is seen as firstborn of is the new creation involving our reconciliation to the Father through Jesus' death and resurrection. In the Revelation Jesus speaks of Himself as being the beginning of the creation of God.

Revelation 3:14: And unto the angel of the church of the Laodiceans write; these things saith the Amen, the faithful and true witness, the beginning of the creation of God; (KJV and most other translations).

The Greek for "beginning" in both Colossians 1:18 and Revelation 3:14 is *arkee*. Greek lexicons show this word means beginning, origin and in some cases ruler. Where this word appears in the NT in conjunction with a genitive expression, which is the way it appears in this passage in Revelation, *arkee* always denotes a beginning or first part of something. In view of what we have seen in the writings of Paul relative to the resurrection of Jesus being associated with our becoming a new creation, it appears Jesus is referring to Himself in the Revelation as the beginning or first part of the new creation God was facilitating for mankind through Christ.

The NIV translated Revelation 3:14 as "the ruler of God's creation." The NET Bible translates it as "the originator of God's creation." "Beginning," however, is the natural expression in view of the Greek genitive grammatical construction found in this passage. The KJV, NKJV, RSV, NAS and most other translations have translated this passage as "the beginning of the creation of God."

In Apostle John's first letter, he speaks of Jesus having been born of God and being the one who keeps others born of God from succumbing to sin.

I John 5:18: We know that anyone born of God does not continue to sin; the one who was born of God keeps him safe, and the evil one cannot harm him.

While the meaning of the phrase "the one born of God" has produced much scholarly debate, it is generally recognized that John is referring to Christ. The NIV has a footnote to this passage that reads, "The one who was born of God. Jesus, the Son of God." The translators recognize it is Jesus who is being referred to as the one born of God who keeps those born of God safe. The RSV actually capitalizes "He," thus showing it as a reference to Jesus. When this passage is seen in the overall Scriptural context of Jesus beginning the process of our spiritual rebirth by He being the first to be granted immortality through His resurrection from the dead, it is not difficult to understand what John is saying.

It is apparent this passage is dealing with spiritual rebirth of the Christian. Jesus became sin for us on the cross and died as a sinner in our stead. Through resurrection Jesus was born to eternal life. We are in the process of being born to eternal life. By Jesus being born to eternal life, He is seen as able to keep those being born safe from the evil one and become a new creation in Christ.

2 Corinthians 5:17: Therefore, if anyone is in Christ, he is <u>a new creation</u>; the old has gone, the new has come!

Galatians 6:15: Neither circumcision nor uncircumcision means anything; what counts is <u>a new creation</u>.

In view of the association seen in Scripture between Jesus being the first to be born from the dead and the new creation that proceeds from that event, we need to see Paul's statement in Colossians 1:16-17 within this context.

Colossians 1:16-17: For by (Greek *ev*) him all things were created: things in heaven and on earth, visible

and invisible, whether thrones or powers or rulers or authorities; all things were created by (ev) him and for him. He is before all things, and in him all things hold together.

The NIV, NET and KJV render the beginning of this passage as "For by him all things were created." The Greek word translated "by" is *ev*. This Greek preposition appears 2,781 times in the NT and is variously translated as in, on, at, with, by and among. Context must determine how it is translated. The context of Colossians chapter one is Christ being the first to be born from the dead and having supremacy in all things. Jesus is repeatedly seen in Scripture as the starting point for establishment of a new creation. In the passage under consideration, Paul is not writing about Jesus being the creator of the physical universe or physical life. This passage is addressing the new creation in Christ that we are invited to participate in. Therefore, this passage should read, "For in him all things were created." This is the translation in the Revised Standard Version, American Standard Version, the New Jerusalem Bible, Concordant Literal New Testament and other translations. Let's look at what Peter wrote:

1 Peter 1:3: Praise be to the God and Father of our Lord Jesus Christ! In his great mercy he has given us new birth into a living hope through the resurrection of Jesus Christ from the dead...

Peter instructs that praise should be directed to the God and Father of Jesus. It is because of the mercy of the God and Father of Jesus we can be born again because the God and Father of Jesus resurrected Him from the dead making Jesus the first fruits of those who slept and the first to be born from the dead to eternal life. Because of this we have opportunity for a new birth as well. This is the central message of the Gospel. This is central to the teaching of Paul, Peter, John and other NT writers. It is in this context we must read Colossians

1:16-17 and realize Paul is not speaking of an incarnated God/man who created the physical universe but is speaking of a human agent of God who died and was resurrected by God to allow for a new creation. This understanding harmonizes with the many Scriptures we have already discussed that identify Jesus, not as God the Son but as the Son of God who through resurrection from the dead became the first born of many brothers (Roman 8:29).

As I have maintained throughout this book, we must look at Scriptures that pertain to the nature of the Father, Son and Spirit within the context of the whole of Scripture. The "all things" created in Jesus (Colossians 1:16-17) is everything connected with the new creation God was and is facilitating through the Christ event. It is in and through Jesus that God is reconciling the world to Himself and making it possible for humanity to be born to eternal life just as Jesus was born to eternal life.

Chapter Sixteen

Philippians, Chapter Two

Philippians 2:5-8: Your attitude should be the same as that of Christ Jesus: Who, being in very nature (Greek *morphe*) God, did not consider equality with God something to be grasped, but made himself nothing (Greek *heauton ekenosen*), taking the very nature (*morphe*) of a servant, being made in human likeness. And being found in appearance as a man, he humbled himself and became obedient to death-- even death on a cross!

It is argued that in Paul saying Jesus is in very nature God, He was of the very essence of God and therefore was God. Some see in this passage the Son emptying Himself of being God in becoming Jesus and returning to being God at the time of His ascension. Several translations render the Greek *heauton ekenosen* as "emptied Himself." For example, the Revised Standard Version translates it this way:

Philippians 2:6-7: who, though he was in the form of God, did not count equality with God a thing to be grasped, but emptied himself, (Greek: *heauton ekenosen*) taking the form of a servant, being born in the likeness of men."

Greek Lexicons show *heauton ekenosen* to mean "to empty or make empty." If Jesus is God, He would be eternal, having neither beginning nor end. How could the Son, if God, empty himself of being God? How could He empty himself of being eternal? The Son could not have emptied himself of being God in order to become the man Jesus. Those who recognize this fact theorize the Son emptied Himself of the glory He eternally had with the Father but did not empty Himself of his deity. It is believed the Son did not give up His divine self but added human nature to His divine nature in becoming the human Jesus. Therefore, Jesus is seen as totally divine and totally human, the "God/man." It is believed when Jesus died, his humanity died but His deity did not die as it isn't possible for an eternally existing God to die. It is believed when Jesus was resurrected He was resurrected as the fully human and fully God Being He was believed to be before the crucifixion.

Here is the problem with this perspective. Scripture teaches the wages of sin is death. Jesus took our sin upon Himself and suffered the death penalty for us. Sin separates one from God. The account of the crucifixion reveals Christ, in taking our sin upon Himself, became separated from God. The Son of God died. He was literally dead for three days and three nights. Jesus plainly says He was dead (Revelation 1:18). Nowhere does Scripture teach the Son of God died only physically. Scripture identifies Jesus dying in totality as the sacrifice for sin.

While it may be possible for God to be both God and man at the same time, this concept appears to be an oxymoron. Since God is immortal and humans are mortal, these two states of being appear to be mutually exclusive. The Scriptures identify God the Father as the only one having intrinsic immortality. The Scriptures show God granting Jesus immorality by resurrecting Him from the dead.

The word translated "nature" or "form" in the passage under consideration is the Greek word *morphe*. This word appears only here in Philippians 2:5-8 and in Mark 16:12 where it is recorded Jesus appeared in a different form to two of His disciples after His resurrection. It should be noted, however, that Mark 16:9-20 does not appear in the earliest of the known Greek manuscripts.

Trinitarian discussion of Philippians 2:5-8 often defines *morphe* as describing the very essence or nature of Jesus. It is concluded that for Jesus to be in the *morphe* of God is to be of the same essence as God. Greek lexicons, however, show *morphe* to define outward appearance. It is used in the Greek literature of the first century to express outward appearance. In the Septuagint, *morphe* is used to show outward appearance. It occurs seven times in the Septuagint and in every case can be seen to mean outward appearance. *Morphe* does not speak to the internal makeup of a person but to ones outward appearance. A recent Greek to English translation of the Septuagint and New Testament Scriptures, the *Apostolic Bible Polyglot*, consistently translates *morphe* as "appearance." For example, in Daniel's account of King Belshazzar seeing the handwriting on the wall (Daniel, chapter five), this translation records his (Belshazzar's) appearance (*morphe*) changed. Obviously his basic human make up did not change. The KJV translates Philippians 2:6-8 in the following manner:

Philippians 2:6-8: Who, being in the form of God, thought it not robbery (Greek *harpagee*) to be equal with God: But made himself of no reputation, and took upon him the form of a servant, and was made in the likeness of men: And being found in fashion as a man, he humbled himself, and became obedient unto death, even the death of the cross.

Some interpret the phrase **"being in the form of God, thought it not robbery to be equal with God: But made himself of no reputation"** as meaning Jesus had equality with God which He thought it not robbery to have. He was willing to give it all up to become a human sacrifice for sin. Greek lexicons show *harpagee* literally means to rob or steal and take by force. The KJV translates it as "robbery" but most translations use the word "grasp." Jesus is seen as not grasping or wanting to take by force equality with God despite being in the form of God which Trinitarians interpret as being the same as being God.

This view is problematic because if Jesus being in the form of God means He is God, why would Paul speak in terms of

Jesus not wanting to rob (steal or take by force) or grasp at being God? This would be tantamount to Jesus seeking to be what He already was. Under Trinitarian thought, Jesus, as God in the flesh, would already have equality with God the Father and wanting or not wanting to have it would be irrelevant. You don't grasp for something you already have.

It is sometimes argued that Paul is speaking in terms of the Son not seeking to retain His equal status with the Father and Spirit but was willing to give up such status to become the human Jesus. If this is the case, what did the Son of God give up in becoming the human Jesus while still remaining fully God? What did He empty Himself of? God is considered omnipotent, omnipresent and omniscient. Did the Son empty himself of any of these qualities? If these are all eternal qualities associated with being God, how could Jesus, as God, empty Himself of such qualities and still be God. If the Son did empty himself of these qualities, He wasn't God in the flesh as claimed. It is these qualities that identify God as God. If Christ was fully God while being fully human He would have had these qualities while in the flesh.

The primary question is what does Paul mean when He writes of Jesus being in the form or appearance of God but taking on the form or appearance of a servant? As already discussed, the Greek *morphe* relates to outward appearance. English words such as endomorphic (a stocky person), ectomorphic (a slim person) and mesomorphic (a big boned, muscular person) are derived from this Greek word. These are all words that describe outward appearance and not the core elements of what makes a human a human.

Some have suggested that because Paul says Jesus was in the form (outward appearance) of God but took the form (outward appearance) of man, it was the outward appearance of God that the Son gave up to take on the outward appearance of the human Jesus. Therefore, Jesus was a human only in outward appearance while His essence remained divine. This was the position of the second century theologian/ philosopher Marcion, a position called Docetism. This position is problematical because the Scriptures show the Son of God died and not that just an outward appearance of the Son of God died.

Throughout the NT it is implicitly and sometimes explicitly stated that Jesus came to reveal the Father. As we have already covered in this book, Jesus was a perfect manifestation of the *logos* of God. As such, Jesus was a perfect representation of the Spirit of the Father. There is no Scriptural reason to believe when Paul writes about Jesus being in appearance as God he is saying Jesus is God in essence and substance. Paul plainly wrote to the Corinthians that the Father was the one and only God. Paul is not telling the Philippians Jesus is God. Paul is saying what Jesus said. Jesus said He was in the Father and the Father was in him. In his teaching and in His demonstration of power, Jesus represented God. He did this because He had a full measure of God's Spirit and God granted Him the wherewithal to be what He was and accomplish what He accomplished.

When Paul tells the Philippians Jesus was in appearance as God, he is talking about the human agent to whom the one and only true God had given extraordinary power and authority. This power and authority was given to Jesus to demonstrate He was indeed the promised Messiah who would become the sacrifice for the sins of humanity and reconcile humanity back to God. Jesus was in the appearance of God because He perfectly represented God in everything He did. Jesus knew He was the promised Messiah and that God had given Him supernatural power and authority as God's agent. Jesus new He was the heir to David's throne. Jesus could have at any time used His granted power to overthrow the Romans and become the king of Israel. When Jesus was being arrested and one of his companions drew his sword and was ready to fight, Jesus said:

Matthew 26:53-54: "Do you think I cannot call on my Father, and he will at once put at my disposal more than twelve legions of angels? But how then would the Scriptures be fulfilled that say it must happen in this way?"

Jesus was apparently given the power of choice, free will and latitude to submit to the crucifixion or dramatically stop the whole process. While praying in the garden before His arrest, He petitioned His Father for a way out of the pending ordeal.

Matthew 26:39: Going a little farther, he fell with his face to the ground and prayed, "My Father, if it is possible, may this cup be taken from me. Yet not as I will, but as you will."

These recorded events in the life of Jesus demonstrate Jesus had His own human will and the God given power to exercise his own will. What he did, however, was to totally submit His will and His granted power and authority to the will and purpose of God His Father. Jesus was willing to humble Himself by emptying Himself of the power He had been granted and totally submit to the will of His Father. It was the power and authority God gave Jesus as the human Messiah that Jesus emptied Himself of in going to the cross to become the sacrifice for sin. Jesus didn't use His power to deliver Himself from the ordeal of the crucifixion. Instead, He laid it all aside and submitted Himself as a powerless human Being in the face of his Jewish accusers and the Roman authority.

2 Corinthians 8:9: For you know the grace of our Lord Jesus Christ, that though he was rich, yet for your sakes he became poor, so that you through his poverty might become rich.

Paul instructed the Philippian Christians to have the same attitude of humility as Christ showed in not seeking power and authority over others but in humility serving others. If Jesus was a God/man as commonly believed, Paul could not have used Him as an example of giving up status in becoming a humble servant. As a God/man, Jesus would have retained his status of deity and would not have truly emptied Himself of anything. If the Son of God is eternal as is the Father, how can it be said the Son of God humbled Himself to the point of the cross (Philippians 2:8)? As an eternal Being, the Son could not die.

It is far more reasonable to see Paul writing about a purely human Son of God who was willing to lay aside the power and authority granted to Him and in humility submit to the will of the Father. In so doing, Jesus provided an example of how we should also in humility submit to one another and to God in obedience to His will.

Paul may have had in mind the comparison between the two Adams. The first Adam was made in the image of God and granted power and authority over creation. This Adam, rather than submitting himself to God in obedience to God's command, sought to become like God by coming to know good and evil (Genesis 3:22). Jesus, who Paul refers to as the second Adam, was granted power and authority but did not seek to become like God but totally submitted to God's will, even to death on the cross.

When Paul writes of Jesus being in the outward appearance of God he is talking about Jesus reflecting attributes of God that God had conferred upon Jesus so He could fulfill God's will. During his ministry, Jesus made it very plain that seeing Him was the same as seeing the Father.

John 14:7-9: If you really knew me, you would know my Father as well. From now on, you do know him and have seen him." Philip said, "Lord, show us the Father and that will be enough for us." Jesus answered: "Don't you know me, Philip, even after I have been among you such a long

time? Anyone who has seen me has seen the Father. How can you say, `Show us the Father'?

Is Jesus revealing Himself here as being God by saying He is in the Father and the Father is in Him? Is Jesus saying that to see Him is to see God? Are we seeing here a mutual indwelling of Father and Son that equates with Father and Son being co-equal, co-eternal and con-substantial? Jesus tells Philip that seeing Him is seeing the Father. We know Scripture identifies the Father as God. Is Jesus telling Philip He also is God and by seeing Him One sees God because God is Father and Son? Remember, in John 17:3, Jesus says the Father is the one and only true God. Is Jesus telling Philip that He (Jesus) is also the one and only true God because He and the Father are one in essence? What about John 1:18?

John 1:18: No one has ever seen God, but God the One and Only, who is at the Father's side, has made him known (NIV).

The NIV translates John 1:18 in such manner as to say the one and only God is Jesus. As discussed in Chapter One, Trinitarians argue that one can see the Father, the Son or the Spirit as the one and only God because the Father, Son and Spirit are seen as indwelling each other and therefore constitute the one and only God. Therefore, when Jesus is quoted as saying the Father is the one and only God (John 17:3), this is not seen as the Son or the Spirit being excluded from this designation. Is this what John is teaching in the passages under consideration? Is John revealing that whether you are speaking of the Father or the Son, you have the one and only God in view because the Father and Son indwell each other? Several other translations of John 1:18 translate this passage similar to that of the NIV.

No man has seen God at any time; the only begotten God, who is in the bosom of the Father, He has explained Him (ASV).

David A Kroll

No one has ever seen God. The only one, himself God, who is in closest fellowship with the Father, has made God known (NET).

No one has ever seen God; the only God, who is at the Father's side, he has made him known (English Standard Version - ESV).

Jesus said the Father is the one and only God (John 17:3). These translations of John 1:18 record John as saying Jesus is also the One and Only God and it is He who has made God known. These translations are apparently derived from a reading of Alexandrian Greek texts that predate the texts most commonly used when translating this passage. These Alexandrian texts have *monogenes Theos* where the word *mono* means only and *genes* means to be born or begotten or, as more recent scholarship has identified, *genes* means kind, type or unique. *Theos* means god. Older English versions use later Greek texts that read *monogenes huios* where *huios* is the Greek word for son. Typical of such translations are the following:

No man hath seen God at any time; the only begotten Son, (*monogenes huios*) which is in the bosom of the Father, he hath declared him (KJV).

No one has ever seen God; the only Son, who is in the bosom of the Father, he has made him known (RSV).

Bosom is from the Greek *kolpos* which literally means "the front part of the body between the arms." In Greek literature it is used both literally and figuratively. New Testament scholar Brian J Wright writes that the reference to being in the bosom of the Father is "an anthropomorphic metaphor for intimacy and fellowship" (page 248, *Revisiting The Corruption Of The New Testament*).

There has been much discussion in scholarly circles as to which Greek manuscripts reflect what John intended. Some

206

argue that since the Alexandrian manuscripts are older, they better reflect what John said as they are closer to the time he wrote his Gospel. It's to be noted that *Theos* instead of *huios* is found not only in ancient Alexandrian texts of the NT but in a variety of other Greek texts and early translations of the Greek into Syriac and Coptic. *Huios*, however, is found in a much wider number of Greek texts than is *Theos,* including some of the later Alexandrian texts. *Huios* is also found in the writings of early church fathers such as Irenaeus, Clement and Tertullian who were writing before the surviving Alexandrian manuscripts were produced. Some scholars believe scribes altered the text to read "*Theos*" in order to promote the belief Jesus was God against a first century teaching known as Adoptionism which taught Jesus was only a man born in the normal way and declared to be the Son of God sometime after His birth.

Some scholars see the Alexandrian renderings of this passage as spurious because these texts virtually say the One and Only God resides in the One and Only God which makes no sense. It is questioned that if the Son is the One and Only God then what does that make the Father? Jesus, Paul and John clearly taught the Father was the one and only God. Can there be two one and only God's? It is also pointed out that the early Alexandrian and later Greek renderings of John 3:16, 18 and 1 John 4:9, all speak of Christ as the only unique Son (*monogenes huios*) of God which indicates this is how John understood the relationship of Christ to God and not that Christ was the one and only unique God (*monogenes Theos*).

In view of the foregoing, it appears John was saying no man has seen God at any time but Jesus, as the one and only uniquely begotten Son of God, has declared Him which is to say has revealed Him. It should be noted that in the passage under consideration, John speaks of Jesus revealing God and God is revealed as the Father. When John says no man has seen God at any time it is the same as saying no man has seen the Father at any time. John sees God as the Father. This is the way God is seen throughout the New Testament. If Jesus is God, as implied in the modern translations cited above, you would have to conclude John is seeing God as Father and Son and then you virtually have God revealing God in this passage or at minimum you have a distinction of God called the Son revealing a distinction of God called the Father.

It is instructive that John clearly states that no man has seen God at any time and He (Jesus), who is in fellowship with the Father, is revealing God, who Jesus consistently identifies as the Father. There is no hint here that Jesus is also God. If Jesus was also God, then it could rightly be said that people seeing Jesus were seeing God which would contradict what John said about no man seeing God.

The weight of internal Scriptural evidence points to John saying *monogenes huios* and not *monogenes Theos*. Translators choosing to use the Alexandrian texts have chosen to ignore the greater number of manuscripts that show *monogenes huios* and, more importantly, have chosen to ignore the weight of internal Scriptural evidence against *monogenes Theos*. In an apparent wish to accommodate Trinitarian theology, these translators have created a modern day orthodox corruption of Scripture. Now let's look at the following passages.

John 10:30: I and the Father are one

John 14:10-11: Don't you believe that I am in the Father, and that the Father is in me? The words I say to you are not just my own. Rather, it is the Father, living in me, who is doing his work. Believe me when I say that I am in the Father and the Father is in me; or at least believe on the evidence of the miracles themselves.

The fourth century theologian Athanasius largely based his Trinitarian theology on his exegesis of John 10:30 and 14:10-11. Athanasius interpreted Jesus as saying his whole Being was in the Being of the Father and the whole Being of the Father was in the whole Being of Himself, the Son.

A contemporary of Athanasius, Hilary, Bishop of Poitiers, in reflecting on John 14:10, wrote: *"Although these Beings do not dwell apart, they retain their separate existence and condition and can reciprocally contain one another, so that one permanently envelopes and is also permanently enveloped by the other whom he yet envelops."*

When Jesus speaks of He being in the Father and the Father being in Him, is He revealing to us that His Being is in the Father and the Father's Being is in Him and, therefore, He and the Father are con-substantial (of the same essence)? Is Jesus talking about an indwelling of mutual substance of Being between He and the Father? Is Jesus telling us He and the Father are the one God?

I submit, on the basis of Jesus' own words, that He is not speaking about reciprocal indwelling of Being when He speaks of He being in the Father and the Father being in Him. Jesus is not addressing substance of Being at all. Jesus is speaking of manifesting the Spirit of God which was reflected in the power and authority Jesus projected during His earthly ministry. Jesus being in the Father and the Father being in Jesus is not a statement of oneness of Being. As discussed in Chapter Seven, it is a statement of oneness of spirit. This is made very evident in the prayer Jesus offered up to the Father on behalf of his followers shortly before His crucifixion.

John 17:20-23, 26: My prayer is not for them alone. I pray also for those who will believe in me through their message, that all of them may be one, Father, just as you are in me and I am in you. May they also be in us so that the world may believe that you have sent me. I have given them the glory that you gave me, that they may be one as we are one: I in them and you in me. May they be brought

to complete unity to let the world know that you sent me and have loved them even as you have loved me. Verse 26: I have made you known to them, and will continue to make you known in order that the love you have for me may be in them and that I myself may be in them.

When Jesus said He and the Father are one (John 10:30), He was not alluding to they being one in Being. When Jesus told Philip He was in the Father and the Father was in Him (John 14:11), He was not teaching He and the Father are a co-equal, co-eternal and con-substantial Being. Jesus is using relational language in showing how He and the Father are of the same mind and spirit. In the passage cited above, Jesus uses the same terminology in speaking of our relationship with Him and the Father as He does in regard to his relationship with the Father. Jesus being in the Father, the Father being in Jesus, we being in the Father and the Father and Jesus being in us are all relational statements pointing to being of like mind and spirit and participating in mutual love. There are multiple dozens of statements in the NT that speak of our being one in spirit with the Father, Jesus and each other.

Trinitarian theology teaches God is a mutual indwelling of Father, Son and Spirit. Therefore, God is seen as one Being in three dimensions or distinctions. The Scriptures, however, show God to be a single and separate Being above all other Beings including the Being Jesus. The concept of mutual indwelling is a valid concept only as it pertains to how the one God who is the Father spiritually indwells the Son and the Son spiritually indwells the Father. This has to do with shared spiritual dynamics, not shared oneness of Being. We humans can share in those same spiritual dynamics through mutual indwelling involving the Father, the Son and us. By participating in mutual indwelling with the Father and the Son we become one with the Father and the Son and they become one with us. This doesn't make us one in Being with the Father or the Son anymore than it makes the Father and Son one Being. We all remain separate entities united by the Spirit of the one God which proceeds from that one God through Jesus and into us.

There is one additional passage in Philippians chapter 2 that is often used as a "proof text" to show that Jesus is *YHWH* and is therefore the one God.

Philippians 2:9-11: Therefore God (*Theos*) exalted him to the highest place and gave him the name that is above every name, that at the name of Jesus every knee should bow, in heaven and on earth and under the earth, and every tongue confess that Jesus Christ is Lord, to the glory of God (*Theos*) the Father.

This statement by Paul appears to be a quote or paraphrase of a passage of Scripture found in Isaiah where *YHWH* is quoted as saying:

Isaiah 45:23: By myself I have sworn, my mouth has uttered in all integrity a word that will not be revoked: Before me every knee will bow; by me every tongue will swear.

In Isaiah 45, *YHWH* is quoted in the first person as saying He is the one and only God. Most of this chapter is devoted to identifying *YHWH* as the one and only God. Because He is the one and only God, He says every knee will bow to Him and confess Him. *YHWH* is identified as Father some fifteen times in the OT. There is nothing in Isaiah 45, or anywhere else in the OT, to suggest *YHWH* is also the Son. Yet, because Paul is using *YHWH's* statement about every knee bowing to Him and every tongue confessing to Him to describe an action connected to Jesus, it is believed Paul must be identifying Jesus as *YHWH*.

Paul writes that God (the Father) exalted Jesus to the highest place and that every knee should bow to Jesus and every tongue confess Jesus is Lord. Paul says all this is done to the glory of God the Father. Paul consistently identifies God (*YHWH*) as the Father in the NT. If Jesus is as much *YHWH* as the Father is *YHWH*, Paul is saying *YHWH* the Father exalted *YHWH* the Son to the glory of *YHWH* the Father.

This is problematic because if *YHWH* the Son is co-eternal, co-equal and con-substantial with *YHWH* the Father, how can it be said *YHWH* the Father is exalting him to the highest place. How could *YHWH*, the Father make the Son to be greater than He already was and always has been. The very language of this passage, and other passages like it, show *YHWH* the Father to be superior and greater than the Son which the Son readily admitted when He said the Father was greater than He. Therefore, Jesus is not *YHWH* but is the exalted Son of *YHWH*.

Paul shows God the Father rewarded Jesus for humbling himself and becoming obedient to the point of being crucified (verse 8). The highest place Jesus was exalted to is shown in other Scriptures as being the right hand of God. *YHWH* the Father does the exalting of Jesus which in itself shows the Father being over the Son in power and authority as has already been shown in a number of other Scriptures. Rather than the passage under consideration showing Jesus is *YHWH*, it shows instead how *YHWH* is superior to Jesus. Applying something to Jesus that *YHWH* said about himself is not a proof that Jesus is *YHWH*. Isaiah shows *YHWH* saying every knee will bow to him because He is the one and only God. Paul shows every knee will bow to Christ because the one and only God (*YHWH*) exalted Him to a position worthy of such worship and not because Christ is the one and only God.

Because of what Jesus accomplished as the Messiah, *YHWH* has exalted Him to His right hand. Therefore, *YHWH* has ordained that Jesus receives the level of respect and worship commensurate with whom the Father has elevated the Son to be. This includes every knee bowing to Christ and every tongue confessing Him as Lord. Jesus was anointed by His Father *YHWH* to be the Lord Jesus Christ, the savior of the world. Jesus is not *YHWH*. He is the anointed of *YHWH*. Paul writes that this is all done to the glory of God the Father (*YHWH*) who Paul consistently identifies as the one and only Most High God.

Chapter Seventeen

"God, your God"

Hebrews 1:8-9, is used as a major support for the proposition Jesus is God in every respect the Father is God short of being the Father.

Hebrews 1:8-9: But about the Son he says, "Your throne, O God, will last for ever and ever, and righteousness will be the scepter of your kingdom. You have loved righteousness and hated wickedness; therefore God, your God, has set you above your companions by anointing you with the oil of joy."

Nearly all English translations take the phrase "Your throne, O God" as a vocative clause in the Greek which means that grammatically it indicates that something or someone is being directly addressed. There are some Greek scholars who see this phrase as a nominative clause and translate it as "God is your throne" implying that God the Father is the source of Jesus' authority. While this is a grammatically acceptable rendering of this phrase, the majority of commentators on this passage see this as a vocative clause referring to Jesus as God.

Scholarship has determined the writer of this passage is quoting from a Psalm written as a wedding song for a Davidic King, most likely Solomon. The writer to the Hebrews sees the Psalm written for Israel's King as applicable to Jesus who God the Father has appointed King over Israel and the entire human race.

Psalm 45:6-7: Your throne, O God, will last for ever and ever; a scepter of justice will be the scepter of your kingdom. You love righteousness and hate wickedness; therefore

God, your God, has set you above your companions by anointing you with the oil of joy.

This psalm is directed to a human king who is called god (*elohim*). Calling human rulers god (*elohim*) is common in OT literature. It is a title applied to one having great power and authority. Kings have great power and authority. Judges are called gods (*elohim*) in Psalm 82. The application of Psalm 45 to Christ is very appropriate as He has been granted great power and authority over angels and all other created beings. This does not mean Christ is God as the Father is God any more than a King in Israel was God as the Father is God even though such Kings were called *elohim*. The evidence that Christ is not God as the Father is God is found in the following quote from Psalm 45.

Hebrews 1:9b: "Therefore God, your God, has set you above your companions by anointing you with the oil of joy."

Here we see the one God addressing Christ as being Christ's God. If Christ is also the one God, we then have the one God addressing the one God which makes no sense at all. When this was written, Jesus was in His glorified state at the right hand of the Father. Yet God is seen as being His God. This clearly shows God to be a separate and distinct Being from Jesus and as such is the God <u>of</u> Jesus. The author continues by writing the following:

Hebrews 1:10-12: He also says, "In the beginning, O Lord, you laid the foundations of the earth, and the heavens are the work of your hands. They will perish, but you remain; they will all wear out like a garment. You will roll them up like a robe; like a garment they will be changed. But you remain the same, and your years will never end."

This is a quote from Psalm 102:25-27 where the Psalmist is addressing *YHWH* as creator and being without end. The

Greek text shows Hebrews 1:10 begins with the word "And." Most English translations begin this passage with the word "And." The phrase "He also says," as found in the NIV, is not in the Greek text. Some theologians believe the word "And" continues the thought seen in verse nine which makes the reference to "Lord" at the beginning of verse ten refer back to God (the Father) who is last mentioned in verse nine and forms a doxology of praise and reverence to God the Father.

Hebrews 1:8-12: But to the Son He says: "Your throne, O God, is forever and ever; a scepter of righteousness is the scepter of Your Kingdom. You have loved righteousness and hated lawlessness; therefore God, Your God, has anointed You with the oil of gladness more than Your companions." And: "You, Lord, in the beginning laid the foundation of the earth, and the heavens are the work of Your hands; They will perish, but You remain; and they will all grow old like a garment; Like a cloak You will fold them up, and they will be changed. But You are the same, and Your years will not fail" (NKJV).

The author begins this passage by using Psalm 45:6-7 to show how God the Father has anointed the Son. The author goes on to quote Psalm 102:25-27 which pays tribute to *YHWH* as creator. As previously discussed, throughout the OT, the Father is identified as the one and only creator God (*YHWH*). Therefore, it is reasonable to believe the author of Hebrews is referencing this Psalm in praise to the creative power and enduring nature of *YHWH* who is the Father and who has given great power and authority and an everlasting kingdom to His Christ (the anointed of *YHWH*). The designation Lord is associated with both God the Father and Jesus in the NT Scripture. In the OT a distinction is made between *Adonai* (*YHWH*) and *adoni* (The Son) as discussed in Chapter Three of this book. That it is *Adonai* as Lord (The Father) being addressed in this passage is confirmed by the overall context of Hebrews, chapter one.

This chapter begins by showing how in the past God spoke to the forefathers through the prophets but has now spoken through his Son, whom he appointed heir of all things, and through whom he made the universe.

Hebrews 1:1-2: In the past God spoke to our forefathers through the prophets at many times and in various ways, but in these last days he has spoken to us by his Son, whom he appointed heir of all things, and through whom he made the universe.

If the Son is *YHWH* God as the Father is *YHWH* God and the Son as *YHWH* God is creator of all things as many believe, why would the Son be appointed heir of all things? Being an heir is to be in a position to inherit what you don't currently own. If the Son is *YHWH*, He would already own all things by virtue of having created all things as the creator God.

It is instructive that the Greek word translated "universe" in Hebrews 1:1-2 in the NIV and "world" in many other translations is *aion*. This Greek word appears 165 times in the New Testament and is variously translated as "world," "age" and "ever." It means a segment of time. It can relate to a long period of time and even time without end (forever), or a short period of time. Context determines it usage. The Greek *kosmos* relates to the world as created and the Greek *oikoumene* refers to the world as inhabited.

The first century church was experiencing transition to a New Covenant age. The writer to the Hebrews shows how Christ, as the one through whom the New Covenant was being facilitated, is superior to angels and the Aaronic Priesthood. God the Father was in the process of creating a New Covenant age through Christ, a process that was consummated in the judgement upon Israel in AD 70 when the temple was destroyed and the means to facilitate the Old Covenant system was eliminated. The last days the writer is referring to are the last days of the Old Covenant age which was about to fade away and be replaced by a New Covenant age facilitated by the Father through Christ (Hebrews 8:13). Hebrews 1:2 is not a reference to God creating the physical universe through Christ. It is the New Covenant age God was making through Christ. Now let's look at verse three.

Hebrews 1:3: The Son is the radiance of God's glory and the exact representation of his being, sustaining all things by his powerful word. After he had provided purification for sins, he sat down at the right hand of the Majesty in heaven.

The Greek word translated radiance in this passage appears only this once in the NT. Its basic meaning is "reflected brightness." Some versions, such as the KJV, translate it as brightness. The writer is saying the Son is the reflected brightness of God. Does being a reflection of something equate with being that something? During His ministry, Jesus expressed to His followers that He was a reflection of His Father when He told them that by seeing and believing in Him one sees the Father. People were not literally seeing the Father. They were seeing the character, will and very mind of the Father represented (reflected) in Christ. In this manner, Jesus was the reflected brightness of God the Father. Jesus was the light that came into the world.

John 12:44-46: When a man believes in me, he does not believe in me only, but in the one who sent me. When he looks at me, he sees the one who sent me. I have come into the world as a light (brightness), so that no one who believes in me should stay in darkness.

The writer to the Hebrews points out that Jesus is the representation of God's Being. This does not mean He is the Being God. The writer speaks of Christ becoming superior to the angels (Hebrews 1:4). Wouldn't the Son already be and always have been superior to the angels if He is God? The writer says because Christ has loved righteousness and hated wickedness; <u>His</u> God will set Him above his companions

Hebrews 1:9: You have loved righteousness and hated wickedness; therefore God, <u>your God</u>, has set you above your companions by anointing you with the oil of joy.

If Jesus is God as God is God, He would already be and always would have been above His companions. The very language of Hebrews 1:4-9, belies Jesus being God as God is God.

The writer of Hebrews 1:3 identifies Jesus as **"the exact representation (image in some translations) of his being" (person in some translations).** "Of his being" refers back to the word God. The word being or person is translated from the Greek word *hypostasis.* The *Arndt, Gingrich and Bauer Greek-English Lexicon of the New Testament and Other Early Christian Literature*, defines *hypostasis* as substantial nature, essence, actual being or reality of something, often as a contrast to what merely seems to be. *Thayer's Greek-English Lexicon* defines *hypostasis* as a setting or placing under as that which has foundation. *Hypostasis* is also defined as confidence, conviction, assurance and steadfastness.

Hypostasis was used by Aristotle and Neo Platonists (third century A.D. followers of the teachings of Plato) to speak of the objective reality of a thing as opposed to its outer form or illusion. *Hypostasis* was used by early Church writers such as Origen and Tatian to denote Being or substantive reality. This Greek word was not always distinguished in meaning from the Greek word *ousia* which means individual substance or essence.

In the formulation of the Trinitarian definition of God by church leaders in the fourth and fifth centuries A.D., *ousia* came to designate God as a single substance in three hypostasis' of Father, Son and Holy Spirit. Athanasius wrote that *ousia* should be used properly of the one Being God while *hypostasis* should be used strictly of the distinct objective reality of each of the divine Persons in their relations to each other. In reflection of this view, Cappadocian theologian Gregory of Nyssa wrote that, *"God is not God because he is Father nor the Son because he is the Son, but because both possess the ousia of the Godhead."* God is seen as one *ousia* expressed in three *hypostases*.

The problem with this concept is seen in looking at the "Lord's Prayer." Jesus instructed His listeners that when they prayed they are to address their Father in heaven. Was Jesus instructing his followers to address only the *hypostasis* of the Father or was He instructing them to address the *ousia* that is God which, under Trinitarian thought, would be Father, Son and Spirit. Since, under Trinitarian theology, God is seen as one *ousia,* it would appear reasonable, within the context of such theology, to conclude that in addressing the Father one is addressing the one *ousia* of Father, Son and Spirit. Yet, there is nothing in Jesus' instruction to remotely suggest such a thing. It would be more reasonable, and certainly consistent with what Christ said about the Father being the one and only true God, that when Christ instructs His listeners to in prayer address their Father, He is instructing them to address the one and only God (one and only *ousia*) who is the Father and only the Father.

Throughout the NT it is evident that when God is being addressed in prayer, He is being addressed as the God of Jesus with no hint of Jesus also being God. In Acts 4:24-27, the people are seen as praying to God and reflecting on Jesus who is seen as the anointed servant of the God they are addressing in prayer. In Ephesians 1:15-16, Paul is seen as praying to the God of Jesus who Paul calls the "glorious Father." In 1 Thessalonians 1:1-3, Paul speaks of praying to God whom he identifies as "our God and Father." In Ephesians 3:14-17, we see Paul kneeling before the Father and asking the Father to grant power to the Ephesian Christians so they will have a greater faith in what Christ has done for them. In Colossians 1:3, we see Paul praying to the God and Father of Jesus. Throughout the NT we see prayer directed to God the Father. We do not see prayer directed to the Son or to the Spirit. This speaks volumes as to who God is.

When Cappadocian theologian Basil was presented with the problems associated with Jesus' instruction to in prayer address the Father as God, he responded by saying that, *"what was common to the Three (Father, Son and Spirit) and what was distinctive among them lay beyond speech and comprehension and therefore beyond analysis or conceptualization."* We are being asked to believe a concept that is beyond speech, comprehension, analysis and conceptualization.

Within Christianity, *hypostasis* became associated with the Greek *prosopon*, which is translated into Latin as *"persona."* The Latin *"persona,"* literally means "mask" or a character played by an actor. Since an actor can play several roles by simply changing masks, this is felt to analogize to one God in three persons or *hypostasis'.*

An actor, however, can only play one role at any given moment. Therefore, this analogy fails to support the Trinitarian concept of God which teaches God is three *persona (hypostasis')* all of the time at the same time. The idea of the actor changing masks to play different roles is much like the Modalistic Model of God taught by the theologian Sabellius in the third century. As discussed in Chapter Twelve, Sabellius taught God is only one person who acts as Father in creating the universe, as Son in redeeming sinners and as Holy Spirit in sanctifying believers. Sabellius viewed the one God playing three different roles at different times in history while retaining single personhood.

Hypostasis appears five times in the NT and in most English translations four out of those five times the word is translated as confidence or assurance which reflects the context of the passage wherein the word is found. Only in Hebrews 1:3 is *hypostasis* translated in such a way as to reflect its meaning of objective or substantive reality.

In view of the meaning ascribed to the word *hypostasis*, when the writer of Hebrews 1:3 says the Son is the radiance or image of God's glory and the exact representation of His Being (*hypostasis*), the writer is saying the Son is the image of the Being (*hypostasis*) that is God. This is the same as saying the Son is the image of the substantial nature, essence, or reality that is God. However, the writer says the one God is *hypostasis* (*ousia* according to Athanasius). The one God is the single objective reality that is God. The writer to the Hebrews sees the Son as the image and representation of the *hypostasis* (objective reality) that is God. God is identified by the Greek word *hypostasis*. How then can it be said the Son is a *hypostasis* of God? This is tantamount to saying the Son is a *hypostasis* of the *hypostasis*. Trinitarianism teaches God's Being (*hypostasis* in Hebrews 1:3) consists of the three *hypostasis'* of Father, Son and Spirit. If the Son is a *hypostasis* of the one *hypostasis* that is God and the one *hypostasis* that is God is actually three hypostasis' of Father, Son and Spirit, the writer is virtually saying the Son is the image of the three *hypostasis'* of Father, Son and Spirit which is to say the Son is the image of Himself.

If, on the other hand, the writer is using the word God in Hebrews 1:3 to mean the Father, then, under Trinitarian thought, the writer would be saying the Son *hypostasis* of the Godhead is the radiance of the glory and the exact representation or image of the Father *hypostasis* of the Godhead. Under Trinitarianism, however, each *hypostasis* of the Godhead has its own attributes that distinguish each *hypostasis* from the other. If the Son has his own attributes as the Son, and the Father has His own attributes as the Father, how can it be said the *hypostasis* called the Son is the exact representation or image of the *hypostasis* that is the Father. Would this not make the Son the same in attributes as the Father and the Father the same in attributes as the Son? What distinction would there be between the Father and Son? If when looking at the Son one sees the Father and when looking at the Father one sees the Son because they are one in Being, where is there any real distinction between the two to justify seeing the Son and Father as *hypostasis's* of the single *ousia* called God?

The truth of the matter is that being the image, engraving or imprinting of something does not make one that something. Scripture tells us we humans are made in the image of God. Yet we obviously are all separate individuals and are not one with God in the Trinitarian sense of being co-equal, un-separated substance. The Greek word for "representation" is *karizomai* and appears just this once in the NT and in Greek means a mark or stamp, such as in engraving, imprinting or etching. The Son is seen as the stamp, engraving or imprinting of the Being (*hypostasis*) that is God. This does not mean the Son is God. When coins are engraved they are not considered one with the engraving device. When stamps are imprinted they are not considered to be the same as the imprinting device. Coins and stamps are an impression of what the engraving or imprinting device does.

Hebrews chapter one does not establish Jesus is God as God is God. Instead we see Jesus reflecting the divine nature and being given superiority over angels and all other Beings. He is granted power, authority and a Kingdom by His God which is in harmony with all other Scripture we have discussed that identify the Father as the one and only Supreme Creator God who is the God of Jesus. In Hebrews 1:3, the Son is seen as sitting down at the right hand of the Majesty in heaven. This clearly shows the superiority of the one God over the Son of this one God. But, you may ask, what about the proclamation Thomas made after being convinced Jesus rose from the dead?

John 20:28: Thomas said to him, "My Lord (*kurios*) and my God (*Theos*)!"

Many Trinitarian apologists consider Thomas statement to be the most profound utterance found in Scripture as to Jesus being God. One commentator calls it the "supreme Christological pronouncement of the fourth gospel."

Was Thomas seeing Jesus as the one and only Supreme Creator God of the universe? As discussed in Chapter Four, the Greek *theos* can be used as a designation for someone other than the one and only Most High Creator God. It can be used as a designation for someone who has or is perceived to have power and authority. Context must be considered in determining how the word God is used in Scripture. Thomas had doubted Jesus had risen from the dead. When Thomas became convinced the crucified Christ had actually risen from the dead he had a virtual epiphany. He now understood this was not an ordinary man. Thomas now understood that the man standing before him was indeed the Christ, the anointed of God. Thomas responded in a euphoric manner and recognized Jesus as his Lord and god which was to recognize Jesus as his master and ruler.

Throughout His ministry, Jesus identified Himself as Lord which is to say master. Jesus never identified Himself as the one and only Supreme God. Jesus identified His Father as being the one and only Supreme God. Paul, John and other of the Apostles identified Jesus as Lord and identified the Father as the one and only Eternal God. If you are going to conclude Thomas is identifying Jesus as being the one and only Most High, Supreme God, you are concluding Thomas is introducing an understanding about Jesus that runs contrary to what Jesus taught and what the Apostles taught regarding who God is versus who Jesus is.

In view of the whole of what Scripture teaches as to who God is versus who Jesus is, it is necessary to conclude Thomas is not using *theos* to identify Jesus as the one and only Supreme, Creator God. Proclaiming Jesus to be God as the Father is God would have run contrary to Thomas' deeply ingrained monotheism. In calling Jesus *theos*, Thomas is expressing great exhilaration at being convinced Jesus is alive. It is a joyous response to what Thomas was experiencing. To take Thomas' statement to be anything more than this is to create serious contradiction within the Scriptures.

It should also be noted that after John records Thomas' reference to Jesus as god, he wrote that what he has written is to demonstrate that Jesus is the Christ, the Son of God.

John 20:31: But these are written that you may believe that Jesus is the Christ, he Son of God, and that by believing you may have life in his name.

Note that John writes "Son of God." In Trinitarian theology, God is Father, Son and Spirit. When John writes that Jesus is the Son of God, there is no indication that in John's mind he understands the word God to include the Son. John is not seeing Jesus as the God He is the Son of. All through the NT we see God identified as the Father and the Father identified as God. Thomas' joyous and exhilarated expression directed at Jesus does not do away with the weight of Scripture that shows there to be only one Supreme God who is the Father and only the Father.

Chapter Eighteen

Is Jesus *YHWH?*

If you have carefully read the material presented to this point, it should be apparent that the Father and only the Father is *YHWH*. Yet many Christians believe Jesus is also *YHWH* and as such is God as much as the Father is God. Some OT passages associated with *YHWH* are seen as being applied to Jesus in the NT and therefore are seen as identifying Jesus as *YHWH*. An example of this approach is seen in Romans 10:13 where it is believed Paul applies a quote from Joel 2:32 to Jesus.

Joel 2:31-32: The sun will be turned to darkness and the moon to blood before the coming of the great and dreadful day of the LORD (*YHWH*). <u>And everyone who calls on the name of the LORD (*YHWH*) will be saved;</u> for on Mount Zion and in Jerusalem there will be deliverance, as the LORD has said, among the survivors whom the LORD calls.

Romans 10:13: "Everyone who calls on the name of the Lord (Greek: *kurios*) will be saved."

In Romans 10:9, Jesus is identified as Lord. **"If you confess with your mouth, 'Jesus is Lord,' and believe in your heart that God raised him from the dead, you will be saved."** Because Jesus is identified as Lord in verse 9, it is believed He is the Lord of verse 13 as well where Paul writes about calling on the name of the Lord. Therefore, the "Lord" of Romans 10:13 is believed to be Jesus and by Paul applying a phrase to Jesus that is applied to *YHWH* in the OT, it is believed Paul is identifying Jesus as *YHWH*.

It is interesting that Peter uses the same quote from Joel in asking his audience to repent and turn to God.

Acts 2:17-21: In the last days, God says, I will pour out my Spirit on all people. Your sons and daughters will prophesy, your young men will see visions, your old men will dream dreams. Even on my servants, both men and women, I will pour out my Spirit in those days, and they will prophesy. I will show wonders in the heaven above and signs on the earth below, blood and fire and billows of smoke. The sun will be turned to darkness and the moon to blood before the coming of the great and glorious day of the Lord. <u>And everyone who calls on the name of the Lord will be saved.</u>'

The Lord to whom one can call on to be saved in the Joel passage is *YHWH* God. When Paul and Peter quote Joel, it is *YHWH* God who is being referenced as the one to call on. Paul, in Romans 3:29, writes of there being one God who is the God of both Jews and Gentiles. In Romans 10:12 he writes of there being one Lord of both Jews and Gentiles. A careful reading of Romans chapter 3 will reveal that it is God the Father who is seen as the facilitator of salvation through his agent Jesus the Christ. In verses 25-30 Paul shows how the one God presented Jesus as the sacrifice for sin and it is through Jesus that the one God justifies both Jews and Gentiles. In Romans 10:9, God is seen as the one who raised Jesus from the dead.

In Romans 10:12 Paul says there is one Lord of both Jews and Gentiles who richly blesses all who call on him. Paul then follows this statement by saying "Everyone who calls on the name of the Lord will be saved." As already discussed in a previous Chapter, Salvation is facilitated by God the Father through Christ Jesus. Scripture shows it is God the Father who blesses us through Christ.

Acts 13:34: The fact that God raised him from the dead, never to decay, is stated in these words: "`I will give you the holy and sure blessings promised to David.'

Ephesians 1:3: Praise be to the God and Father of our Lord Jesus Christ, who has blessed us in the heavenly realms with every spiritual blessing in Christ.

When taking the whole of Scripture into account, it appears reasonable to conclude that when Paul and Peter quote Joel's statement about calling upon the name of the Lord to be saved, it is God the Father, who is being referenced. Even if it is the Lord Christ being referenced in Romans 10:12-13, it does not mean Christ is the one and only Most High, Supreme LORD God.

As we have already discussed in this book, Paul distinguishes between the one God who is the Father and the one Lord who is the Christ, the anointed of the Father. A careful examination of the Scriptures will reveal it is the LORD (*YHWH*) God the Father who through His Lord Christ has facilitated salvation for both Jews and Gentiles. Jesus is the anointed Lord through whom the Most High LORD does his work. Jesus is called Lord throughout the NT in his role as the appointed and anointed agent of the one God who is the Father. Jesus is called Lord because He was made Lord by the one and only Supreme LORD, God the Father (Acts 2:36). Jesus is Lord in His capacity as the <u>anointed of *YHWH* God</u>, not because he <u>is</u> *YHWH* God. Only the Father is intrinsically LORD. No one made the Father LORD. The Father has eternally existed as the Supreme LORD of all including being the LORD God of Jesus. Jesus is seen as receiving His Lordship from the Father. The Supreme LORD, who is the Father and who is the source of salvation, is seen as facilitating His salvation through the one He made Lord (Acts 2:36). Jesus is the mediator of salvation. Paul plainly said, **"For there is <u>one God</u> and one mediator <u>between</u> God and men, the man Christ Jesus" (1 Timothy 2:5).**

The Father is the Supreme, Most High LORD (*YHWH*) God Almighty. Jesus is the Lord Christ, the begotten and anointed of *YHWH* God. Jesus is the LORD's lord as we saw in our examination of Psalm 110:1 in Chapter Three. Since the Greek Scriptures use only the one word *kurios* to designate Lord, context must be the determining factor as to what Lord is being referenced in any given passage. For example, in Luke's account of the birth of Jesus, Luke writes:

Luke 1:32: He will be great and will be called the Son of the Most High. The Lord God will give him the throne of his father David.

Here it is obvious the "Lord God" is referring to the Most High God (*YHWH*) who is the Father and is seen as distinct and superior to the one to be called the Son. In Luke 2:26, the Son is referred to as the Lord's Christ which is to say the anointed of the Most High LORD (*YHWH*) God. Here the word Lord is obviously referring to the Father. The word Lord (*kurios*) occurs nearly twenty times in Luke chapter 2 and by context can be seen to refer to God the Father. The very language of Luke, chapter 2 shows seeing Jesus as *YHWH* God to be a scripturally untenable position.

NT writers apply many sayings from the OT to Christ. Often such sayings are seen to have a different meaning in their OT context. We will examine examples of this in Chapter Nineteen when we consider Matthew 1:23 and Isaiah 7:14. One example is when Joseph was told to escape to Egypt with Mary and the Christ child and return after the death of Herod. Matthew sees this as a fulfillment of a past historical event recorded in Hosea where the prophet speaks of Israel being called out of Egypt (Hosea 11:1/Matthew 2:14-15). Matthew uses a fulfilled event associated with Israel and applies it to Christ. In the NT, writers often see fulfillment of OT events in events current to them in the NT. Applying OT events to Christ doesn't mean there is equivalent meaning between the OT and NT events. Taking statements associated with *YHWH* in the OT and applying them to Christ in the NT doesn't mean Christ is *YHWH*.

Because *YHWH* is seen as savior in Scripture and Jesus is seen as savior in Scripture doesn't mean Jesus is *YHWH* any more than Jesus being called out of Egypt means Jesus is Israel because Israel being called out of Egypt is applied to Christ in the NT. If it is Jesus who Paul says to call on for salvation in Romans 10:13, it is not because Jesus is *YHWH* but because He is the facilitator of *YHWH's* salvation. Jesus perfectly represents *YHWH*. Calling on the name of the Lord Jesus for salvation is calling on the name of *YHWH's* agent for salvation. Jesus is the intermediary between *YHWH* and man as Paul wrote to Timothy. When my son represents me in a business deal, he acts on my behalf and facilitates my intentions. My son acts as an intermediary. A vender dealing with my son is virtually equivalent to the vender dealing with me. This doesn't mean my son is me.

Language applied to *YHWH* in an OT context which is applied to Jesus in a NT context does not equate *YHWH* with Jesus. Use of similar language in different contexts and in association with different individuals does not translate into those individuals being the same individual. To assume such is the case is to assume the thing to be proved and amounts to a Non Sequitur argument where the conclusion does not follow from the premise. For example, Paul's statement in 1 Corinthians 10:22 about arousing the Lord's jealousy is a phrase found in association with *YHWH* in several OT passages. Because it is believed Paul is using this saying in association with the Lord Christ, some conclude this identifies Christ as *YHWH*. It is concluded Jesus is *YHWH* because similar language is used in association with *YHWH* in the OT. Does arousing Jesus to jealousy identify Him with *YHWH* because *YHWH* is shown as being aroused to jealousy?

In Proverbs 6:34, the writer shows a husband to be aroused to jealousy over his wife becoming involved in adultery. In Acts 5:17, the high priest and his associates were aroused to jealousy over the success of Peter healing the sick. In Acts

13:45, the Jews were aroused to jealousy because of what Paul was doing. No one would conclude these folks were aroused to jealousy because *YHWH* is seen as being aroused to jealousy and therefore they are *YHWH*. In 2 Corinthians 11:2, Paul says, **"I am jealous for you with a godly jealousy."** Does Paul having a godly jealously mean he is the Lord God or the Lord Christ?

In Psalm 24:1 it is written, **"The earth is the LORD's, (*YHWH's*) and everything in it, the world, and all who live in it."** In 1 Corinthians 10:25-26, Paul is dealing with the issue of foods sacrificed to idols and says, **"Eat anything sold in the meat market without raising questions of conscience, for, 'The earth is the Lord's, and everything in it.'"** Because Paul references Christ a number of times in this chapter, some believe Paul is applying the statement from Psalm 24 to the Lord Jesus in 10:26 and this identifies Jesus as *YHWH* since it is *YHWH* who is seen as possessor of the earth in Psalm 24.

A careful reading of the entirety of 1 Corinthians 10 will reveal Paul speaks both of God and Jesus as Lord in this passage. Since the earth is seen as belonging to *YHWH* in Psalm 24 and *YHWH* is referenced in a similar manner in Exodus 9:29, I would lean toward Paul referencing the Father in 10:26 as the Father is seen as the *YHWH* who is creator of heaven and earth. On the other hand, *YHWH* has given great power, authority and glory to Jesus which includes rulership over the earth. Therefore, Jesus could be seen as possessor of the earth. This doesn't make Jesus *YHWH* any more than Jesus being savior equates Him with *YHWH*. Jesus is who He is because *YHWH* has granted Him the wherewithal to be who He is and not because He is *YHWH*.

It is critical we look at the whole of Scripture in determining the relationship between *YHWH* as LORD and Jesus as Lord. Jesus is the appointed and anointed Lord of the Supreme LORD God Almighty. Jesus and *YHWH* are not the same Lord as is clearly seen in our examination of Psalm 110 and dozens of other Scriptural passages we have discussed. Statements directed to *YHWH* in the OT and used in association with Jesus in the NT do not identify Jesus as *YHWH*.

Chapter Nineteen

Seeing Things in Context

There are a number of Scriptural passages that are used as "proof texts" to establish the Doctrine of the incarnation and Trinity. A "proof text" is a passage of Scripture taken by itself to establish a particular point of doctrine. "Proof texting" is a dangerous way to establish doctrine. While specific passages of Scripture can provide helpful information in the establishment of a doctrine, it is vital that such passages are examined and compared to what the whole context of Scripture reveals as to a particular doctrinal issue. In this chapter we will examine Scriptural passages often used as "proof texts" (texts that prove) Jesus is God as God is God.

Scripture #1: Matthew 1:23: Behold, a virgin shall be with child, and shall bring forth a son, and they shall call his name Emmanuel, which being interpreted is, God with us (KJV).

This statement about Mary's son being called Emmanuel which means "God with us" is often seen as straightforward evidence Jesus is God. If His name is "God with us," He must be God. Let's examine this conclusion by studying the original context from which Matthew's statement is taken.

Isaiah 7:14. Therefore the Lord himself shall give you a sign; Behold, a virgin shall conceive, and bear a son, and shall call his name Immanuel.

Isaiah chapter seven shows Ahaz was king of Judah. Kings Rezin of Aram and Pekah of Israel were in alliance and came up to fight against Ahaz and Judah. The Lord, through Isaiah, told Ahaz this alliance would not succeed against Ahaz and

Judah. It's recorded the Lord then gave a sign to Ahaz to show him the alliance would not succeed. The sign is that a virgin shall conceive and bear a son who will be named Immanuel which in Hebrew means, "God is with us" or "God with us." In referring to this son who would be called Immanuel, Isaiah went on to say the following:

Isaiah 7:15-16: He will eat curds and honey when he knows enough to reject the wrong and choose the right. But before the boy knows enough to reject the wrong and choose the right, the land of the two kings you dread will be laid waste.

Isaiah 8:3-8: Then I went to the prophetess, and she conceived and gave birth to a son. And the LORD said to me, "Name him Maher-Shalal-Hash-Baz. Before the boy knows how to say `My father' or `My mother,' the wealth of Damascus and the plunder of Samaria will be carried off by the king of Assyria." The LORD spoke to me again: "Because this people has rejected the gently flowing waters of Shiloah and rejoices over Rezin and the son of Remaliah, therefore the Lord is about to bring against them the mighty floodwaters of the River -- the king of Assyria with all his pomp. It will overflow all its channels, run over all its banks and sweep on into Judah, swirling over it, passing through it and reaching up to the neck. Its outspread wings will cover the breadth of your land, O Immanuel!"

The sign given to Ahaz was directed to Ahaz and the house of David (Judah). The naming of the child Immanuel relates to the events at hand in Isaiah's time. The context of Isaiah 7 and 8 clearly shows the son spoken of is a boy living at that time and behaving in a certain way relative to the two kings being laid waste. The son being named Immanuel (God with us) doesn't mean this boy was God. Ahaz was given a sign from God that God would intervene on his behalf to defeat the alliance. The sign was the boy named Immanuel. God was telling Ahaz He would be with him and his people.

Matthew is using this OT event to show that through Jesus, God would be with His people Israel. Just as the son born to the prophetess and called "God with us" was not actual God, neither was the son born to Mary actual God but signified God as being with His people Israel. Israel never viewed the promised Messiah as an incarnation of the one God. There was no thought in Israel's theology that Messiah would be actual God. Such a conclusion would run contrary to everything Israel understood about God and Messiah. Matthew is not seen as introducing a new concept of God by saying the one God of Israel was going to be incarnated in the son born to Mary. While the religious leaders of the first century rejected Jesus as Messiah, many of the people saw Jesus as a great prophet through whom God had come to help His people and in this respect God was with them.

Luke 7:16: They were all filled with awe and praised God. "A great prophet has appeared among us," they said. "<u>God has come to help his people</u>."

Scripture #2: Matthew 3:3: This is he who was spoken of through the prophet Isaiah: "A voice of one calling in the desert, `Prepare the way for the Lord, make straight paths for him.'"

The "he" Matthew refers to is John the Baptist. The quote is taken from Isaiah 40:3 where the word Lord is translated from the Hebrew *YHWH*. John is seen as making straight paths for *YHWH*.

Isaiah 40:3: A voice of one calling: "In the desert prepare the way for the LORD (*YHWH*); make straight in the wilderness a highway for our God (*Elohim*)."

Because Isaiah speaks of preparing the way for *YHWH* and a highway for our *Elohim*, it is believed Matthew is telling us John the Baptist is preaching a message of preparation for the coming of *YHWH Elohim*. Since it is Christ who came, it is believed Christ is *YHWH Elohim*. Jesus, however, sheds more light on what Isaiah said. In speaking about John the Baptist, Jesus said this:

Matthew 11:10: This is the one about whom it is written: "I will send my messenger ahead of you, who will prepare your way before you."

The key to understanding this passage is to determine who the "I" is and who the "you" and "your" is. The "I" appears to be *YHWH* speaking and the "you" and "your" appear to be referring to Jesus. *YHWH* is speaking of sending a messenger to prepare the way for the coming of the Christ (*YHWH's* anointed one). *YHWH* is not speaking of John preparing the way for His (*YHWH's*) coming. This prophecy has to do with John preparing the way for the coming of the anointed of *YHWH* and not a coming of *YHWH* Himself. In calling people to repentance, John was acting as *YHWH's* agent to prepare and establish the conditions and environment *YHWH* wanted to be extant for the arrival of His anointed.

The focus here is not on the person who was coming but on a messenger preparing the way for the person who was coming by turning people back to *YHWH*. Jesus is the recipient of this preparation. It allows Jesus to begin His ministry among people who have begun to turn to God. In essence, *YHWH* is preparing the way for His anointed through the efforts of John. This is what Jesus is saying in the Matthew 11:10 quote. Mark's rendering of what Isaiah wrote shows this as well.

Mark 1:2: It is written in Isaiah the prophet: "I (YHWH) will send my messenger (John) ahead of you (Jesus), who will prepare your (Jesus') way"

Isaiah is saying that *YHWH* will send a messenger ahead of Jesus to prepare a way for Jesus. If Jesus is *YHWH*, this passage would have to read: "**I (*YHWH*) will send my messenger (John) <u>ahead of you (*YHWH*),</u> who will prepare your (*YHWH's*) way.**" As can be seen, such a reading makes no sense. It should be evident John the Baptist was *YHWH Elohim's* agent to prepare the way for the appearance of the <u>anointed</u> of *YHWH,* not the appearance of *YHWH.* In Luke 2:26, Jesus is referred to as the Lord's Christ which is to say Jesus is the anointed <u>of</u> *YHWH* and not that Jesus <u>is</u> *YHWH* (see my discussion of Psalm 110:1 in Chapter Three).

Scripture #3: **Matthew 9:2-6: Some men brought to him a paralytic, lying on a mat. When Jesus saw their faith, he said to the paralytic, "Take heart, son; your sins are forgiven." At this, some of the teachers of the law said to themselves, "This fellow is blaspheming!" Knowing their thoughts, Jesus said, "Why do you entertain evil thoughts in your hearts? Which is easier: to say, `Your sins are forgiven,' or to say, `Get up and walk'? But so that you may know that the Son of Man has authority on earth to forgive sins. . . ." Then he said to the paralytic, "Get up, take your mat and go home."**

It is believed only God can forgive sin and since Jesus had authority to forgive sin, Jesus must be God. What is overlooked is the scripturally stated reason Jesus had authority to forgive sin and do all that He did.

Matthew 9:8: When the crowd saw this, they were filled with awe; and they praised God, <u>who had given such authority to men.</u>

God the Father gave the man Jesus extraordinary power and authority on earth to do many things that could not be done by other men. Jesus turned water into wine, walked on water, calmed a raging storm, fed thousands of people from a few morsels of food, healed the sick, raised the dead and forgave sin. Matthew recorded the reaction of the people when they saw how Jesus healed the paralytic.

God had given great authority to the man Jesus. Jesus was God's unique human agent sent to facilitate His will on earth. The authority granted to Jesus included He being able to give power and authority to His disciples. The Scriptures show Jesus giving authority to His disciples to heal the sick. In Luke we read, **"When Jesus had called the Twelve together, he gave them power and authority to drive out all demons and to cure diseases" (Luke 9:1).** After His resurrection He even gives them authority to forgive sin.

John 20:21-23: Again Jesus said, "Peace be with you! As the Father has sent me, I am sending you." And with that he breathed on them and said, "Receive the Holy Spirit. If you forgive anyone his sins, they are forgiven; if you do not forgive them, they are not forgiven."

The ability to forgive sin or do anything else Jesus gave his disciples power and authority to do did not make those disciples God or equal with God. It did not make them equal with Christ. What we are seeing here is granted power and authority. God granted power and authority to Jesus which included giving Jesus the ability to grant power and authority to others. The fact Jesus did everything His Father empowered Him to do does not make Him equal to His Father anymore than Jesus empowering His disciples made them equal with Him.

Athanasius, in his treatise entitled, *"The Incarnation of the Word of God,"* written in the early fourth century, argued that Jesus must be God because only God could make the blind see, cast out demons, turn water into wine, walk on water and raise the dead. What Athanasius failed to mention was that Peter, James, John and Paul also performed great supernatural acts. This didn't make these men God. Peter raised Dorcas from the dead. The power of God manifested in Apostle Peter was so pronounced that in Acts 5:15, it is implied that even the shadow of Peter passing over someone was enough to facilitate healing. These men were imbued with power and authority because God gave it to them. This did not make them equal with God. Why should it be assumed Jesus was equal with God because he performed miracles? In **Acts 19:11-12** we read, **"God did extraordinary miracles through Paul, so that even handkerchiefs and aprons that had touched him were taken to the sick, and their illnesses were cured and the evil spirits left them."** Did this make Paul God?

Look at what God did through Moses. Moses turned the water of the Nile River into blood. He brought plagues of frogs, gnats, flies, locusts, darkness and hail upon the people of Egypt. He brought a plague upon the animals of Egypt and took ashes from a furnace, threw them into the air and caused boils to break out on the Egyptian people. Finally He brought about the death of the firstborn of Egypt. Moses wasn't God. Moses was a servant of God through whom God did many mighty works. In like manner, Jesus was a servant of God through whom God did mighty works.

Scripture makes it clear God the Father granted Jesus great power and authority. It does not follow from this that Jesus is co-equal, co-eternal and con-substantial with the one granting Him such authority and power. Jesus plainly said that all He did came from the Father and it was the Father doing the works through Him (John 5:19). The Apostles did great works by the power of God the Father. The source for their power was the same source from which Jesus received power. The great works Jesus did were enabled by the power of God the Father. That same power that flowed from the Father into Jesus flowed from Jesus to the Apostles. The one and only Supreme God is the source of the power and authority displayed by Christ and the Apostles. Their exercise of God's power doesn't equate with their being the source of that power.

Scripture #4: John 5:16-18: So, because Jesus was doing these things on the Sabbath, the Jews persecuted him. Jesus said to them, "My Father is always at his work to this very day, and I, too, am working." For this reason the Jews tried all the harder to kill him; not only was he breaking the Sabbath, but he was even calling God his own Father, making himself equal with God.

Here we see the Jews accusing Jesus of breaking the Sabbath and also making Himself equal with God by calling God His Father. Keep in mind it is the Jews who are accusing Jesus of breaking the Sabbath and making Himself equal with God. Jesus never admitted to breaking the Sabbath and neither did He ever claim to be equal with the Supreme, Most High God. Jesus answered the Jews by saying the following:

John 5:19: Jesus gave them this answer: "I tell you the truth, the Son can do nothing by himself; he can do only what he sees his Father doing, because whatever the Father does the Son also does."

Trinitarianism teaches the Son is a person or distinction of a Triune God and is God as the Father and Spirit is God. It is believed "God the Son" became incarnate in a human body and was God in the flesh. Trinitarianism, also teaches there is no separation in the Triune God. All three distinctions of the Triune God are equal in every way except that of being each other. Because they indwell each other, they are a single Being.

This perspective of God is problematical for the doctrine of incarnation. If there is no separation in God and God is a single Being, how can it be said the Son distinction of the one God became incarnate in Jesus? If there is no separation in God, God as Father, Son and Spirit would have to incarnate Jesus. If there is no separation in God, how can it be said God incarnated Jesus through the Son? The Scriptures consistently speak of the Son of God. How can the Son be of God if the

Son is God? I am the son of my father John. As the son of my father John, I am a separate individual from my father John and certainly not of the same Being as my father.

As previously pointed out, we consistently read in the Scriptures of the Son of God and the Spirit of God. Since it is the Father who is consistently identified as God in Scripture, this is the same as saying the Son of the Father and the Spirit of the Father. You do not find in Scripture any reference to the Father of God which would be equivalent to saying the Father of the Father. This should be very instructive as to who God actually is. Jesus spoke of His Father being in heaven and consistently related to His Father as a separate Being. Jesus plainly said He could do nothing by Himself. If Jesus is co-equal with the Father, why is he dependent on the Father for everything He does?

Since Jesus is seen as totally God and totally man in Trinitarian thought, it is argued His dependence on the Father is only a dependence necessitated by His humanity. Yet, the consistent Scriptural view is that the Father, as the one and only Supreme God, is superior to the Son, always has been and always will be (1 Corinthians 11:3 and 15:28). Jesus plainly said the Father is greater than He (John 14:28). Jesus clearly said the Father is the only true God (John 17:3). Jesus never said He was the one God or that He was equal with God. The Jews, in accusing Jesus of making Himself equal with the Father, were as mistaken in this accusation as they were in accusing Jesus of breaking the Sabbath because He healed on the Sabbath. All of NT Scripture teaches us Jesus related to the Father as his superior, both during His earthly ministry and after His ascension.

Scripture #5: Romans 9:5: Theirs are the patriarchs, and from them is traced the human ancestry of Christ, who is God over all, forever praised! Amen.

Is Paul identifying Jesus as God in this passage? Greek manuscripts of the NT do not contain punctuation. Punctuation was added by the translators based on their understanding of the context in which a word or passage is found. Interpretation, as well as doctrinal predisposition, has always played a role in determining how translators transfer meaning from one language into another. This is especially true of ambiguous passages. Romans 9:5 can be punctuated either with a period or a comma after the word Christ depending on what the translator feels the writer is saying. While a number of translations place a comma after the word Christ, others do not. For example, the Revised Standard Version has it this way:

"to them belong the patriarchs, and of their race, according to the flesh, is the Christ. God who is over all be blessed for ever. Amen."

How can we know what is the correct way to punctuate this passage? Looking at Paul's letter to the Romans as a whole, it will be seen Paul always distinguishes between Jesus Christ and God. The word God (Greek *Theos*) appears 153 times in Romans in addition to its appearance in 9:5. In all these 153 occurrences, it can be clearly seen Paul associates the word God with the Father. This pattern is seen overwhelmingly in all of Paul's letters. Therefore, it appears extremely unlikely Paul changes his manner of expression by suddenly calling Jesus God when in every other instance he associates God with the Father.

A number of commentators have focused attention on what appears to be a doxology at the end of 9:5. Doxologies are closing statements, hymns or prayers directed to the praise of God. Paul's statement in 9:5, **"God who is over all be blessed (Greek: *ulogeetos*) for ever. Amen" (RSV)** is seen as a clear doxology in the same vain as others found in the writings of Paul. Paul's use of the Greek *ulogeetos* is instructive. He consistently uses this word in praise to God the Father in his writings. If Paul is using this word in reference to Christ in 9:5, it would be a noted departure from the manner in which he uses this word in the rest of his writings. Here are some examples of doxologies and Paul's use of *ulogeetos.*

2 Corinthians 1:3: Praise (ulogeetos) be to the God and Father of our Lord Jesus Christ, the Father of compassion and the God of all comfort.

2 Corinthians 11:31: The God and Father of the Lord Jesus, who is to be praised (ulogeetos) forever, knows that I am not lying.

Ephesians 1:3: Praise (ulogeetos) be to the God and Father of our Lord Jesus Christ, who has blessed us in the heavenly realms with every spiritual blessing in Christ.

In view of Paul's consistent use of doxologies in praise to God the Father, it is very unlikely Paul suddenly uses a doxology in praise to "God the Son." As previously pointed out, nowhere does Paul use the phrase "God the Son" nor is this phrase found anywhere in Scripture. Paul consistently writes in terms of the "God and Father of our Lord Jesus."

It should be noted, however, that even if it could be shown Paul is calling Jesus God, this would not necessarily mean Jesus is the one and only God in a Triune relationship of Father, Son and Spirit. It is a common tendency on the part of Trinitarians to draw such a conclusion when viewing Scriptures that may reference Jesus as being God. As previously discussed, there is nothing inherent in the Hebrew *elohim* or the Greek *theos* that requires these words be limited to only identifying the one and only God. These words are used to identify angels, prophets, judges, Kings of Israel and even possibly Satan (2 Corinthians 4:4). These words are used to identify individuals having, or having been granted, power, authority and leadership. Concluding that Jesus is God as the Father is God should not be done strictly on the basis of Scriptural passages where Jesus appears to be called God. We must look at the whole of Scripture when examining apparent references to Jesus as God.

Scripture #6: Titus 2:11-14: For the grace of God that brings salvation has appeared to all men. It teaches us to say "No" to ungodliness and worldly passions, and to live self-controlled, upright and godly lives in this present age, while we wait for the blessed hope--the glorious appearing <u>of our great God and Savior, Jesus Christ</u>, who gave himself for us to redeem us from all wickedness and to purify for himself a people that are his very own, eager to do what is good.

I discussed this passage in Chapter Eight in association with "Sharp's Rule" but want to revisit this discussion here because of its importance to the thesis of this book. The NIV translates verse 13 of this passage in such manner as to show there to be one subject (God) and that subject to be Jesus Christ, seen as the great God and Savior who's appearing is anticipated. Other translations show two subjects and therefore could be read with God being one referent and Jesus being another.

"Looking for that blessed hope, and the glorious appearing of <u>the great God</u> <u>and our</u> Saviour Jesus Christ (KJV).

"Looking for the blessed hope and appearing of the glory of <u>the great God</u> <u>and our</u> Saviour Jesus Christ (ASV).

As previously discussed, scholars are divided as to how best to render this passage. Some see it referring only to Christ and some see it referring separately to God the Father and to Jesus Christ. The presence of the Greek *kai* (and) between the first noun (God) which is proceeded by the definite article *tou* (the) and the second noun (Jesus) preceded by no article has led some to conclude that God and Jesus are being identified as the same person in this passage. It is believed that if Jesus

244

is to be identified as separate from God a definite article would precede His name. Others cite Scriptural passages with similar Greek grammar construction where a definite article precedes the first noun but not the second noun and where context clearly shows two different individuals being referenced.

Those who believe this passage refers only to Jesus believe Jesus is identified as *YHWH*. Verse 14 of this chapter speaks of how Christ gave Himself to redeem us and purify a people for His very own. Since the OT speaks of God (*YHWH*) as Savior and redeemed people are spoken of as being God's possession, it is felt that similar language in the NT testifies of Jesus being *YHWH*. However, Jesus plainly says that those given to Him were given to Him by God His Father. This shows Jesus being the subordiant agent of the Father unto whom the Father has given a redeemed people. In praying to the Father Jesus said:

John 17:6-7: I have revealed you to those whom you gave me out of the world. They were yours; you gave them to me and they have obeyed your word. Now they know that everything you have given me comes from you.

It is important we look at the entire context of Paul's letter to Titus in order to understand what Paul is saying in the passage under consideration. Paul begins his letter by writing, **"Paul, a servant of God and an apostle of Jesus Christ" (Titus 1:1).** He goes on to write that the preaching entrusted to him is by the **"command of God our Savior" (Verse 3).** He continues his greeting to Titus by writing, **"Grace and peace from God the Father and Christ Jesus our Savior" (Verse 4).** Paul proceeds to give instruction in Christian living and concludes this instruction by writing, **"so that in every way they will make the teaching about God our Savior attractive" (Titus 2:10).** Paul then makes the comments quoted above in Titus 2:11-13. Paul finishes his letter by continuing to instruct in matters of Christian living and then writes the following:

Titus 3:4-6: But when the kindness and love of God our Savior appeared, he (God) saved us, not because of righteous things we had done, but because of his (God's) mercy. He (God) saved us through the washing of rebirth and renewal by the Holy Spirit, whom he (God) poured out on us generously through Jesus Christ our Savior.

As Paul consistently does in his letters, he begins by distinguishing between God and Christ (Titus 1:1). In his greeting to Titus, he also distinguishes between God the Father and Christ Jesus as Savior (Verse 4). In verse 3 he writes about preaching by the "command of God our Savior." In Titus 2:10, Paul writes of practicing proper behavior in order to make the teaching of God our Savior attractive. In Titus 3:4-6, it is evident Paul is referring to the Father in speaking of the "love of God our Savior" which He generously poured out through Jesus Christ our Savior.

In chapter one of a letter to Timothy, Paul clearly distinguishes between God and Jesus by saying he is an apostle by "the command of God our Savior and Christ Jesus our hope." In chapter two of this letter the context shows it is the Father Paul calls God our Savior in distinction from the man Jesus who is seen as a mediator between the Father and men. Jude also writes in terms of God our Savior in distinction from Jesus as Lord. Both Paul and Jude write in terms of God the Father being the one God.

1 Timothy 1:1-2: Paul, an apostle of Christ Jesus by the command of God our Savior <u>and</u> of Christ Jesus our hope. Grace, mercy and peace from God the Father and Christ Jesus our Lord (2b).

1 Timothy 2:3-5: This is good, and pleases <u>God our Savior</u>, who wants all men to be saved and to come to a knowledge of the truth. For there is <u>one God</u> and one mediator <u>between</u> God and men, <u>the man Christ Jesus</u>,

Jude 1:25: to <u>the only God </u>our Savior be glory, majesty, power and authority, <u>through</u> Jesus Christ our Lord, before all ages, now and forevermore! Amen.

In the passages we have been reviewing it is evident both God the Father and Christ Jesus the Son are seen as Savior. The phrase "God our Savior" appears seven times in the NT. In four of these passages (Titus 3:4-6, 1 Timothy 1:1-2, 2:3-5 and Jude 1:25), it can be seen by context it is God the Father who is being referred to as "God our Savior." The most definitive passage is 1Timothy 2:3-5, where the phrase "God our Savior" refers to the one and only God in distinction from the man Jesus. Titus 3:4-6 is also definitive in identifying "God our Savior" as the one who gives us salvation through Jesus. In view of Paul's use of "God our Savior" in clear association with the Father in Titus 3:4-6 and 1 Timothy 1:1-2 and 2:3-5, it is reasonable to conclude Paul is referring to the Father as God our Savior in Titus 1:3 and 2:10 as well when he writes about preaching at the command of God our Savior and making the teaching about God our Savior attractive.

The whole focus of the salvation message is that God the Father loves us and because He loves us He provided for our deliverance from eternal death through the Christ event. Scripture clearly shows salvation comes from God the Father and is facilitated through Jesus. Therefore, God the Father is our ultimate Savior and Jesus is the agent through whom the Father's salvation is accomplished. Therefore, when Paul writes of waiting for the "blessed hope--the glorious appearing of our great God and Savior, Jesus Christ," he is in all likelihood referring to the Father as the Great God who facilitates salvation through Jesus (Titus 2:13). Paul writes in Titus 2:11 that the grace of God that brings salvation has appeared to all men. Paul's reference to the grace of God in this passage is a reference to the grace of the Father. Now let's examine Hebrews 2:9-10.

David A Kroll

The majority of surviving Greek texts renders Hebrews 2:9-10, to show it is by the grace of God that Christ became the author of salvation. We know it is the grace of God the Father being spoke of because the whole of Scripture shows it is God the Father who has facilitated salvation through Christ Jesus. Remember, Christ Jesus means anointed Savior. Salvation is derived and flows from God the Father through his anointed facilitator of salvation, Christ Jesus.

Hebrews 2:9-10: But we see Jesus, who was made a little lower than the angels, now crowned with glory and honor because he suffered death, so that by the grace of God (The Father) he might taste death for everyone. In bringing many sons to glory, it was fitting that God (The Father), for whom and through whom everything exists, should make the author of their salvation perfect through suffering.

I mentioned that the majority of extant Greek manuscripts say "that by the grace of God." It's to be noted, however, that several very ancient manuscripts of the NT Scriptures read "that apart from God" in place of "the grace of God." This variant was acknowledged by Origen as the reading present in the majority of manuscripts of his day. It is quoted in this manner by various Christian writers down to the eleventh century and is rendered as such in some Greek to Latin translations. Some scholars, such as Bart Ehrman, believe there is strong evidence for seeing this variant as what the writer to the Hebrews actually wrote. If this is the case, it gives further evidence to Jesus and God being separate entities and not *homoousios*.

Scripture #7: 2 Peter 1:1-2: Simon Peter, a servant and apostle of Jesus Christ, To those who through the righteousness of our God and Savior Jesus Christ have received a faith as precious as ours: Grace and peace be yours in abundance through the knowledge of God and of Jesus our Lord.

I discussed this passage in Chapter Eight in relationship to "Sharp's Rule" but want to add to that discussion here because of its relevance to the overall focus of this book.

It should be noted that while the majority of Greek manuscripts show "of our God (*Theos*) and Savior Jesus Christ," there are nine extant manuscripts that show "of our Lord (*Kurios*) and Savior Jesus Christ." A review of Peter's epistle reveals the phrase "Lord and Savior" is more in sync with who Peter understands Christ to be as he uses the phrase "Lord and Savior" four times in this epistle (1:11, 2:20, 3:2,18).

It is instructive that in verse 2 is found the exact same grammatical construction where Peter says, **"through the knowledge of God and of Jesus our Lord."** Here a definite distinction is made between God and Jesus because Jesus is identified as Lord in distinction from God. What is of greater significance in our quest to determine what Peter is saying is the fact Peter clearly distinguishes between Jesus and God the Father in all his other writings. He refers to Jesus twelve times as Lord and forty-five times to God as Father. There is no reference to Jesus as God found in Peter's writings other than the possible reference in 1 Peter chapter one. The weight of references to the Father as God and the one single possible reference to Jesus as God makes it highly unlikely Peter is calling Jesus God in verse one.

As discussed in Chapter Eight, the Greek grammatical construction of "our God and Savior Jesus Christ" is the same as in Titus 2:13 except here the writer does not refer to God as the "great God." The same grammatical construction is repeated in 2 Peter 1:11 where Peter writes, **"and you will receive a rich welcome into the eternal kingdom of our Lord and Savior Jesus Christ."** In this verse, one person is clearly in view, namely Jesus Christ.

The grammatical construction found in 2 Peter 1:1-2 and in Titus 2:13 does allow for having just one person in view. It also allows for having two persons in view and is so rendered in a number of translations of 2 Peter 1:1-2 such as in the following:

"to them that have obtained like precious faith with us through the righteousness of God and our Saviour Jesus Christ" (KJV).

"to them that have obtained a like precious faith with us in the righteousness of our God and the Saviour Jesus Christ:" (ASV).

"to those who are chancing upon an equally precious faith with us, in righteousness of our God, and the Savior, Jesus Christ" (Concordant Literal New Testament).

Apostles Paul and Peter refer to God as Father 99% of the time and only on a few occasions is there a possible reference to Jesus as God. Such tremendous disparity in the way the word God is used by these Apostles in association with the Father as opposed to the Son is instructive to say the least. Therefore, it is vitally important we consider the whole of Scripture in determining how its authors use the word God in association with Jesus in the few instances where the Greek grammar allows for such association.

Scripture #8: Jude 1:4-5: For certain men have secretly slipped in among you – men who long ago were marked out for the condemnation I am about to describe – ungodly men who have turned the grace of our God into a license for evil and who deny our only Master and Lord, Jesus Christ. Verse 5: Now I desire to remind you (even though you have been fully informed of these facts once for all) that Jesus, having saved the people out of the land of Egypt, later destroyed those who did not believe (NET).

The NET translators, as do the ESV translators, show Jesus as the one who saved the people out of the land of Egypt. They have chosen this rendering because the Greek *Ihsous* (Jesus) appears in a small number of early Greek renderings of verse 5. The majority of Greek manuscripts have *Kurios* (Lord) and some have *Theos* (God). Most English translations appear to use manuscripts that have *Kurios* and thus show the Lord as having saved the people. It is sometimes argued that because Jude initially refers to Jesus Christ as Lord, it is the Lord Jesus Christ who is being referred to as the one who saved the people out of Egypt. We know from the OT that it was *YHWH* who delivered the Israelites out of Egypt (Exodus 20:2).

I think I have sufficiently demonstrated in the material already presented that *YHWH* is the Father and only the Father and Jesus, the Son, is not *YHWH*. Therefore, I will not cover that same ground again. Scholars have clearly demonstrated that there are many variants in the Greek Biblical manuscripts where scribes involved in copying the manuscripts changed wording to reflect a particular theological point of view. A number of references to Jesus have been altered to show Him to be God. A must read for anyone interested in the dynamics associated with these alterations is the book, *The Orthodox Corruption Of Scripture* by Bart D Ehrman.

Since the majority of Greek manuscripts do not have *Ihsous* in Jude 1:5, and since we know it is *YHWH* who delivered the Israelites out of Egypt and since I believe I have adequately demonstrated and will continue to demonstrate that Jesus is not *YHWH*, I will have to conclude that when Jude writes of the Lord delivering His people he is speaking of God the Father. I will also have to conclude that the NET and ESV translators of Jude are choosing Greek manuscripts that represent their conviction Jesus is God and are not taking into account the whole of Scripture in establishing their theology.

Scripture #9: Acts 20:28: Keep watch over yourselves and all the flock of which the Holy Spirit has made you overseers. Be shepherds of the church of God (*Theos*), which he bought with his own blood (NIV).

Since it is Jesus who shed His blood, some believe this passage says God shed his blood and so Jesus must be God. Some Greek manuscripts substitute *Kurios* for *Theos* in this passage and thus render the passage as "church of the Lord." The ASV apparently used a Greek text showing *Kurios* instead of *Theos*.

Take heed unto yourselves, and to all the flock, in which the Holy Spirit hath made you bishops, to feed the church of the Lord which he purchased with his own blood (ASV).

It should be noted that "church of the Lord (*Kurios*)" is a variant rendering as it is evident that *Theos* is the word found in the oldest Greek manuscripts and "church of the Lord" is found nowhere else in the NT whereas "church of God" is found twelve times and is also attested too in the writings of the early church fathers. The NASV has changed the rendering to "church of God."

Some commentators have pointed out that the literal translation of the Greek at the end of this passage is "with the blood of his own." The phrase "his own" is felt to be a reference to the Son and therefore the passage is sometimes translated as "with the blood of His own Son."

Take heed to yourselves and to all the flock, in which the Holy Spirit has made you overseers, to care for the church of God which he obtained with the blood of his own Son (RSV).

Watch out for yourselves and for all the flock of which the Holy Spirit has made you overseers, to shepherd the church of God that he obtained with the blood of his own Son (NET).

As can be seen, there are several different ways of translating this passage depending on the Greek manuscript used and the manner in which the Greek construction is understood. The "church of God" rendering is found in the older Alexandrian texts. Theologian Bart Ehrman believes the variant readings found in Greek texts are a reflection of the continuing battle in the early centuries of the Church over how to understand the relationship between the Father and the Son. There were the Adoptionists who believed Jesus was not deity and became the Son of God during His earthly ministry. On the opposite end were the Patripassianists (type of Modalism) who believed God was only the Father and this God who is Father took on humanity and appeared as Jesus Christ to shed His blood for the sins of mankind.

Ehrman believes the textual variant of "church of the Lord" was an attempt to moderate the Patripassianist view that God the Father became Jesus and shed his blood. Some later Greek manuscripts are seen to further adjust the passage to read "the church of the Lord <u>and</u> God." In the oldest Greek manuscripts the end of this passage is rendered "the blood of his own" while in later texts, including most modern Greek texts, the rendering is "his own blood" thus making "his own" refer back to God. What it appears we are seeing is that over the centuries, copiers (scribes) of the Greek text made adjustments of the Greek text to reflect what those in positions of Church leadership promoted as orthodox. What appears to be the case, as Ehrman points out, is that at times adjustments were made one way and at other times adjustments were made the other way in order to counter what were considered unorthodox teachings.

In the case of Acts 20:28, it appears that "church of God" and "the blood of his own" is what the author intended as this is the rendering found in many of the oldest manuscripts and is also in harmony with other Scriptures. This would permit the passage to say that God purchased the church through the shedding of the blood of His own Son. This would harmonize well with I John 1:7 where God's Son Jesus is seen as shedding

His blood for sin. Yet in most of the more recent Greek texts, we see the rending "his own blood." This appears to be a deliberate "adjustment" to support the idea that the reference to God in this passage is a reference to Jesus and therefore tacitly provides support for Incarnational and Trinitarian theology.

All this raises the obvious question as to how much has orthodoxy influenced the transmission of Scripture versus Scripture being allowed to influence and determine orthodoxy? This is a very delicate dynamic and it should instruct us to be very careful in how Scripture is used to establish doctrine, especially a doctrine as foundational as the nature of the Father, Son and Spirit. It is very apparent that Greek texts differ in their rendering of certain passages and English and other language translations taken from such Greek texts will reflect such differences. Historically, translators have had to make choices as to what texts to use. It is evident from the variance seen in renderings; choices are often made on the basis of what is orthodox theology at the time. This, however, does not ensure that the rendering chosen is that which best reflects the thinking of the original author.

Scripture #10: 1 Timothy 3:16: And without controversy great is the mystery of godliness: God was manifest in the flesh, justified in the Spirit, seen of angels, preached unto the Gentiles, believed on in the world, received up into glory (KJV).

The KJV translation of this passage suggests Jesus is God as it speaks of God (*Theos*) being manifest in the flesh and we know it is Jesus who was manifested in the flesh. *Theos* is found in a Greek Byzantine text along with a few other Greek manuscripts. The King James translators apparently used these texts in providing this rendering.

This rendering is sometimes used by Trinitarians as a "proof text" to show Jesus is God. Yet the oldest Greek Manuscripts do not show *Theos* but a different Greek construction that doesn't say God was manifest in the flesh but that "he" or "who," was manifest in the flesh. Most scholars believe this is referring to the Christ who was manifest in the flesh. In ancient Greek manuscripts, copyists abbreviated the word Theos (God) with the Greek letters theta and sigma with a line drawn over the top to indicate it was an abbreviation. The Greek theta looks like a 0 with a line running horizontally through the middle. In the early fifth century manuscript called Codex Alexandrinus, it was determined the 0 in this passage did not have a line running through it and the line above it had been added at a later time. This meant the letter was not theta but omicron which when combined with sigma means who or he. Most modern translations render this passage using the word "He" as referring to Christ as seen in the following renditions.

Beyond all question, the mystery of godliness is great: He appeared in a body, was vindicated by the Spirit, was seen by angels, was preached among the nations, was believed on in the world, was taken up in glory (NIV).

And we all agree, our religion contains amazing revelation: He was revealed in the flesh, vindicated by the Spirit, seen by angels, proclaimed among Gentiles, believed on in the world, taken up in glory (NET).

Without any doubt, the mystery of our religion is very deep indeed: He was made visible in the flesh, justified in the Spirit, seen by angels, proclaimed to the gentiles, believed in throughout the world, taken up in glory (New Jerusalem Bible).

Even though the New Jerusalem translation was made by Catholic scholars who are Trinitarians, they chose to use Greek texts they felt were closer to the original even if it didn't necessarily support Trinitarian doctrine as do the texts used by the KJV translators. The Simple English paraphrased Bible says it this way:

We must agree that the secret of our faith is great: Christ appeared in a human body. He was shown to be right by the Spirit. He was seen by angels. He was preached among the nations. He was believed in the world. He was taken up to heaven.

Trinitarian theologian Thomas F Torrance writes that this passage *"came to play a central and important role in formulating the doctrine of the Trinity"* (*The Christian Doctrine of God: One Being Three Persons*, page 74). This is felt to be the case because Paul speaks of the "mystery of godliness" which is believed to relate to the Trinitarian nature of God. Is Paul talking about the Trinitarian nature of God? Paul writes that Christ appeared in a human body which is to say the anointed of God was a human. He manifested righteousness in all He did and said which is what the Greek word translated "vindicated" in the NIV and justified in the KJV means. Angels ministered unto him at the time of His temptation in the wilderness and in the garden of Gethsemane. He was preached among the nations and many believed in Him. He ascended to his God and Father. There is nothing here to suggest Jesus is God as God is God or that God is a Trinity of Father, Son and Spirit.

The Greek word translated mystery in this passage is *mysterion*. It does not mean something that can't be understood but something that is understood as private knowledge held by an individual or group. The discussion in 1 Timothy chapter three is all about qualifications to be an elder or deacon in the Church of God. This information was private to the internal structure of the Church and had to do with how potential leaders in the Church were to relate to God.

The Greek word translated "godliness" in the KJV and NIV is *eusebeia* which means devotion and piety toward God. Paul is concluding his discussion of qualifications for elders and deacons by saying the knowledge of devotion and piety is great. He proceeds to list various dynamics of the Christ event as demonstration of this knowledge of devotion and piety. This passage has nothing to do with defining God as a Trinity.

Scripture #11: Matthew 28:19: Therefore go and make disciples of all nations, baptizing them in the name of the Father and of the Son and of the Holy Spirit.

Trinitarians often point to Matthew 28:19 as proof of the Trinitarian nature of God. Trinitarians believe these statements show a mutual indwelling of Father, Son and Spirit which makes them the one single Being God. Jesus is understood to be saying "in the name of God who is Father, Son and Holy Spirit."

Matthew 28:19 is commonly used as a baptismal protocol in the Christian community. What is of interest is that this baptismal protocol is not found to have been used by the early Church. All Scriptural references to baptism show baptism being done only in the name of Jesus. Here are a few examples:

Acts 2:38: Peter replied, "Repent and be baptized, every one of you, <u>in the name of Jesus Christ</u> for the forgiveness of your sins. And you will receive the gift of the Holy Spirit.

Acts 10:48: So he ordered that they be <u>baptized in the name of Jesus Christ.</u>

Acts 19:5: On hearing this, they were <u>baptized into the name of the Lord Jesus.</u>

One reason we see the early church not following the baptismal protocol found in Matthew 28:19 may be that this formula was never uttered by Jesus. Eusebius (260 to 340 AD),

Bishop of Caesarea, was a prolific writer of church history up to his time and often quoted Scripture in his writings including Matthew 28:19. Eusebius never quotes Matthew 28:19 as it appears in modern translations but always finishes this verse with "in my name." He shows Jesus saying that baptism was to be done in His name. Eusebius was quoting from manuscripts that are no longer extant. Our modern translations are taken from later Greek manuscripts. In view of this and the Scriptures repeatedly showing baptism being only done in the name of Jesus, it would appear that the baptismal protocol found in modern translations of Matthew 28:19 is suspect. On the other hand, there is mention of this protocol in the *Didache*, a manual of Christian living which dates from the early second century and which was regarded as canonical Scripture by Clement of Alexandria and Origen.

In view of a mixed perspective as to the authenticity and application of the Matthew 28:19 passage, it should be used with caution in the establishment of doctrine. Since this passage has to do with the doctrine of baptism, any application of this passage to other doctrinal perspectives should be done with even greater caution. Therefore, the use of this passage as a "proof text" for the Trinity can only be employed provided there is ample support for the Trinitarian position within the whole of Scripture. It is the thesis of this book that such broad Scriptural support for the Trinity does not exist, while on the other hand, there is broad Scriptural support for a non-Trinitarian position.

Even if the Matthew 28:19 passage is a valid recording of a protocol Christ gave relative to baptism, such baptism protocol doesn't establish the Father, Son and Spirit as coequal, coeternal and consubstantial indwelling distinctions of a Trinitarian God.

Scripture #12: 2 Corinthians 13:14: May the grace of the Lord Jesus Christ, and the love of God, and the fellowship of the Holy Spirit be with you all.

Trinitarians see this passage as identifying God as Father, Son and Spirit. Is this the case? It can be seen throughout his writings that Paul uses the word God to designate the Father and the word Father to designate God. So it can safely be said that in this passage Paul is distinguishing between the Lord Jesus and God the Father as he does in 1 Corinthians 8:6 where he clearly says the Father is the only God in distinction from Jesus being Lord. The words Jesus Christ and God are capitalized in the Greek text of this passage whereas Holy Spirit is not capitalized as is the case throughout the Greek NT. I will discuss the subject of the Holy Spirit in a later chapter.

In 1 Timothy 5:21, Paul says, **"I charge you, in the sight of God and Christ Jesus and the elect angels...."** No one would conclude from this statement that God, Jesus Christ and angels are in some kind of Trinitarian relationship. It appears a real stretch to conclude Paul's remarks to the Corinthians reflects his belief God is a Trinity. Sometimes 1 Corinthians 12:4-6 is used as evidence for God being a Trinity.

1 Corinthians 12:4-6: There are different kinds of gifts, but the same Spirit. There are different kinds of service, but the same Lord. There are different kinds of working, but the same God works all of them in all men.

This entire chapter is dealing with the gifts of the Spirit. Verse four speaks of the Spirit as being from God and it is through the Spirit that is from God that various gifts are seen as given to members of the Church. In Chapter Twenty-Three of this book it will be shown that the Spirit is the power and intrinsic attributes of the one and only God which He shares and distributes throughout his creation. As such, the Spirit is not a distinction of a Trinitarian Godhead but the very core of God's nature.

When one carefully examines Scriptures that are purported to give evidence to support the Trinitarian concept of God, it can be seen these Scriptures do not provide such evidence.

When these Scriptures are examined side by side with the many passages we have studied that provide straightforward, unambiguous evidence as to the Father being the one and only Supreme God, it should be apparent the weight of Scriptural evidence clearly shows God the Father as separate and superior to the Son and the Son as a subservient agent of this God.

Scripture #13: John 12:40-41: He has blinded their eyes and deadened their hearts, so they can neither see with their eyes, nor understand with their hearts, nor turn--and I would heal them." Isaiah said this because he saw Jesus' glory and spoke about him.

Trinitarians believe John's statement about Isaiah seeing Jesus' glory is associated with Isaiah seeing the glory of *YHWH* as recorded in Isaiah chapter six. Therefore, it is believed Jesus is identified as *YHWH*.

Isaiah 6:1-3: In the year that King Uzziah died, I saw the Lord (*Adonai*) seated on a throne, high and exalted, and the train of his robe filled the temple. Above him were seraphs, each with six wings: With two wings they covered their faces, with two they covered their feet, and with two they were flying. And they were calling to one another: "Holy, holy, holy is the LORD (*YHWH*) Almighty; the whole earth is full of his glory."

Isaiah 6:9-10: He said, "Go and tell this people: "Be ever hearing, but never understanding; be ever seeing, but never perceiving.' Make the heart of this people calloused; make their ears dull and close their eyes. Otherwise they might see with their eyes, hear with their ears, understand with their hearts, and turn and be healed."

Let us examine the text of Isaiah chapter 6 from where John quotes Isaiah and determine whether the conclusion that Isaiah is seeing *YHWH* as Jesus is a valid conclusion.

Isaiah 6:1: In the year that King Uzziah died, I saw the Lord (*Adonai*) seated on a throne, high and exalted, and the train of his robe filled the temple.

Isaiah, during the reign of King Uzziah of Judah, had a vision of *Adonai*, which is seen throughout the OT as synonymous with *YHWH*. To say *Adonai* is to say *YHWH*. In 6:2-3, *YHWH* is clearly identified as the Being seen by Isaiah. It is recorded that seraphs were calling to one another: **"Holy, holy, holy is the LORD (*YHWH*) Almighty; the whole earth is full of his glory."** In 6:8, Isaiah hears the voice of *YHWH* asking **"Whom shall I send? And who will go for us?"** Isaiah answers: **"Here am I. Send me!"** We then see *YHWH* giving to Isaiah the message He wants Isaiah to take to the people of Judah as recorded in 6:9-10.

The context of Isaiah 6 is Isaiah seeing the glory of *YHWH* and responding to *YHWH's* request for someone to go to the people of Judah and tell them it is because of their ever hearing and never understanding and ever seeing and never perceiving, that their cities will be destroyed. Isaiah volunteers to take this message to Judah. Biblical history shows the Babylonians invaded Judah and destroyed their cities and took them into captivity. In John 12:40, John paraphrases Isaiah's quote of *YHWH's* message to the people and applies it to the Israelites of Jesus' day. History shows first century Israel was judged when the temple and the city of Jerusalem were destroyed by the Romans in A.D. 70 and many were taken into captivity.

Because John paraphrases Isaiah 6:9-10 and goes on to say, **"Isaiah said this because he saw Jesus' glory and spoke about him,"** it is believed Isaiah was seeing the glory of Jesus when he speaks of seeing the glory of *YHWH* in Isaiah 6:1. Did Isaiah record what God said in 9-10 because he saw the glory of *YHWH*? No he did not. Is there an association between Isaiah seeing the glory of *YHWH* in 6:1 and John saying Isaiah saw Jesus' glory? No there is not and here is why:

When John writes that **"Isaiah said this because he saw Jesus' glory and spoke about him,"** John is not alluding to Isaiah 6:1. Isaiah did not see the glory of Jesus in 6:1. Isaiah saw the glory of Jesus in Isaiah 53. John is referring back to what Isaiah said in Isaiah 53:1 which John quotes in John 12:38. It is in Isaiah 53 where Isaiah saw the glory of Jesus.

John 12:38b: Lord, who has believed our message and to whom has the arm of the Lord been revealed?

Isaiah 53:1: Who has believed our message and to whom has the arm of the LORD (*YHWH*) been revealed.

It is John's quote of Isaiah 53:1 in John 12:38 that is associated with John's statement in 12:41 when he said, "Isaiah said this because he saw Jesus' glory and spoke about him." It is in Isaiah 53 where Isaiah sees the glory of Jesus and speaks about Him. Isaiah 53 is an overview of the first coming of Christ. In this chapter, Isaiah writes about Christ growing up, being despised and rejected by men, taking on himself our infirmities, pierced for our transgressions, oppressed and afflicted and being led like a lamb to the slaughter. Isaiah writes that upon completing His sufferings, Christ is glorified in that He receives life and a portion among the great.

It is in Isaiah 53 that the prophet speaks about Jesus and sees His glory. John 12:38, is a direct quote from Isaiah 53:1. Because it is in Isaiah 53 where Isaiah sees the glory of Jesus and speaks about Him, it should be evident John's statement in 12:41 is associated with Isaiah 53 and not Isaiah 6:1

Rather than John 12:41 showing Jesus is *YHWH*, it shows just the opposite. Isaiah 53 shows Jesus as the suffering servant of *YHWH* and not that Jesus is *YHWH*. Isaiah 53:1 speaks of the arm of the LORD (*YHWH*). Isaiah 53:2 speaks of Christ growing up before him. Who is the "him"? The "him" is *YHWH* who is referred to in verse one. The arm of *YHWH* is Christ. In Isaiah 53:10, the prophet writes the following:

Isaiah 53:10: Yet it was the LORD's (*YHWH's*) will to crush him and cause him to suffer, and though the LORD (*YHWH*) makes his life a guilt offering, he will see his offspring and prolong his days, and the will of the LORD (*YHWH*) will prosper in his hand.

Isaiah is showing it was *YHWH's* will to crush Jesus and make His life a guilt offering and that the will of *YHWH* will prosper in his hand. If Jesus is *YHWH*, this passage makes no sense whatsoever. Isaiah is showing *YHWH* as the God of Jesus and not that Jesus is *YHWH*. Isaiah 53 offers strong evidence that Jesus is not *YHWH* but the servant of *YHWH* through whom *YHWH's* will is carried out.

Scripture #14: Jeremiah 23:5-6: "The days are coming," declares the LORD (*YHWH*), "when I will raise up to David a righteous Branch, a King who will reign wisely and do what is just and right in the land. In his days Judah will be saved and Israel will live in safety. This is the name by which he will be called: The LORD (*YHWH*) Our Righteousness.

The righteous branch of David is generally believed to be a reference to Christ. Therefore, it is believed Christ is being called "The Lord (*YHWH*) Our Righteousness," and therefore Christ is *YHWH*. Since the Trinitarian God is seen as the one God *YHWH* and is an indwelling of Father, Son and Spirit, this passage is seen as *YHWH* the Father speaking about *YHWH* the Son in a Trinitarian relationship of Father, Son and Spirit.

Is this passage of Scripture saying Christ is *YHWH*? We have *YHWH* declaring He will raise up to David a righteous branch who will be called "The Lord (*YHWH*) Our Righteousness." Under the Trinitarian perspective we would have to conclude *YHWH* the Father is raising up *YHWH* the Son as a righteous branch of David. In view of all we have already covered in this book as to how Jesus is the agent of *YHWH* the Father; it is much more congruent with the rest of Scripture to see Christ called "*YHWH* Our Righteousness" as a title showing He is the representative of *YHWH Elohim* and not Himself *YHWH Elohim*. This would be similar to Christ being called Emanuel (God with us) where Christ wasn't literally God but was God's representative as we discussed earlier.

Something or someone being called a certain name doesn't mean they are literally what that name signifies. In Jeremiah 33:16, Jerusalem is called, "The LORD (*YHWH*) Our Righteousness." Jerusalem is not literally *YHWH*. The OT shows many titles for *YHWH* and these titles are used by OT characters in many ways to show *YHWH's* involvement in their lives. Abraham called the mountain upon which he was going to sacrifice Isaac, "The Lord (*YHWH*) will provide" (Genesis 22:14). Obviously the mountain wasn't *YHWH*. Moses built an altar and called it "the LORD (*YHWH*) is my banner" (Exodus 17:15). Obviously the altar wasn't *YHWH*. Gideon built an altar and called it "The Lord (*YHWH*) is our peace" (Judges 6:24). The altar wasn't *YHWH*.

Scripture reveals Jesus is the righteousness <u>of</u> *YHWH* and not that Jesus <u>is</u> *YHWH*. Jesus was a reflection of the perfect righteousness that characterizes *YHWH*. Jerusalem is called "The LORD (*YHWH*) Our Righteousness" because *YHWH* would display His righteousness there in the person of Christ Jesus. This doesn't make Jerusalem or Jesus *YHWH* but the vehicle through which *YHWH's* righteousness is revealed.

Scripture #15: 1 Timothy 1:17: Now to the King eternal, immortal, invisible, the only God, be honor and glory for ever and ever. Amen.

Some believe because he is addressing "the King," Paul is identifying Jesus as the "only God" in this passage. Is this the case? Paul begins his letter to Timothy by saying, **"Paul, an apostle of Christ Jesus by the command of God our Savior and of Christ Jesus our hope" (Verse one).** Paul distinguishes between God as savior and Christ Jesus as our hope. In verse two, Paul again distinguishes between God and Christ when he writes, **"Grace, mercy and peace from God the Father and Christ Jesus our Lord."** In verse eleven Paul speaks of the **"glorious gospel of the blessed God, which he entrusted to me."**

As previously discussed, Paul, in his writings, identifies the Father as the one and only God. Also, as previously discussed, Scripture identifies God the Father as King and the facilitator of salvation through His anointed agent Christ Jesus. In Colossians chapter one it is God the Father who is seen as invisible. Jesus, in speaking of the Father, shows Him to be invisible when He said that no man has seen God at any time.

In view of the foregoing, there is every reason to believe Paul is speaking of God the Father as the only God in 1 Timothy 1:17. Paul's statement appears to be another one of his doxologies. As discussed in our review of Romans 9:5, doxologies are closing statements, hymns or prayers directed to the praise of God. Rather then 1 Timothy 1:17 identifying Jesus as God, it is further establishing Paul's understanding that it is the Father who is the one and only God.

Scripture #16: 1 John 5:7: For there are three that bear record in heaven, the Father, the Word, and the Holy Ghost: and these three are one (KJV, NKJV).

This passage is first found in manuscripts of the Latin Vulgate which was a fourth century translation of the Greek NT into Latin. In the Greek manuscripts that contain this passage it appears it was translated from the Latin into the Greek. It is not found in any manuscripts that predate the Vulgate. It was these post Vulgate Greek manuscripts that translators used to produce the KJV, NKJV and other English translations. Therefore, this passage is found in these English versions of the NT. Scholars have since determined this passage is a deliberate scribal insertion into the NT text in an apparent effort to give Scriptural support to the doctrine of the Trinity. This passage is no longer included in translations of John's epistle (See NIV, RSV, ASV, NET, ESV, etc.).

Chapter Twenty

Did Jesus Pre-exist?

We have examined dozens of Scriptures and Scriptural passages that show there is one God whose name is *YHWH* and who is identified as Father throughout Scripture. We have seen that Jesus, as the Son of this God, is not co-equal with this God but was begotten by this God at a specific time in history for a specific purpose which He effectively fulfilled. Upon such fulfillment, Jesus was elevated by this God to the highest place in the universe, next to God Himself.

Trinitarian theology teaches the Son has always existed as a distinction of a Trinitarian God of Father, Son and Spirit. Trinitarians will point to a number of Scriptures that it is felt give evidence to the pre-existence of the Son. Let us consider these Scriptures.

John 13:3: Jesus knew that the Father had put all things under his power, and that he had <u>come from God</u> and was <u>returning to God</u>.

John 17:4-5: I have brought you glory on earth by completing the work you gave me to do. And now, Father, glorify me in your presence with the glory I had with you <u>before the world (Greek *kosmos*) began.</u>

John 17:24: Father, I want those you have given me to be with me where I am, and to see my glory, the glory you have given me because you loved me <u>before the creation of the world.</u>

John 3:13: No one has ever gone into heaven except the one <u>who came from heaven</u>--the Son of Man.

John 6:62: What if you see the Son of Man ascend to <u>where he was before</u>!

John 20:17: Jesus said, "Do not hold on to me, for I have not yet <u>returned to the Father.</u> Go instead to my brothers and tell them, `<u>I am returning to my Father</u> and your Father, to my God and your God."'

These statements by Jesus appear to say He had glory with the Father and was loved by the Father before the world began. While these statements don't say anything about the Son being God, they appear to indicate He pre-existed. I believe I have established through our discussion to this point that the Son is not God as God is God. The Son is not co-equal, co-eternal and of the same substance as the God identified as *YHWH* and Father throughout Scripture. If the Son did not eternally exist, was the Son created by God at some point in eternity past prior to his birth some 2000 yeas ago? The fourth century theologian Arius taught that the Son was created at some point in the distant past before the creation of the universe. This teaching led to much controversy and resulted in formulation of the Nicene Creed and the eventual formulation of the Doctrine of the Trinity which sees Jesus as having always existed as God in a Trinitarian relationship of Father, Son and Spirit.

To this very day there are religious groups who believe the Son pre-existed, not as an eternal god, but as a created Being. Jehovah's Witnesses believe the archangel Michael became Jesus. They draw this conclusion based on associations between Jesus and Michael found in Scripture. Let's look at these associations presented by Jehovah's Witnesses.

1 Thessalonians 4:16: For the Lord himself will come down from heaven, with a loud command, with the voice of the archangel and with the trumpet call of God, and the dead in Christ will rise first.

Since Michael is identified in Scripture as an archangel (Jude 1:9) and Jesus is seen as coming down from Heaven with the voice of the archangel, it is believed Jesus is Michael. Michael, however, is not mentioned in the 4:16 passage. Paul doesn't identify any particular archangel. Paul speaks of the voice of the archangel. No definition is provided as to what that means. Using this passage to prove Christ is Michael is highly speculative. The main Scriptural passage used to establish Michael as Christ is found in Daniel.

Daniel 12:1: At that time Michael, the great prince who protects your people, will arise. There will be a time of distress such as has not happened from the beginning of nations until then. But at that time your people--everyone whose name is found written in the book--will be delivered.

This passage is believed to parallel statements made in the Olivet Discourse (Matthew 24) as to conditions extant at the return of Christ and consequently it is believed the prince spoken of in Daniel 12 is the Christ that is seen returning in the Olivet Discourse. Michael, however, is not mentioned in the Olivet Discourse and is only mentioned twice in the entire NT (Jude 1:9, Revelation 12:7). Neither reference shows Michael to be Christ. Sound evidence for Michael being Christ is completely lacking in Scripture which makes the validity of this perspective extremely unlikely.

In what respect is the human Jesus to be seen ascending and descending heaven? Scripture speaks of Jesus coming down from heaven. Jesus did come down from heaven in so much as the heavenly Father personally begat Jesus in the womb of Mary. He ascended to the Father after completing His Father's mission and received the honor and glory that had been ordained for him since before creation.

As discussed in Chapter Thirteen, the Scriptures indicate Jesus was crucified from the foundation of the world (Revelation

13:8). Paul speaks of the grace that was given to us in Christ Jesus before the beginning of time (2 Timothy 1:9). Jesus speaks of the Kingdom having been prepared for us since the creation of the world (Matthew 25:34). Paul told the Ephesian Christians that God chose us in him (Jesus) before the creation of the world (Ephesians 1:4).

As previously discussed, there is found in Scripture a good deal of proleptic language. This is language that treats things that have not as yet happened as though they already did happen. Please review my discussion of this linguistic technique in Chapter Thirteen. Let's now look more closely at some of the Scriptural passages cited from the Gospel of John.

John 13:3: Jesus knew that the Father had put all things under his power, and that he had come from God and was <u>returning to God</u>.

The NIV translation of John 13:3 gives the impression that Jesus was returning to the Father. The word "returning" is translated from the Greek *hupago* which means to withdraw oneself, depart or simply to go somewhere. There is nothing in the definition of *hupago* that means to return to somewhere you were before. The KJV translates it as "went." The NKJV and RSV translate it as "going." The Greek for "had come" is *exerkomai*, which means to come forth or proceed. Jesus had proceeded from the Father in so much that God directly facilitated His human birth. Now Jesus was about to depart from the world and go to be with His God and Father.

John 20:17: Jesus said, "Do not hold on to me, for I have not yet <u>returned to the Father.</u> Go instead to my brothers and tell them, `<u>I am returning to my Father</u> and your Father, to my God and your God.'"

The NIV translation incorrectly uses the word "return" in place of "ascend" in their rendering of John 20:17. Most translations use the word "ascend" which is the correct translation of the Greek *anaaino* which means to go upward. There is nothing in the meaning of this Greek word that suggests returning to where you were before. The word simply means to go up and is used in this manner some eighty-one times in the NT narrative.

Do Scriptures that speak of Jesus being sent by God and coming down from heaven prove the Son pre-existed? John 1:6 records that John the Baptist was sent from God. This doesn't mean John the Baptist pre-existed because God sent him. In a prophecy about John, the prophet Malachi quotes God as saying: "See, I will send you the prophet Elijah before that great and dreadful day of the LORD comes" (Malachi 4:5). Does this mean John, as represented by Elijah, was sent from heaven to earth?

In Acts 7:37, Stephen speaks of God sending a prophet like Moses which is an allusion to the sending of Jesus. In Exodus 3:12 it is recorded God sent Moses and yet Moses did not pre-exist. OT Scripture speaks of God sending his servants the prophets (Jeremiah 7:25). Where these servants in heaven with God before being sent to earth?

While it is true there are dozens of Scriptural passages in the NT that say Jesus was sent by God, it is also true that it was a common Hebrew and Aramaic idiom to say that something or someone came down from God or down from heaven when God was the cause. This doesn't mean there was a literal coming down but an identification of God as the cause or source of a particular occurrence. Even though the NT was written in Greek, the thoughts and idioms are often Hebrew or Aramaic as this was the language spoken by the people.

In John, chapter six, Jesus used a great deal of figurative language. He said He was living bread that came down from heaven. He said His followers had to eat His flesh and drink His blood. After hearing these things, it is recorded that many of His disciples no longer followed Him. It is apparent they concluded Jesus was not creditable. Jesus then asked the twelve if they too were going to leave. Peter answered, **"Lord, to whom shall we go? You have the words of eternal life. We believe and know that you are the Holy One of God"** (John 6:68-69).

It is instructive that the twelve saw Jesus as the Holy One of God. Never do we read of anyone relating to Jesus as coming down from heaven as God. Never do we see Jesus called God the Son. Even if one were to conclude that statements saying Jesus was sent by God and came down from heaven meant Jesus was a pre-existent Being, such statements would not be evidence that Jesus, as the Son of God, is God. Jesus said, **"Just as the living Father sent me and I live because of the Father, so the one who feeds on me will live because of me"(John 6:57).** This statement, as do so many others found in the NT, clearly shows Jesus received His life from the Father which, as pointed out in Chapter Twelve, precludes Jesus being ontologically one with the Father.

The few Scriptural passages that appear to indicate pre-existence for the Son must be considered within the broader context of the many Scriptural passages that show the Son had His beginning as the human Jesus nearly 2000 years ago in a small town called Bethlehem. The Scriptures reveal Jesus to be the Son of God and not God the Son. Jesus is seen as the fulfillment of prophecies pointing to a son of Abraham and David becoming a savior to Israel. Scripture shows Jesus became the Son through His supernatural birth and not that He already was the Son. Luke said the **"holy one that will be born will be called the Son of God."** Jesus is called the Son of God because He was directly conceived by God. The conception of the Son was in the plans of the Father from the beginning. Jesus is proleptically seen as having glory with the Father, a glory that is realized upon His crucifixion, His resurrection and His ascension to the Father as seen in Daniel.

Daniel 7:13-14: "In my vision at night I looked, and there before me was one like a son of man, coming with the clouds of heaven. He <u>approached</u> the Ancient of Days and was <u>led into his presence.</u> <u>He was given</u> authority, glory and sovereign power; all peoples, nations and men of every language worshiped him. His dominion is an everlasting dominion that will not pass away, and his kingdom is one that will never be destroyed.

It is after His ascension to His God and Father that Jesus is given the glory that was ordained for him from the beginning of God's plan and purpose to facilitate salvation for the human creation. Jesus was God's human agent who is seen as a descendant of Abraham and David with a human genealogy (Matthew chapter one and Luke chapter three) and born of a human mother. While it is certainly evident Jesus' birth came about as the result of supernatural intervention, it is also evident Jesus experienced a begettal which by definition shows He experienced a beginning. Jesus was able to be tempted and Jesus was able to die and did die. All this is witness to Jesus' complete humanity and not to He being a mixture of humanity and Divinity. Jesus is not alive because He always was alive or because He was created to be forever alive at some point before the creation of the universe. The begotten Son of God is forever alive because God, His Father, made him forever alive through resurrection from the dead. Jesus is the first human to be born from the dead to eternal life. He is the first fruits of all those who had died. Because of this great event, humanity is assured of resurrection to life.

Chapter Twenty-One

Jesus in the Revelation

Revelation 1:1-2: "The revelation of Jesus Christ, which God gave him to show his servants what must soon take place. He made it known by sending his angel to his servant John, who testifies to everything he saw--that is, the word (*logos*) of God and the testimony of Jesus Christ.

John writes that God gave Jesus the Revelation. Since God is commonly used throughout the NT to designate the Father, we can assume John sees the Father as giving the Revelation to Jesus. As discussed in Chapter Six, the word (*logos*) of God is the thoughts of God expressed in speech and creative activity. John writes of testifying to the word (*logos*) of God and the testimony of Jesus Christ. John makes a distinction between the *logos* of God and Jesus. This shows the *logos* of God is not Jesus as is often claimed. Trinitarians will argue that when John writes it is God who gave Jesus the Revelation, it is God as Father giving the Revelation to Jesus within the Trinitarian relationship of Father, Son and Spirit. The following passage dispels such a notion.

Revelation 1:4-6: John, To the seven churches in the province of Asia: Grace and peace to you from him who is, and who was, and who is to come, and from the seven spirits before his throne, <u>and</u> from Jesus Christ, who is the faithful witness, the <u>firstborn from the dead</u>, and the ruler of the kings of the earth. To him who loves us and has freed us from our sins by his blood, and has made us to be a kingdom and priests to serve his <u>God and Father-</u>-to him be glory and power for ever and ever! Amen.

In this passage John gives greetings from "him who is, and who was, and who is to come" and from the seven spirits before his throne <u>and</u> from Jesus Christ who is identified as the firstborn from the dead who has made us a kingdom of priests to serve <u>His</u> <u>God and Father</u>. Here we see distinction not only between the Father and Jesus but between <u>God</u> and Jesus. If distinction was only being made between the Father and Jesus, it could possibly allow for some kind of single Being, indwelling relationship as found in Trinitarianism. Distinction, however, is made between <u>God</u> and Jesus. John is clearly saying that the Being who is to be praised is both God and Father <u>of</u> Jesus, not just the Father of Jesus. If God is seen as the God of Jesus, how can Jesus be that same God? Remember, we are seeing Jesus after His ascension. Jesus still relates to God as <u>His</u> God after he has ascended to God. In Revelation 3:12, Jesus is quoted four times as referring to God as His God. Therefore, to postulate that God and Jesus are a single Being and equally God is a virtual oxymoron.

Revelation 3:12: Him who overcomes I will make a pillar in the temple of <u>my God.</u> Never again will he leave it. I will write on him the name of <u>my God</u> and the name of the city of <u>my God</u>, the new Jerusalem, which is coming down out of heaven from <u>my God</u>; and I will also write on him my new name.

Distinction is made between the one associated with the throne before which are seven spirits and the person Jesus. Who is associated with the throne? In chapter four is a description of the throne on which sits the Lord God Almighty who is characterized as "who was, and is, and is to come."

Revelation 4:2b, 8b: before me was a throne in heaven with someone sitting on it. Verse 8b: "Holy, holy, holy is the Lord God Almighty, who was, and is, and is to come."

In Revelation chapter five, the one who sits on the throne is seen as handing the scroll to Jesus Christ who is represented by a lamb. In chapter eleven, the Lord God Almighty is identified as "the one who is and who was."

Revelation 5:6-7: Then I saw a Lamb, looking as if it had been slain, standing in the center of the throne; ---- He came and took the scroll from the right hand of him who sat on the throne.

Revelation 11:16-17: And the twenty-four elders, who were seated on their thrones before God, fell on their faces and worshiped God, saying: "We give thanks to you, Lord God Almighty, the One who is and who was, because you have taken your great power and have begun to reign.

It is apparent the one who sits on the throne is the Lord God Almighty. The one sitting on the throne is seen as interacting with the Lamb (Jesus) in various ways throughout the Revelation.

Revelation 7:10: And they cried out in a loud voice: "Salvation belongs <u>to our God</u>, who <u>sits on the throne</u>, <u>and</u> to the Lamb."

Revelation 12:10b: Now have come the salvation and the power and the kingdom of our God, and the authority <u>of his</u> Christ.

Revelation 20:6c: but they will be priests of God <u>and</u> of Christ and will reign with him for a thousand years.

Christ is seen as separate from the Lord God Almighty who sits on the throne and is identified as the Christ <u>of</u> God. Therefore, Jesus is not one and the same God who sits on the throne as the Lord God Almighty. It is the Lord God Almighty who is seen as "him who is, and who was, and who is to come." Therefore, this title is not referring to Jesus. Since God the Father is seen as the God and Father <u>of</u> Jesus in 1:5, it should be apparent Jesus is the servant of the Lord God Almighty who sits on the throne.

Some believe Revelation 1:8 refers to Jesus as the Alpha and the Omega and "him who is, and who was, and who is to come, the Almighty." Therefore, Jesus is believed to be the Almighty God no less than the Father.

Revelation 1:8: "I am the Alpha and the Omega," says the Lord God, "who is, and who was, and who is to come, the Almighty."

In this passage reference is made to the "Almighty" as the "who is, and who was, and who is to come." This title is associated with the Lord God Almighty who sits on the throne (compare Revelation 4:2 and 4:8c). In Revelation 5:6-7, the one who sits on the throne is seen as separate from the Lamb (Jesus). Therefore, it should be apparent the Almighty of 1:8, the Lord God Almighty of 4:2 and 8c and the one who sits on the throne in 5:6-7 is the same Being and a different Being from the one seen as the Lamb. Since the Lord God Almighty is identified in Scripture as the Father, He who sits on the throne is God the Father and is the Alpha and the Omega of 1:8. Since it is the Father and not the Lamb (Jesus) who sits on the throne, Revelation 1:8 is speaking of the Father and not Jesus. In Revelation 21:5-7 the one who sits on the throne is specifically identified as the Alpha and the Omega.

Revelation 21:5-7: He who was seated on the throne said, "I am making everything new!" Then he said, "Write this down, for these words are trustworthy and true." He said to me: "It is done. I am the Alpha and the Omega, the Beginning and the End. To him who is thirsty I will give to drink without cost from the spring of the water of life. He who overcomes will inherit all this, and I will be his God and he will be my son."

In this passage it is the one seated on the throne who will be the God of those who overcome and they will be his sons. Since the Scriptures speak often of we becoming sons of God the Father and since becoming a son implies a Father/son relationship, it is evident we become sons of God the Father which further verifies that the one seated on the throne is God the Father who is the Lord God Almighty and the God and Father of Jesus.

Trinitarians point to Revelation 22:12-13 referring to Jesus as the **"Alpha and Omega, the First and the Last, the Beginning and the End,"** as Jesus being *YHWH*.

Revelation 22:12-13: "Behold, I am coming soon! My reward is with me, and I will give to everyone according to what he has done. I am the Alpha and the Omega, the First and the Last, the Beginning and the End."

In Revelation 11:16-18 the Lord God Almighty (*YHWH*) is seen as being worshiped on his throne and is identified as the "one who is and who was." He is also seen as bringing reward to his servants (verse 18). In Matthew 6:1-4, reward is seen as derived from the Father. As already discussed, the Lord God Almighty is the Alpha and Omega sitting on the throne and is seen as separate from the lamb (Jesus) and as the God (*YHWH*) of Jesus throughout the Revelation. Therefore, references to the coming of Jesus must be seen in the context of Jesus acting as the agent of His God (*YHWH*) and Father. Matthew writes that Jesus comes in the glory of the Father. It is the Father who facilitates reward and judgement through the Son. The Son is seen as coming in the presence of God the Father.

1 Thessalonians 3:13: May he strengthen your hearts so that you will be blameless and holy in the presence of our God and Father when our Lord Jesus comes with all his holy ones.

God the Father is seen as the one coming through His agent Christ Jesus. Jesus, as the "Alpha and the Omega, the First and the Last, the Beginning and the End," as seen in Revelation

22:12-13, is Jesus coming as the representative of His God and Father and as such is given these titles. Application of these titles to Jesus does not define Jesus as being the one He consistently calls <u>His</u> God.

YHWH is identified as the first and last in Isaiah 44:6 and 48:12. In Isaiah 44:6, *YHWH* is identified as the Almighty and the one and only God. It should be apparent from our discussion to this point that *YHWH*, as the "first and the last" and the one and only God, is the God and Father <u>of</u> Jesus which precludes Jesus being this same God. Therefore, Jesus is not the first and the last in the same manner as *YHWH* is. Any reference to Jesus as the "first and the last" must be seen in the broader context of who God is versus who Jesus is.

In Revelation 1:17 and 2:8, Jesus is seen to be the "first and the last." Do these passages identify Jesus as *YHWH*? In both these passages Jesus associates being the first and the last with His death and resurrection and not as being without beginning or end as is true of *YHWH*. Jesus died. Jesus is identified as the Lamb of God (*YHWH*) slain for the sins of the world and not as the Almighty God who sits on the throne as the Alpha and Omega. In Revelation 1:18 Jesus is quoted as saying **"I am the Living One; <u>I was dead</u>, and behold I am alive for ever and ever!"** In Revelation 2:8, John speaks of Christ who died and came to life again. As previously discussed, God can't die.

The designation, "first and last" is being applied in two different ways in the Revelation. In relation to the one who sits on the throne, it signifies the eternally existing *YHWH*, the one and only Almighty God the Father. In the case of Jesus, it signifies His death and His resurrection to eternal life through *YHWH* who is the God and Father <u>of</u> Jesus.

The very language of the passages we have considered from the Revelation should make it clear Jesus is not God but is the glorified servant of God. If you carefully read the entire Revelation and pay careful attention to the flow of narrative, it will become abundantly clear God and Jesus are separate Beings and not separate persons of the same Being. Jesus is not the *YHWH* who sits on the throne but is the anointed of *YHWH* who sits on the throne. God the Father is the Eternal Almighty Creator God and Jesus is the resurrected Son of this God unto whom this God has granted eternal life, great power, authority and glory.

Chapter Twenty-Two

The Melchizedek Issue

Because of the manner in which Melchizedek is portrayed in Scripture, some believe Melchizedek is one and the same with a pre-incarnate Christ. It is believed it was Jesus Christ who appeared to Abraham as the priest Melchizedek.

Genesis 14:18-20: Then Melchizedek king of Salem brought out bread and wine. He was priest of God Most High, and he blessed Abram, saying, "Blessed be Abram by God Most High, Creator of heaven and earth. And blessed be God Most High, who delivered your enemies into your hand." Then Abram gave him a tenth of everything.

Melchizedek is seen as bringing bread and wine. Bread and wine were used by Christ to represent his body and blood at the Passover meal He shared with His disciples prior to His crucifixion. Melchizedek, as priest of the Most High God, is seen blessing Abraham. Abraham is seen as giving a tenth of everything to Melchizedek. In Psalm 110:4, the LORD (*YHWH*) is seen as declaring to the lord (*adoni*), **"You are a priest forever, in the order of Melchizedek."** As earlier discussed, *adoni* pertains to Christ and *YHWH* is God the Father.

The writer to the Hebrews discusses the issue of Christ becoming a priest after the order of Melchizedek.

Hebrews 5:5-6, 9-10: So Christ also did not take upon himself the glory of becoming a high priest. But God said to him, "You are my Son; today I have become your Father." And he says in another place, "You are a priest forever, in the order of Melchizedek." Verse 9-10: Once made perfect, he became the source of eternal salvation for all who obey

him and was designated by God to be high priest in the order of Melchizedek. Hebrews 6:20: He has become a high priest forever, in the order of Melchizedek.

Hebrews 7:1-4: This Melchizedek was king of Salem and priest of God Most High. He met Abraham returning from the defeat of the kings and blessed him, and Abraham gave him a tenth of everything. First, his name means "king of righteousness"; then also, "king of Salem" means "king of peace." Without father or mother, without genealogy, without beginning of days or end of life, like the Son of God he remains a priest forever. Just think how great he was: Even the patriarch Abraham gave him a tenth of the plunder! Verse 8: In the one case, the tenth is collected by men who die; but in the other case, by him who is declared to be living.

The writer explains the name Melchizedek means "king of righteousness" and "king of Salem" means "king of peace." Some believe "king of righteousness" and "king of peace" are designations applied to Christ in Scripture. These designations, however, only appear in Scripture in association with Melchizedek. The statements, **"Without father or mother, without genealogy, without beginning of days or end of life, like the Son of God he remains a priest forever"** and **"by him who is declared to be living"** are seen by some as referring to Christ since Christ is believed to reflect the properties here associated with Melchizedek. The Greek for "remains" and the Greek for "is living" are both in the present tense and therefore signify an ongoing existence for Melchizedek.

In view of all this, Melchizedek is believed to have existed eternally and since the Son of God is believed to have existed eternally (without beginning of days or end of life) and the writer says, **"like the Son of God remains a priest forever,"** it is believed Melchizedek and Christ are one and the same.

The phrase, "without genealogy" is translated from the Greek word *agenealogeetos*. Thayer's Greek to English Lexicon defines this word as "*of whose decent there is no account,*" which means there is no recorded genealogy. The Greek for "without Father" is *apithia* and according to Thayer's Lexicon means, "*whose father is not recorded in the genealogies.*" The phrase, "without mother" is the Greek *ameetor* which Thayer's defines as "*born without a mother*" and "*whose mother is not recorded in the genealogy.*" Jesus has a recorded genealogy and a mother of record as found in Matthew and Luke. Since Jesus has a recorded genealogy and mother of record and Melchizedek does not, it becomes problematical that Melchizedek and Christ are one and the same. The Scripture says he was like the Son of God in relation to being a priest forever and not that he was the Son of God. The relationship between Melchizedek and Christ is further defined in Hebrews 7:14-17.

Hebrews 7:14-17: For it is clear that our Lord descended from Judah, and in regard to that tribe Moses said nothing about priests. And what we have said is even more clear if another priest like (after the similitude) Melchizedek appears, one who has become a priest not on the basis of a regulation as to his ancestry but on the basis of the power of an indestructible life. For it is declared: "You are a priest forever, in the order of Melchizedek."

The Greek word translated "like" ("similitude" in the KJV and "likeness" in many other versions) is *homoioteta*. This word indicates being similar or like something but not being identical with that something. Melchizedek represented an eternal priesthood that can never die out. The writer compares this to the temporal priesthood under Moses that had to be continually replenished as priests died. The writer did not say Jesus is Melchizedek but that Jesus' priesthood is similar to Melchizedek's. The writer speaks of another priest like Melchizedek appearing, one who becomes a priest, not on the basis of ancestry but on the basis of living forever. Christ is

David A Kroll

seen as becoming this priest. Becoming a priest presupposes not having been a priest at some time in the past.

Melchizedek was a priest. If Jesus was Melchizedek, He would already be the priest Melchizedek. He would not have to become the priest Melchizedek or a priest like Melchizedek. The writer clearly shows that Jesus became a priest like Melchizedek. It is contradictory to conclude Jesus became who He already was. Some will argue the Son set aside being Melchizedek when He became the human Jesus. As already discussed, the idea that the Son was able to divest Himself of eternal properties or add temporal properties to eternal properties to become the human Jesus and still die as the eternal God is highly problematical.

It is much more Scriptural to conclude that Jesus, as the humanly begotten Son of God the Father, became a priest in the order of Melchizedek upon completing His earthly mission. This happened in association with His receiving authority, power and glory and an everlasting Kingdom as pictured in Daniel. Admittedly, this doesn't define or identify Melchizedek other than what we see in Genesis and Hebrews. To conclude, however, that Melchizedek is Jesus, the Son of God, runs contrary to what we see the writer to the Hebrews recording and therefore becomes nothing more than speculations based on assuming the thing to be proved.

Those who hold to the position that Christ is Melchizedek often hold to the position Christ is *YHWH*. In Psalm 110:1-4, *YHWH* is seen as addressing Christ (*adoni*). As covered in Chapter Three, the Hebrew *adoni* is not a reference to deity but to man unto whom power and authority is granted. This passage of Scripture shows *YHWH* granting *adoni* the right to be at His right hand and declaring *adoni* to be a priest forever in the order of Melchizedek. If *YHWH* is granting *adoni* (Christ) authority and power and declaring *adoni* to be a priest in the order of Melchizedek, how can Christ be *YHWH*? Trinitarian's often argue that Scriptures showing *YHWH* speaking to the Son are showing *YHWH* the Father speaking to *YHWH* the Son in a Trinitarian indwelling of Father, Son and Spirit. Psalm 110 makes this argument untenable in so much as *YHWH* is not addressing Jesus as *Adonai* (Lord) but as *Adoni* (lord). *YHWH* is not addressing Jesus as *YHWH* but as a glorified servant of *YHWH* to whom *YHWH* has granted great power and authority and the privilege of being at *YHWH's* right hand as a priest.

In Genesis 14:18-20, Melchizedek is called the priest of God Most High. In Luke 1:31-35, Mary is told she will be with child and give birth to a son, who will be called the Son of the Most High. Throughout Scripture, the Most High is identified as *YHWH*. There can only be one Most High. Melchizedek is shown as a priest of the Most High and Jesus is called the Son of the Most High. This clearly shows both Melchizedek and Jesus are subservient to *YHWH* who alone is the Most High God. *YHWH*, as the Most High God, is not God the Son but is the God of the Son as has been clearly shown throughout this discussion.

Chapter Twenty-Three

The Holy Spirit

Inclusion of the Holy Spirit in the Trinitarian concept of God did not materialize until the Council of Constantinople in AD 381. The tenets of the Constantinople Creed pertaining to our discussion are as follows:

We believe in one God, the Father Almighty, Maker of heaven and earth, and of all things visible and invisible. And in one Lord Jesus Christ, the only-begotten Son of God, begotten of the Father before all worlds (aeons), Light of Light, very God of very God, begotten, not made, being of one substance with the Father; by whom all things were made; who for us men, and for our salvation, came down from heaven, and was incarnate by the Holy Ghost of the Virgin Mary, and was made man; And in the Holy Ghost, the Lord and Giver of life, who proceedeth from the Father, who with the Father and the Son together is worshiped and glorified.

The Holy Ghost (Spirit) is described as the Lord and Giver of life, who proceeds from the Father and who with the Father and the Son together is worshiped and glorified. Since this Creed identifies the Spirit as a "who," it is apparent the Spirit is viewed as a person as is the Father and the Son. It is interesting that the Spirit is seen as proceeding from the Father. Trinitarianism sees the Spirit as indwelling the Father and Son and the Father and Son indwelling the Spirit. How then can it be said the Spirit proceeds only from the Father? Would not the Spirit also proceed from the Son if it mutually indwells the Father and the Son? If the Spirit is God as God is God, isn't the Creed virtually saying God proceeds from God? Since there is no causation seen between the three distinctions of the Trinitarian Godhead, how could the Spirit proceed from the Father without the Father being the source or cause of the Spirit?

Athanasius taught the Son and the Spirit are both of the Being of the Father and not of the Person of the Father in the Trinitarian Godhead. How can it be said the Son and Spirit are of the Being of the Father within the Trinitarian formulation? There is no Being of the Father according to the Trinitarian construct. There is only the Being of Father, Son and Spirit.

I agree with Athanasius that the Son and Spirit are of the Being of the Father, but not as distinctions of a Trinitarian Godhead as was formulated under Athanasius' influence in the fourth century. The Being of the Father is the one and only Most High, Supreme Being called God. The Spirit is of this Being and proceeds from this Being. The Son is also of this Being and was begotten by this one and only Supreme Being as the man Jesus some 2000 years ago. The Son receives Spirit from the Father and we receive Spirit from the Father through the Son.

The primary argument offered by Trinitarians for the Holy Spirit being God is the Spirit's close association with God and Christ as seen throughout the Scriptures. The Spirit is seen as exerting influence in a great number of ways and always doing so in association with the Father and/or the Son. The Spirit is seen as active in creation, in the affairs of Israel, in the Prophets, in Jesus Christ, the Apostles and the New Testament Church. The Holy Spirit is seen in association with the manifestation of power, wisdom, understanding, judgement, love and truth.

The words Spirit and Holy Spirit appear hundreds of times in the Scriptures. In Hebrew the word for spirit is *ruah* and in Greek the word for spirit is *pneuma*. These words have the same basic meaning. They mean air. More specifically these words denote the movement of air as in breath or wind. Scripture speaks of the Spirit of God, the Spirit of Christ, the spirit of life, the spirit in man and the spirit in a variety of other ways. The Scriptures often show the Spirit as speaking, teaching, helping, interceding, guiding and doing many other such things. Therefore, Trinitarians view the Spirit as a person and believe only a person could be said to do what the Spirit is said to do. For example, the Spirit teaches convicts, is truth, guides, speaks, hears, restrains, sanctifies and even appears to think. The following Scriptures provide some examples of what the Spirit does.

John 14:26: But the Counselor, the Holy Spirit, whom the Father will send in my name, will teach you all things and will remind you of everything I have said to you.

John 16:8: When he (the Holy Spirit) comes, he will convict the world of guilt in regard to sin and righteousness and judgment:

John 16:13: But when he, the Spirit of truth, comes, he will guide you into all truth. He will not speak on his own; he will speak only what he hears, and he will tell you what is yet to come.

Acts: 16:6: Paul and his companions traveled throughout the region of Phrygia and Galatia, having been kept by the Holy Spirit from preaching the word in the province of Asia.

1 Peter 1:2: Who have been chosen according to the foreknowledge of God the Father, through the sanctifying work of the Spirit

1 Corinthians 2:10: but God has revealed it to us by his Spirit. The Spirit searches all things, even the deep things of God.

Such activity of the Spirit has led many to conclude the Spirit has personality and must be a distinct person like the

Father and the Son. Others believe the recorded activity of the Spirit reflects the mind and power of God at work in His creation. References to the Spirit teaching, convicting, guiding, speaking, hearing, restraining, sanctifying, and so forth, are seen as personifications of the Spirit. To personify something is to give that something a figurative life (personhood) of its own. One dictionary definition of personify is to be "the perfect example of something." Another definition is "to perfectly represent something."

In Scripture, we find attributes such as wisdom and understanding represented as having a life of their own. In the Proverbs, wisdom is personified as a woman and is said to speak, cry out, raise her voice, reprove, laugh and so forth. Wisdom is seen as being loved, having a mouth, having a house and offering bread and wine (See Proverbs chapters one, four, eight and nine). Yet we all know that wisdom is not a person but an attribute of mind. The Spirit of God is seen as doing many things. Upon close examination, the Spirit of God is seen as the mind and power of God expressing all that God is. It is His knowledge, understanding and wisdom. It is his power and authority. It is His love, mercy, righteousness and justice. It is the outward manifestation of all that God is. The Scriptures actually identify God <u>as</u> Spirit.

John 4:24: God is spirit, and his worshipers must worship in spirit and in truth.

The human spirit is the manifestation of all that humans are. The body without the spirit has no expression of thought or will. The body without the spirit is dead. Spirit is the life of the living physical body. In Genesis 2:7 it is recorded God breathed (Hebrew *ruah)* into man and man became a living soul. Spirit gives life. God is Spirit and is inherent life. Because God is life He is the source of all other life including the life of Jesus as Jesus plainly said (John 5:26). Our human life comes from God and is subject to death. God's will is that we be reborn to eternal life. Eternal life comes from the Father through Jesus who was the first to be reborn to eternal life (Colossians 1:18, Revelation 1:5, 1 Corinthians 15:20).

God is manifested in the world and in us through His Spirit. It is called Holy Spirit because it is from God who is holy. Sinning against the Spirit is the same as sinning against God and vice versa. When Ananias and his wife lied about the money, they are seen as lying to the Holy Spirit and this is seen as lying to God.

Acts 5:3-4: Then Peter said, "Ananias, how is it that Satan has so filled your heart that you have lied to the Holy Spirit and have kept for yourself some of the money you received for the land? Didn't it belong to you before it was sold? And after it was sold, wasn't the money at your disposal? What made you think of doing such a thing? You have not lied to men but to God."

Trinitarians believe that in their lying to the Holy Spirit, Ananias and his wife lied to a distinction of the one God called the Holy Spirit and that is how it can be said they lied to God. The Holy Spirit, however, is seen in Scripture as proceeding from the Father as even the Constantinople Creed states. If the Holy Spirit is God as the Father is God, to say the Holy Spirit proceeds from God the Father is to say God proceeds from God which makes no sense at all. Apostle Paul shows God gives of His Spirit.

1 Thessalonians 4:8: Therefore, he who rejects this instruction does not reject man but God, who gives you his Holy Spirit.

Scripture repeatedly speaks in terms of the Spirit of God, not the Spirit as God. It is the Spirit of God which is seen as working in us to facilitate eternal life and behavior in line with the will of God the Father.

Romans 8:11: And if the Spirit <u>of him</u> who raised Jesus from the dead is living in you, he who raised Christ from the dead will also give life to your mortal bodies through his Spirit, who lives in you.

2 Corinthians 1:21-22: Now it is God who makes both us and you stand firm in Christ. He anointed us, set his seal of ownership on us, and put <u>his Spirit</u> in our hearts as a deposit, guaranteeing what is to come.

Ephesians 2:21-22: In him the whole building is joined together and rises to become a holy temple in the Lord. And in him you too are being built together to become a dwelling in which God lives by <u>his Spirit</u>.

Ephesians 3:16: I pray that out of his glorious riches he may strengthen you with power through <u>his Spirit</u> in your inner being.

1 John 4:12-14: No one has ever seen God; but if we love one another, God lives in us and his love is made complete in us. We know that we live in him and he in us, because he has given us of <u>his Spirit</u>. And we have seen and testify that the Father has sent his Son to be the Savior of the world.

The last quote above is especially revealing in that it clearly shows it is the Father's Spirit given to us that results in God the Father living in us and we living in God the Father. John states no one has ever seen God. We know it is the Father John is speaking of because John makes this same statement in his Gospel where by context it can be seen he is referring to the Father (John 1:18). Trinitarianism teaches God is a mutual indwelling of Father, Son and Spirit. If this is the case, when John speaks of God dwelling in us he must be saying Father, Son and Spirit dwell in us. John, however, is not saying this. He is saying it is the Father who dwells in us through indwelling of the Father's Spirit. While it is true the Scripture also speaks of Christ dwelling in us and the Spirit of Christ dwelling in us, Scripture also clearly shows the Spirit proceeds from the Father through Christ and into us. The Father and only the Father is the unoriginate source of the Spirit.

It is instructive that the salutations found at the beginning of fourteen of the letters found in the NT documents all speak of grace and peace from God the Father and the Lord Jesus Christ. These greetings never include the Spirit. If the Spirit is a distinction or person of a Trinitarian Godhead, it seems rather strange the Spirit is not included in these salutations (See Romans 1:7, 1 Corinthians 1:3, 2 Corinthians 1:2, Galatians 1:3, Ephesians 1:2, Philippians 1:2 Colossians 1:2-3, 1 Thessalonians 1:1, 2 Thessalonians 1:2, 1 Timothy 1:2, 2 Timothy 1:2, Titus 1:4, Philemon 1:3, 2 Peter 1:2). Furthermore, we see James seeing himself as a servant of God and the Lord Jesus. John sees us having fellowship with the Father and with His Son. The Spirit is not mentioned.

James 1:1: James, a servant of God and of the Lord Jesus Christ, To the twelve tribes scattered among the nations: Greetings.

1 John 1:3: We proclaim to you what we have seen and heard, so that you also may have fellowship with us. And our fellowship is with the Father and with his Son, Jesus Christ.

If God is an indwelling of co-eternal, co-equal and con-substantial distinctions of Father, Son and Spirit, it appears rather odd that these men fail to include the Spirit when writing of their associations with the Father and the Son.

Let's now look at what Paul said about the spirit in man compared to the Spirit of God.

1 Corinthians 2:11: For who among men knows the thoughts of a man except the man's spirit within him? In the same way no one knows the thoughts of God except the Spirit of God.

Just as the thoughts of man's spirit are not separated or distinct from man, neither are the thoughts of God's Spirit separate or distinct from God. Just as the spirit in man is the very manifestation of man's thoughts and actions, so the Spirit of God is the very manifestation of what God thinks, does and virtually is. Just as man has spirit which is not a separate or distinct person from himself, so the Father, as the one and only God, has Spirit which is not a separate or distinct person from Himself. The Spirit of God is intrinsic to the very Being of God and is not a distinction within the Being of God having its own characteristics. Scripture plainly shows the Spirit of God interacts with our human spirits which are intrinsic to our humanity.

Romans 8:16: The Spirit itself beareth witness with our spirit, that we are the children of God (KJV).

The Scriptures show God is able to distribute His Spirit throughout the universe. It is by His Spirit the universe is sustained. This can be analogized to the sun distributing its light and heat through millions of miles. The light and heat are not the sun but are a manifestation of what the sun is. God's Spirit is a manifestation of what God is and it is distributed throughout the universe and is expressed in thousands of ways including the various personifications found in Scripture. It is through God's Spirit Mary became impregnated with Jesus. Let's look at what the angel told Mary as recorded by Luke.

Luke 1:35: The Holy Spirit will come upon you, and the power of the Most High will overshadow you. So the holy one to be born will be called the Son of God.

Is the angel distinguishing between a person called the Holy Spirit and the power of the Most High? Scripture clearly identifies the Most High as the Father. So we know it is through the power of the Father Mary became impregnated. The word "The" before Spirit is not in the Greek of Luke 1:35. In the Greek Scriptures, "Holy Spirit" often appears without the article "the." The angel is telling Mary Holy Spirit will come upon her. Trinitarians believe the Father used the distinction of God called the Holy Spirit to incarnate Jesus. It is sometimes said that if the Holy Spirit is a person, then the Holy Spirit was the Father of Jesus and not God the Father. The very language of this passage should tell us that Holy Spirit and the power of the Most High are one and the same. Holy Spirit proceeds from the Father as power and word and not as a person distinct from the Father. Therefore, God the Father is the Father of Jesus, not through the action of a person called the Holy Spirit, but through the action of the Father's power and word which is Holy Spirit.

Jesus told the disciples to stay in Jerusalem until they were clothed with power from on High. Here again the Spirit is seen to be associated with the power of God the Father and not some third person of a Triune God.

Luke 24:49: I am going to send you what my Father has promised; but stay in the city until you have been clothed with power from on high.

David sees God's Spirit defused throughout the universe and equates God's Spirit with God's presence. There is nothing here to suggest the Spirit of God is a person of a Triune Godhead. The Spirit of God is seen as the ubiquitous presence of God.

Psalm 139:7: Where can I go from your <u>Spirit</u>? Where can I flee from your <u>presence</u>? If I go up to the heavens, <u>you</u> are there; if I make my bed in the depths, you are

there. If I rise on the wings of the dawn, if I settle on the far side of the sea, even there your hand will guide me.

Spirit is regularly seen in Scripture to signify power, mind and presence. In Luke 1:17, John the Baptist is seen as coming in the spirit and power of Elijah. No one would conclude the spirit of Elijah was a person. Paul wrote to Timothy that God has given us a spirit of power, love and sound mindedness (2 Timothy 1:7). These are all attributes of God's Spirit with no hint of them coming from and through a third person of a Trinity. Paul said this to the Romans:

Romans 8:9: You, however, are controlled not by the sinful nature but by the Spirit, if the Spirit of God lives in you. And if anyone does not have the Spirit of Christ, he does not belong to Christ.

Here it is indicated our behavior can be controlled by the Spirit of God rather than the sinful nature. Is God's Spirit a person of a Triune God living in us and controlling our behavior or is it the Father's power providing us with the ability to avoid sin? The Spirit of God is equated with having the Spirit of Christ. As covered in a previous Chapter, the Father gave Jesus a full measure of His Spirit so Jesus could exercise complete control over temptation to sin. We have access to the Spirit of the Father just as Christ did. Christ made such access available through His death, resurrection and ascension to the Father from whom He sent the Spirit beginning with the Day of Pentecost as recorded in Acts chapter two.

As discussed above, the Apostles greetings to the Churches are always sent from two persons, the Father and the Son. Never is the Holy Spirit included in such greetings. If God is a Trinity of Father, Son and Spirit, why is the Spirit never included in these greetings? Worship is seen as directed to both the Father and the Son in Scripture but never to the Spirit. Trinitarians will say Scripture does direct worship to the Spirit because God is Father, Son and Spirit so when you worship God you worship the Spirit. This approach assumes the Trinity to be valid and is a case of assuming the thing to be proved, which is a dangerous way to argue anything.

Paul's benediction at the end of his second letter to the Corinthians is often seen as supporting the Trinitarian concept of God. Here Jesus, God (The Father) and the Holy Spirit are simultaneously mentioned. It is questioned how there can be fellowship of the Holy Spirit if the Holy Spirit is not a person.

2 Corinthians 13:14: May the grace of the Lord Jesus Christ, and the love of God, and the fellowship of the Holy Spirit be with you all.

Trinitarians believe this passage identifies God as being the three distinctions of Father, Son and Spirit. Paul's use of the word God is seen as Paul referring to the Father. Paul does use the word God to mean the Father throughout his writings as context will clearly reveal. Paul frequently uses the phrase "God the Father" in contrast to Jesus as Lord. Nowhere, however, does Paul, or any other NT author, use the phrase God the Son or God the Spirit. Paul's frequent use of "God the Father" and total lack of using the phrase God the Son or God the Spirit should tell us who it was Paul believed God to be. In view of what Scripture says about the Father as the source of the Spirit, it should be evident when Paul writes of the fellowship of the Holy Spirit being with us, he is not speaking of the Spirit as a person of a Trinitarian Godhead but as the very power and mind of God the Father dwelling in us.

The Greek word translated "fellowship" in the NIV rendition of 2 Corinthians 13:14 (communion in some translations) is *koinonia* and has the overall meaning of associating, sharing or participating in something. We know from the Scriptures that both the Father and the Son are identified as Beings we can have fellowship (association) with (1 John 1:3). The Scriptures do not identify the Spirit as having Being or being a person of a Triune Being called God. We have fellowship with the Being of the Father and the Being of the Son through the power of the Spirit which proceeds from the Father through the Son and into and through us.

When Paul speaks of the Corinthians sharing or participating in the Holy Spirit, he is not speaking of them fellowshipping with a person called the Holy Spirit. Paul is telling the Corinthians the same thing he told Timothy. To have fellowship or communion with the Holy Spirit is to experience the power, love and sound mindedness that characterize the Holy Spirit of God. The Holy Spirit proceeds from the Father and participates with our human Spirit to provide a way of thinking and behaving reflective of the Spirit of God.

As previously discussed, the Scriptures often speak of the Spirit of God or the Spirit of Christ. If the Spirit is a distinction in a presumed Godhead of three co-eternal, co-equal and con-substantial persons, how can the Spirit be of God and of Christ? Trinitarians will argue that all three persons of the "Godhead" dwell in each other thus allowing for the Spirit to be of the Father and of the Son. While the Son is seen to dwell in the Father and the Father in the Son, there is no Scriptural hint of the Father and Son dwelling in the Spirit which would have to be the case if there is a mutual indwelling of Father, Son and Spirit. While the Son and Spirit are seen as of the Father, nowhere is the Father or Son seen as being of the Spirit. Scripture clearly shows the Spirit proceeds from the Father who shares it with the Son who in turn shares it with us.

Scripture records that when the disciples would have to appear before government officials, Jesus told them they would be given the words to say. A comparison of the three accounts of what Jesus said gives evidence to the Spirit proceeding from the Father through the Son and into the disciples.

Matthew 10:20: For it will not be you speaking, but the Spirit of your Father speaking through you.

Luke 21:15: For I (Christ) will give you words and wisdom that none of your adversaries will be able to resist or contradict.

Mark 13:11c: Just say whatever is given you at the time, for it is not you speaking, but the Holy Spirit.

The very language of Scripture shows the Spirit acting in ways not coherent with seeing the Spirit as a distinct identity in a Trinitarian union of Father, Son and Spirit. Scripture shows the Spirit to be God's influence upon our lives and yet an influence that can be mitigated by our human ability to exercise free choice. The Spirit can be quenched and fanned into flame. Paul shows the Spirit to be dynamics of power, love and self-discipline. Scripture consistently shows the Spirit of God to be dynamics of mind and power.

1 Thessalonians 5:19: Do not quench the Spirit (RSV).

2 Timothy 1:6-7: For this reason I remind you to fan into flame the gift of God, which is in you through the laying on of my hands. For God did not give us a spirit of timidity, but a spirit of power, of love and of self-discipline.

The Spirit of God is the power and mind of God in action. In **Isaiah 40:13** the prophet says, **"Who hath directed the spirit (Hebrew: *ruah*) of the LORD (*YHWH*), or being his counselor hath taught him" (KJV)**? Apostle Paul quotes this passage when he says, **"Who has known the mind of the Lord? Or who has been his counselor?" (Romans 11:34).** In the Septuagint, the Greek word *nous* is used to translate the Hebrew *ruah*. This word in the Greek means the faculty of intellect, perceiving, understanding, feeling, judging, determining and so forth. Paul is apparently quoting

298

the Septuagint translation of Isaiah 40:13 where *nous* is used to define the Hebrew *ruah*. *Nous* is appropriately translated into English as "mind." It is apparent the Septuagint translators understood the Spirit to be the mind of God and rendered *ruah* as *nous* which is defined as dynamics of cognitive function.

Spirit is power and cognitive function. In the case of God it is supreme power and cognitive function. To the extent we embrace the dynamics of God's Spirit is the extent to which we represent the will and purpose of God in our lives. Jesus was the perfect representation of the dynamics that characterize the Spirit of God. The Father gave Jesus a full measure of His Spirit. This enabled Jesus to be in perfect harmony with the will and purpose of the Father. In His glorified state, Jesus is in such perfect unity with the Father who is Spirit that Paul spoke of Jesus as being Spirit.

2 Corinthians 3:17: Now the Lord is the Spirit, and where the Spirit of the Lord is, there is freedom. And we, who with unveiled faces all reflect the Lord's glory, are being transformed into his likeness with ever-increasing glory, which comes from the Lord, who is the Spirit.

Some believe Paul is here referring to the Spirit as Lord and in so doing identifies the Spirit as a distinction of the Trinitarian Godhead. The context of 2 Corinthians, shows the Lord Paul is talking about is Jesus. Paul says "the Lord, who is the Spirit." In Trinitarian theology, the Son is not the Spirit and the Spirit is not the Son. They are seen as separate distinctions of the Triune Godhead. Therefore, Trinitarian theology would not allow for the Lord to be the Spirit. When Paul speaks of the Lord (Christ) as Spirit, he cannot be identifying the Spirit as a distinction of a Trinitarian Godhead. It is more reasonable to conclude Paul is seeing Jesus as the perfect reflection of the Spirit of the Father. Christians can also reflect the Spirit of the Father by embracing and exercising the dynamics of the Spirit of God as Jesus did. This is what it means to be transformed by the Spirit.

Greek Nouns and Pronouns:

Readers of the NT often see the pronouns "he" and "his" used in association with the Spirit as indicating the Spirit is a person. As pointed out previously, in the Greek language nouns have what is called gender where some nouns are considered masculine, some feminine and some neuter. For example, the Greek for the word sword is in the feminine gender. The Greek for wall is masculine, for door feminine, and for floor neuter. In Greek, male and female gender designations are applied to persons, places and things. The neuter gender is generally applied to things such as objects, forces, abstractions and so forth but can be found in association with persons and places. Neuter nouns can also be given personification.

The Greek language also has three kinds of pronouns associated with these genders. When a pronoun appears with a noun having a masculine, feminine or neuter gender, the pronoun must match the gender designation of the noun. For example, a masculine noun takes a masculine pronoun such as "he," "who," "whom," or "his." A neuter noun takes a neuter pronoun such as "it," "itself," or "which." The Greek *pneuma*, translated Spirit in the NT, is neuter and takes the pronoun "it" or "which." Translators of the NT Greek to English often use a masculine pronoun to identify the Spirit (*pneuma*) and thus abandon the grammatical requirements of the Greek language. A good example of this is found in the book of Acts.

Acts 5:32: We are witnesses of these things, and so is the Holy Spirit, whom (Greek "o") God has given to those who obey him.

In this passage the word "Spirit" is neuter. The Greek pronoun "o" is translated "whom" but should be translated "which" in order to be consistent with Greek grammar requirements. If you look at Acts 5.32 in a Greek interlinear translation where Greek words are translated into their equivalent English words you will find "*o*" translated as "which." In interlinear translations the translator must adhere to the grammar requirements of the language. Use of masculine pronouns in association with the grammatically neuter "Spirit" is misleading and unwarranted. It gives the false impression the Greek language is showing the Spirit to be a person which the language is not doing.

The use of gender in the Greek language does not establish the meaning of a noun. Meaning of a noun must be established by other knowledge associated with the noun. This being said, it is instructive that the neuter gender in Greek generally applies only to things such as objects, forces, abstractions and so forth. It is not generally used in association with persons. This alone places into serious question the concept of the Spirit being a person.

As already discussed, the Spirit is defined as power and cognitive function which proceed from God the Father. This is how the Spirit is identified in both the Old and New Testaments. Scripture clearly shows all things are created and sustained by and through the Spirit of God. As already discussed, God and Spirit are so closely associated that God is actually called Spirit. Because Jesus had a full measure of the Father's Spirit, He also is described as Spirit in Scripture.

Scriptural passages in John, chapters fourteen and fifteen are often offered as evidence the Holy Spirit is a person and not just the manifestation of the mind and power of God. In these passages Jesus tells the disciples that He would send them another Counselor (Greek *parakletos*) who is identified as the Holy Spirit. Since the Counselor, as the Holy Spirit, is referred to as he, him and whom, it is believed the Holy Spirit is a person.

John 14:16-17: And I will ask the Father, and he will give you another Counselor (Comforter in KJV, Helper in NKJV) to be with you forever—the Spirit of truth. The

David A Kroll

world cannot accept him, because it neither sees him nor knows him. But you know him, for he lives with you and will be in you (NIV).

John 14:26: But the Counselor, the Holy Spirit, whom the Father will send in my name, will teach you all things and will remind you of everything I have said to you.

John 15:26: "When the Counselor comes, whom I will send to you from the Father, the Spirit of truth who goes out from the Father, he will testify about me.

John 16:7-8: But I tell you the truth: It is for your good that I am going away. Unless I go away, the Counselor will not come to you; but if I go, I will send him to you. When he comes, he will convict the world of guilt in regard to sin and righteousness and judgment.

John 16:13-15: But when he, the Spirit of truth, comes, he will guide you into all truth. He will not speak on his own; he will speak only what he hears, and he will tell you what is yet to come. He will bring glory to me by taking from what is mine and making it known to you. All that belongs to the Father is mine. That is why I said the Spirit will take from what is mine and make it known to you.

The Greek *parakletos* is of masculine gender and, therefore, requires a masculine pronoun. It is grammatically necessary to use the pronouns him, he, his and whom in these passages. However, just as the neuter gendered Greek *pneuma* does not establish the personhood or non-personhood of Spirit, neither does the masculine gendered *parakletos* establish the personhood or non-personhood of Counselor. As stated above, the Greek masculine gender is associated with persons, places and things. When this gender is associated with a noun, it doesn't by itself tell you what the noun means. That must be determined by other information.

302

In the passages cited above, the Counselor is identified as the Holy Spirit and the Spirit of Truth. It is the masculine gendered *parakletos* that is being discussed and so using the personal pronouns of he, him and whom in association with the Spirit is perfectly legitimate as Spirit relates to *parakletos*. Even in John 16:13-15, were Jesus speaks of the Spirit of truth, He is still talking about the *parakletos* and therefore identifying the Spirit as a "he" (Greek pronoun *ekeinos*) is appropriate. Some insist that since the word Spirit is being modified by the pronoun *ekeinos* in this passage, it shows personhood for the Spirit. This is simply not the case. While *ekeinos* is a masculine pronoun and is used in association with the Spirit (Greek pneuma) in John 16, it no more establishes *pneuma* as a person than it establishes *parakletos* as a person. Greek genders and their associated pronouns do not by themselves establish the meaning of a word.

In view of the dynamics associated with gender in the Greek language and the fact that gender does not establish the meaning of a noun, a personhood for the Holy Spirit cannot be established on the basis of grammar. This is acknowledged by Greek scholars. It is further pointed out that in John 15:26, the Counselor is seen as going out from the Father (proceeding from the Father in the KJV). According to Trinitarian theology, the Holy Spirit is distinct from the Father in the Trinitarian Godhead. If this is the case, why is it seen as proceeding from the Father? The answer is that the Father is the one and only Supreme God who alone has intrinsic Spirit of mind and power and this Spirit flows from the Father to all of His creation.

Throughout the Scriptures the Son is spoken of as of God, the Spirit is spoken of as of God but nowhere is the Father spoken of as of God. The Father is never spoken of as of God because the Father is God and the Son and Spirit are not this God but of this God. The Son is seen as of the Father in being directly begotten by the Father and the Spirit is seen as of the Father as the Father's power, thought, emotion, creativity and all other personal attributes manifested by the Father's Spirit. The Spirit of God is virtually what God is, just as the spirit in man is virtually what man is. In neither case does spirit exist as its own person in distinction from the Being with whom it is associated.

Chapter Twenty-Four

Summary

The Biblical Scriptures provide us with a clear understanding that God is not Father, Son and Spirit. Both Old and New Testaments identify God as the Father and only the Father. In the Hebrew Scriptures, God is seen as *YHWH*, the self existent one, and is identified as Father some fifteen times. In the Greek Scriptures, Jesus, Paul, Peter, John and other authors of Scripture clearly identify the Father as the one and only God.

Scripture identifies Jesus as the promised Messiah to Israel who became the Son of God through supernatural conception in the womb of Mary some 2000 years ago. Jesus fulfilled His ministry, was crucified and through resurrection was born again to eternal life. Jesus was the first fruits of those who had died. Scripture clearly shows Jesus was the first to be born from the dead to eternal life. Jesus plainly said He was dead. The Son was not God incarnate which is to say He eternally existed and could not die. The Son of God clearly died. He is alive because the Father resurrected Him, not because He eternally existed (Acts 2:24, 5:30-31, Romans 6:9-11, 1 Corinthians 15:20, Colossians 1:18, 1 Peter 1:3, Revelation 1:5, 1:18).

The Spirit is of the Father. It is not one of three distinctions or persons of a Triune God where it is co-equal and con-substantial with the Father and the Son. The Spirit of God the Father is the power and creative activity of God the Father. It is manifested throughout the universe. It is manifest in the Son and in you and me. While the Spirit is at times seen as personified in Scripture, it is not a person or distinction of God. It simply is the mind and power of God the Father.

The word of God is not a person called the Son but is the virtual speech of the Father. It is the Father's expressed thought, will and purpose which is manifested through the power of His Spirit. When Apostle John writes that the word became flesh in the person of Jesus, John is saying the word of the Father was manifested in the conception of Jesus through the Father's Spirit. Because of what Jesus accomplished in becoming the savior of the human race, God the Father elevated Jesus to His right hand and gave Him great power, authority and glory.

Trinitarian theologians use the Greek word *perichoresis* to describe a mutual indwelling of Father, Son, and Spirit. The Father, Son and Spirit are believed to participate in a three-way reciprocity. While the three are seen as having properties of their own as distinctions of the one God, the three are seen as inseparable. Though distinction can be seen in their activities they are considered to be one in both Being and activity. The three are seen as always acting together. The Father is not the Father apart from the Son and the Spirit, the Son is not the Son apart from the Father and the Spirit and the Spirit is not the Spirit apart from the Father and the Son. It is believed there is oneness of activity between them within their *homoousial* (single substance), *perichoretic* (mutual indwelling) and *hypostatic* (distinction of Being) existence as Father, Son and Spirit.

Trinitarian theology teaches all humanity is centered in the *homoousial, perichoretic* and *hypostatic* existence of Father, Son and Spirit. It is sometimes stated there is no God behind the back of Jesus. Jesus is believed to be God as God is God and when we look at Jesus we see God which is to say we see Father, Son and Spirit. It is maintained God reveals Himself through Himself, a concept originally formulated by the theologian Irenaeus and more recently developed by theologian Karl Barth. Therefore, it is believed Jesus had to be God in order for God to reveal Himself through Himself.

Scripture shows, however, that God has and does reveal Himself in many ways. God revealed Himself to Moses in a burning bush. No one would conclude the burning bush was God. God was revealed to Israel through Moses. No one would conclude Moses was God. The power, will and purpose of God were constantly revealed to Israel and other nations through the prophets. No one would conclude these prophets were God. We consistently see in the OT Scriptures God revealing Himself through the prophets and others for the explicit purpose to have the people know that "I am *YHWH*." Jesus was a prophet (Acts 3:22) and as such had the Spirit of God by which He revealed God as His Father and our Father and his God and our God (John 20:17). Jesus did not have to be God to reveal God.

Theologians, such as the late Thomas F Torrance, teach that all Christian doctrine is to be formulated within the framework of the Trinity and incarnation. It is believed all humanity is centered in the Trinity and through participation in this Trinitarian union of Father, Son and Spirit we have relationship with God.

The Scriptures, however, say nothing about humanity being centered in a *homoousial, perichoretic* and *hypostatic* union of Father, Son and Spirit. Christ taught we are to be centered in the Father. Jesus plainly said the Father is the one and only God and it is the Father who we are to be reconciled to and with whom we are to have a relationship. While such relationship is facilitated through Christ, it is, nevertheless, a relation with the one and only God who is the Father, not a God who is Father, Son and Spirit. Scripture teaches we become adopted sons of the Father. Paul wrote to the Galatians that God the Father sent His Son to redeem us so we may receive full rights as His (The Father's) sons. Because we are sons, God gives us His Spirit whereby we acknowledge God as our Father. This is the same Spirit whereby Christ acknowledged God as His Father. This is why Paul can say God sends the Spirit of His Son into our hearts. It is the same Spirit the Father gave to His Son. Being a son of God equates to being a son of the Father. Nowhere in Scripture are we identified as sons of the Son of God or the Spirit of God.

Galatians 4:4-6: But when the time had fully come, God sent his Son, born of a woman, born under law, to redeem those under law, that we might receive the full rights of sons. Because you are sons, God sent the Spirit of his Son into our hearts, the Spirit who calls out, "Abba, Father."

As did Paul and other of the Apostles, Jesus also consistently directs attention to the Father in His teachings. While the Scriptures show Jesus as being worshiped and at times prayed to, we find Jesus directing worship and prayer to the Father (Matthew 6:6, John 4:23). While we pray to the Father in the name of Jesus, we still pray to the Father. This says a lot about who the one and only God is and where our relational focus should be.

While the concept of *perichoresis* does not define God as a mutual indwelling of Father, Son and Spirit resulting in singleness of Being, it is a useful concept in defining the spiritual relationship between God, Christ and humanity. Jesus spoke of His being in the Father and the Father in Him and of our being in the Father and the Father being in us. All this is seen as accomplished through the Spirit of the Father which proceeds from the Father through Christ and to us. This mutual indwelling pertains to spiritual oneness. The mutual indwelling between the Father and the Son and between the Father and us has nothing to do with being one in Being. Being one in spirit does not mean oneness of Being. We do not become one in Being with the Father by having the Spirit of the Father dwell in us and neither does Christ. Jesus having the Father's Spirit dwell in Him does not make Him ontologically one with the Father anymore than it makes us ontologically one with the Father. The indwelling passages found in Scripture all have to do with spiritual dynamics of singleness of mind, purpose, thought and will and not singleness of Being.

308

The Worship of Jesus:

Because Jesus is seen as being worshiped in NT Scriptures, it is commonly believed Jesus must be as much God as the Father is God. It is believed the Hebrew *Shema* prohibits worship of anyone other than the one God. (See Chapter Two for a discussion of the *Shema*). It is believed first century monotheistic Jewish Christians could not have worshiped Jesus if they didn't believe Him to be the one God as much as the Father is the one God. Does the *Shema* prohibit worship of anyone other than God?

The *Shema* doesn't address worship. The Shema simple states that God is one and is to be loved with all your heart soul and strength. Jesus identified who the One God of the *Shema* is. Jesus plainly said the Father is the one and only true God (John 5:44 and 17:3). Jesus upheld the *Shema* (Mark 12:29). Apostle Paul upheld the tenets of the *Shema* (1 Corinthians 8:6, 1 Timothy 2:5). In the *Shema*, God the Father is seen as a stand alone Deity who alone is *YHWH Elohim*. Scripture identifies *YHWH* alone as the Most High God over all the earth and above all other gods.

Psalm 97:9: For you, O LORD (YHWH) are the Most High over all the earth; you are exalted far above all gods.

Psalms 83:18: Let them know that you, whose name is the LORD (*YHWH*), that <u>you alone</u> are the Most High over all the earth.

Scripture teaches there is only one Most High God and that God is *YHWH*. The monotheism represented in the *Shema* is violated if someone worships someone other than *YHWH* as the one and only Most High God. In worshiping Jesus, we are not worshiping the Most High God. We are worshiping the Son of the Most High God.

Luke 1:35: The angel answered, "The Holy Spirit will come upon you, and the power of the Most High will

overshadow you. So the holy one to be born will be called the Son of God.

As discussed throughout this book, Jesus identifies himself as the Son of the one and only true God and not that He also is the one and only true God. Jesus identifies himself as the Christ (anointed one) of the one and only God. As discussed several times in this book, nowhere in Scripture will you find the phrase God the Son or God the Spirit. You only find God the Father. The *Shema* prohibits worship of someone as the one and only God who is not the one and only God. The *Shema* does not prohibit the worship of someone who is not the one and only God but is considered worthy of worship. Worship of Jesus is not worship of the Most High God. Therefore, worship of Jesus and Jesus accepting worship is not a violation of the *Shema*.

We worship the Father commensurate with who He is and who He is, is the one and only Most High God over all reality. We worship Jesus commensurate with who he is and who He is, is the resurrected and glorified one and only directly begotten Son of the one and only Most High God. As discussed and demonstrated throughout this book, being the resurrected and glorified Son of God does not equate with being that God. While it is not permissible to worship anyone but *YHWH* as the one and only God, it is permissible to worship others commensurate with whom they are.

Worship is an act of respect and reverence toward one having authority, power, and a certain status. In the Hebrew Scriptures we find worship being directed not only to God but to men of position and power. The Hebrew word commonly used in the OT for worship is *hithpael* which means to prostrate one self. It was a way of doing homage to a superior. While this word is primarily seen in association with the worship of God in the OT, it is also seen in association with the worship of Kings and others. We see David prostrating himself before King Saul and the Israelites doing *hithpael* to both God and King David.

1 Samuel 24:8: Then David went out of the cave and called out to Saul, "My lord the king!" When Saul looked behind him, David bowed down and prostrated (*hithpae*l) himself with his face to the ground.

1 Chronicles 29:20: Then David said to the whole assembly, "Praise the LORD your God." So they all praised the LORD, the God of their fathers; they bowed low and fell prostrate before the LORD <u>and</u> the king.

We find Bathsheba doing *hithpael* to David. Ruth did *hithpael* to Boaz. The Shunammite women, whose son the prophet Elisha raised from the dead, did *hithpael* to Elisha. We find dozens of such occurrences in OT Scripture. Worship in Scripture is not something limited to God. Worship can be directed to others commensurate with their level of qualification for such worship.

In the Greek Scriptures we see the word *proskuneo* translated "worship." This word is equivalent to the Hebrew *hithpael* in meaning and is used almost exclusively in association with the worship of God and Jesus but is also seen in Revelation 3:9 as applied to members of the church at Philadelphia.

Revelation 3:9: I will make those who are of the synagogue of Satan, who claim to be Jews though they are not, but are liars--I will make them come and fall down (*proskuneo*) at your feet and acknowledge that I have loved you.

The Father is the only one worthy of being worshiped as the Supreme, Most High God because the Scriptures show Him to be the one and only Supreme God. Jesus is worthy of worship because of His status as the one and only begotten Son of the one and only Supreme God. Our worship of the Father and Jesus is a response to who they are. Our worship of them is commensurate with who they are. We worship

311

the Father as the one and only self existent Eternal Creator God. We worship the Son as the anointed of this stand alone Supreme God. Because we worship Jesus doesn't mean He is the Supreme God. Jesus was worshiped by the Magi that came to Bethlehem not because they thought He was the Supreme God but because they knew He was the prophesied King of Israel. Therefore, they paid Him the appropriate homage. God the Father and Jesus the Son of God the Father are worthy of worship commensurate with who they are. Paul makes plain who they are.

I Corinthians 8:6: Yet for us <u>there is but one God, the Father</u>, from whom all things came and for whom we live; and <u>there is but one Lord, Jesus Christ,</u> through whom all things came and through whom we live.

1Timothy 2:5: For there is <u>one God</u> and one mediator <u>between</u> God and men, the man Christ Jesus.

Some believe when Paul, in 1 Corinthians 8:6, says Jesus is the one Lord, Paul is identifying Jesus as the LORD of the *Shema* since the *Shema* says, **"Hear, O Israel: the LORD (*YHWH*) our God, the LORD (*YHWH*) is one."** It is believed Paul is reformulating the *Shema* to reveal the identity of the one God as being both the Father and the Son. Therefore, it is believed Jesus is identified with the LORD (*YHWH*) of the *Shema*. Those who take this position read 8:6 as, "There is but one *YHWH* the Father and one *YHWH* Jesus Christ."

This approach assumes the thing to be proved which is that Father and Son are equally *YHWH*. Paul clearly says the Father is the one God and Jesus is the one Lord. Jesus, as the one Lord, is clearly distinguished from the Father who is identified as the one God. Paul makes this distinction throughout his writings and clearly shows the Son is not the Father's equal but is subservient to the Father (I Corinthians: 11:3, 15:27-28). Both the Father and the Son are identified as Lord in Scripture. The

Father is the one Supreme Creator LORD God (*YHWH Elohim*) while Jesus is Lord Christ (The anointed of the Father).

In Chapter Fourteen, I asked the question, Is Jesus Divine? Let's return to that question. As pointed out in Chapter Fourteen, to be divine involves exceeding the bounds of normal humanity and manifesting supernatural attributes. The Son of God, as the human Jesus, demonstrated supernatural attributes more than any other human. He did this not because He was God in the flesh but because the one and only Most High God granted Him supernatural attributes. To a lesser extent, God granted supernatural attributes to Apostles Peter, Paul and others as witnessed by their miracle working activity. This did not make these men the Most High God or entitle them to be worshiped as the Most High God. They understood all praise and worship for humanly performed supernatural activity belonged to the Supreme God. When Paul facilitated the healing of a man crippled from birth, the people began to offer sacrifices to Paul and Barnabas believing them to be gods come down to them in human form. Paul quickly dismissed such activity and said the credit for what they did should be directed **"to the living God, who made heaven and earth and sea and everything in them" (Acts 14:8-15).** Even though Paul and Barnabas displayed divine activity, they were quick to reveal the source of such divine activity. Jesus did the same thing throughout His ministry and even after His ascension He continued to identify the source of His power and glory as the Father who He continued to relate to as His God.

During His ministry, Jesus consistently directed praise for what He did to His Father God. Jesus plainly said He could do nothing on His own. All that He did He did because God the Father enabled Him. God gave Jesus supernatural powers beyond anything given to any other human. While Scripture shows Jesus being worshiped, there is no evidence such worship directed to Jesus was directed to Him as the One and Only Most High God. Worship of Jesus as the One and Only

God would have run totally contrary to the *Shema* which Jesus showed identified God as a single, undifferentiated Being. Nothing in the *Shema* identifies God as being differentiated as Father, Son and Spirit.

During His ministry, Jesus gave no hint of being one with the Father in Being. Jesus plainly said the Father was the one and only true God (John 5:44 and 17:3). Worship directed toward Jesus during His earthly ministry was in response to recognition of Him being the promised King of Israel. As previously discussed, when the Magi worshiped Jesus at his birth they didn't do so because they thought He was the Eternal God.

After the death, resurrection and ascension of Jesus, His God and Father granted Him great power, authority and glory. Within the context of who God the Father has made Jesus to be, Jesus is worthy of being worshiped as a god provided we remain cognizant of the fact the Father is the One and Only Most High Supreme God from whom all power and authority flows. *YHWH* is this God and there is no other God like *YHWH* (See my discussion of Psalm 82:1-7 and John 10:30-36 in Chapter Fourteen).

When we consider what Jesus accomplished on our behalf as the totally obedient and subservient agent of the One and Only Most High God and how His God and Father elevated Him to high status because of what He accomplished, it should be apparent Jesus is worthy of great worship as our glorified Savior and Lord. This does not in any way compromise the monotheism of Scripture which is based on the exclusive worship of only one Being as the Supreme God, a God who is the power over all reality including the reality that is Christ Jesus. Worship of the Son is not equal to worship of *YHWH*. The belief that worship of Jesus undermines monotheism if Jesus isn't *YHWH* does not square with the Scriptures.

I have presented a number of straightforward Scriptural quotes from Jesus, Paul, John and others who identify the Father as the one and only Supreme God. I believe it is clear Scriptures such as these that must define our understanding of who God is in relation to who Jesus is. These are core statements made by the men we look to for formulation of Christian doctrine. These are foundational statements that must define our understanding of who the Father and the Son are in relationship to each other. Scriptures that appear on the surface to say something different as to the relationship between God and Christ must be examined in light of the clear and concise core Scriptures that show there to be one Unitarian, undifferentiated God who is the Father. Such Scriptures present straightforward, unambiguous evidence showing the Father to be the one and only Most High God.

We have examined dozens of Scriptural passages that have been used by Trinitarians to say Jesus is God as God is God. Upon careful examination of these Scriptural passages, they do not provide clear evidence of Jesus being God as God is God. In many cases they provide strong evidence Jesus is not God as God is God. On the other hand, we have examined dozens of Scriptural passages that provide undeniable evidence that the Father is the one and only Most High, Supreme Creator God and the Son is the prophesied and begotten Messiah of this one and only Most High, Supreme Creator God.

Trinitarian theologians readily admit their three in one and one in three concept of God is a mystery that cannot be comprehended. Typical of admissions to that effect are the following statements taken from the book we quoted from earlier, *The Christian Doctrine of God, One Being Three Persons*, by the renowned Trinitarian theologian Thomas F Torrance.

"Both the generation of the Son and the procession of the Spirit are incomprehensible mysteries which are not explicable through recourse to human modes of thought. Hence, as

David A Kroll

Athanasius and Gregory of Nazianzen insisted, we must set aside all analogies drawn from the visible world in speaking of God, helpful as they may be up to a point, for they are theologically unsatisfactory and even objectionable, and must think of 'Father' and 'Son' when used of God as imageless relation. 'Father,' Gregory pointed out, is the name of the relation in which the Father stands to the Son, and the Son stands to the Father, but as such it is an ineffable relation which exceeds and transcends human powers of imagination and conception, so that we may not read the creaturely content of our human expressions of 'father' and 'son' analogically into what God discloses of his own inner divine relations. Hence Gregory Nazianzen like Athanasius insisted that thy must be treated as referring imagelessly, that is in a diaphanous or 'see through' way to the Father and the Son without the intrusion of creaturely forms or sensual images into God. Thus we may not think of God as having gender nor think of the Father as begetting the Son or the Son as the begotten after the analogy of generation or giving birth with which we are familiar among creaturely beings" (Page 157-158).

"In response to his Word we cannot help but use human language in speaking of God, but in itself it is far from adequate or proper. The ultimate truth to which we seek to give theological expression when, following Holy Scripture, we call God 'Father and Son' is hidden in the mystery of God's transcendent Being. That is holy ground upon which we dare not try to intrude through human speculation. Karl Barth went as far as to write about this: 'We do not know what we are saying when we call God Father and Son. We can say it only in such a way that on our lips and in our concepts it is untruth. For us the truth we are expressing when we call God Father and Son is hidden and unsearchable' " (Page 159).

"As Karl Barth once wrote: 'In our hands even terms suggested to us by Holy Scripture will prove to be incapable of grasping what they are supposed to grasp.' However, as

316

Cyril of Alexandria one said, 'when things concerning God are expressed in language used of men, we ought not to think of anything base, but to remember that the wealth of divine Glory is being mirrored in the poverty of human expression' " (page 173).

In response to the above quotes, let me say the following: The Christian theological system is based on the Biblical Scriptures which are a collection of documents believed to have come about as a result of the leading of the Spirit of God. It is recognized that authors of Scripture use a great deal of analogy, metaphor, rhetorical exaggeration (hyperbole) and figurative language in their writings. Analogy is showing something to be like something else. It involves the drawing of parallels. Metaphor is using the non-literal to represent the literal. Metaphor often uses symbols to represent the real thing. Hyperbole is the use of language in exaggerated ways to make a point. There is much use of all three of these forms of communication in the Scriptures, especially in the prophetic writing.

While it is true the authors of Scripture frequently used these forms of speech, much of what is written in Scripture is straightforward in its communication to us of information vital to our understanding of who the Father , Son and Spirit are. If this were not the case, we would flounder in an endless sea of speculative interpretation as to what the Scriptures are teaching us. Language is for the purpose of communicating information. Words are meant to communicate their common and accepted meaning. When reading the Scriptures, we must consider the words used by its authors to contain the normal and accepted meaning germane to such words unless context suggests something different.

For example, we see the word "begotten" used in Scripture to signify a moment in time beginning. This is the common and normal way this word is used and understood as seen by its use in both secular and sacred context. Therefore, there is no reason to use this word to signify an eternal (without beginning) event. Such usage is completely outside of the normal usage of this word. Mr. Torrance writes that we can't define begetting or begotten in terms of how those words are used in describing human activity and yet sees nothing wrong with defining these words in ways totally contrary to their normal meaning.

The Arian controversy of the fourth century centered on how the Son came to be. Arius believed the Son had a moment in time beginning. His opponents believed the Son was eternally begotten (had no beginning). Fourth century theologians could have avoided much conflict if they simply would have recognized that to become begotten is to have a beginning in time. Having a beginning in time involves something or somebody coming into existence that was not previously in existence.

When the Scriptures tell us God is immortal and those same Scriptures tell us Jesus died, I have no reason to conclude the Jesus who died is the immortal God as such a conclusion is totally out of line with the normal and accepted meaning of the word immortal and the word death. When Jesus says His Father is the one and only true God, I have to believe "one and only" means "one and only" and not that "one and only" includes two additional entities.

The Scriptures do not present the relationship between the Father, Son and Spirit as a great mystery that can't be understood. As previously discussed, the Greek word translated mystery in the NT does not mean something that can't be understood but something that is understood as private knowledge held by an individual or group to whom understanding has been given. Paul consistently uses this word in relation to revealed knowledge, not hidden knowledge. Here is just one example of this.

Romans 16:25-27: Now to him who is able to establish you by my gospel and the proclamation of Jesus Christ, according to the revelation of the <u>mystery</u> hidden for long

ages past, but <u>now revealed</u> and made known through the prophetic writings by the command of the eternal God, so that all nations might believe and obey him-- to the only wise God be glory forever through Jesus Christ! Amen.

God being a Trinity is truly a mystery that cannot be understood because it presents a construct of God that does not square with the Scriptural revelation of who the Father, Son and Spirit are in relation to each other. Formulation of the Trinity is founded on the use of words outside their normal and accepted usage resulting in ambiguous and confusing theology.

I want it to be clear that if the Biblical Scriptures clearly revealed God to be a single Being of single undivided substance and yet differentiated in three Persons or distinctions, I would have no problem accepting such revelation as paradoxical as such a concept of God may appear to be. If the Scriptures clearly revealed the immortal God died, I would have no problem accepting such revelation as contradictory as such a teaching would be to human reasoning. The Scriptures, however, do not reveal such a paradoxical and contradictory God. The Scriptures reveal God is an intrinsically immortal, undifferentiated Unitarian Being who is incapable of dying. This God of immeasurable power is the source of all things and purposed from the beginning to provide a totally mortal human sacrifice to atone for the sin of mankind. That sacrifice was the man Jesus, begotten through the Spirit of the Father who, upon completing His earthly mission, ascended to His God and Father and received great power and glory which had been ordained for Him from the beginning.

The doctrine of the Trinity, as is true of all Christian doctrine and propositions of all kinds, must be able to stand up to falsification. Falsification is the presentation of evidence that contradicts what is believed to be true. I believe the Scriptures falsify the doctrine of the Trinity by presenting God as Unitarian and not Trinitarian. I have identified and discussed multiple

319

dozens of Scriptural passages that falsify the doctrine of the Trinity. Here is just a sampling of the Scriptural passages used in this book that provide such falsification. John 5:43-44, 17:3, 14:28, 5:26, 20:17, Romans 3:29-30, 16:25-27, Revelation 1:5-6, 1 Corinthians 8:4-6, Ephesians 4:4-6, 1 Timothy 2:5, Galatians 1:3-5, 1 Corinthians 11:3, 15:27-28, 1 John 5:20, Mark12:29-30, Psalm 103.

The very language of the NT Scripture is evidence Jesus was not viewed as the eternal God but as the appointed servant of the eternal God. When Jesus and the Apostles are quoted as saying the Father is the one and only true God, they are not speaking in code which can be deciphered to mean Jesus and the Spirit are also the one and only true God. Apostle Peter's Pentecost sermon shortly after Jesus had ascended to the Father emphatically shows who Jesus is versus who God is.

Acts 2:22-24: Men of Israel, listen to this: Jesus of Nazareth was <u>a man accredited by God</u> to you by miracles, wonders and signs, <u>which God did among you through him</u>, as you yourselves know. This <u>man was handed over to you by God's set purpose and foreknowledge</u>; and you, with the help of wicked men, put him to death by nailing him to the cross. But <u>God raised him from the dead</u>, freeing him from the agony of death, because it was impossible for death to keep its hold on him.

There is no hint in anything Peter said to indicate he believed or anyone else believed Jesus was God as God is God. Jesus is shown to be a man accredited by God through miracles God did through Him. His crucifixion is seen as occurring as a result of God's will and purpose to have Jesus die. Jesus, the Son of God, died! The man Jesus was dead. God raised Him from the dead. If we allow the Scriptures to instruct us as to who Jesus was during his presence on planet earth, it becomes abundantly clear Jesus was a totally human man ordained by God to accomplish a special purpose. Upon completion of that purpose, God made Jesus immortal and elevated Him to great glory.

The Jesus of Scripture is not an incarnation of the eternal God. The Jesus of Scripture is a totally human man through whom the eternal God accomplished His purpose to have a human sacrifice atone for human sin. Jesus is alive, not because He is the immortal God but because the immortal God resurrected Him from the dead.

I know the Trinitarian concept of God is entrenched in the Christian consciousness. I know what I have written in this book runs contrary to what is believed by the majority of Christian theologians, ministers and members of the Christian community. Many will see my conclusions as revisionary, radical and heretical. Some will accuse me of promoting a low Christology versus the high Christology generally seen in Evangelical Christianity. Some will see what I have written as a minimalistic interpretation of Christian theology. Others may accuse me of reviving the Arian controversy of the fourth century. Some will simply conclude that the historical leadership of the Church could not possibly be wrong on an issue as important as the nature of the Father, Son and Spirit.

In reality, all such responses are irrelevant. The only thing relevant is what the Scriptures are actually teaching as to the nature of the Father, Son and Spirit. I ask you to carefully and objectively consider what the Scriptures reveal regarding the issues dealt with in this book and resist the urge to simply pigeonhole the position presented as being without merit.

The Christian community has been shown to be wrong before on major issues. For centuries the leadership of the Christian Church believed and taught the sun revolved around the earth and used various Biblical Scriptures to support this belief. When evidence was presented that the earth revolves around the sun, such evidence was denounced by Church leadership and those advancing such evidence were condemned. It took a considerable amount of time for the Church to embrace the evidence that the earth does indeed revolve around the sun.

I urge you to carefully and objectively examine what I have written. Be careful to evaluate what has been presented within the context of <u>the whole of Scripture</u>. When all the Scriptures that bear on this issue are carefully examined and studied in their relationship to each other, I believe there is a preponderance of evidence for the conclusions I have drawn. If it can be demonstrated that the many Scriptures I have presented that identify the Father as the One and Only Supreme, Most High God can fit into a Trinitarian construct of God, I will be happy to examine such evidence. I only ask that responses to what I have written be constructive, comprehensive and evidence based and not just sectarian or knee-jerk emotional reactions to the material presented. I can be reached through <u>www. theologicalperspectives.com</u>.

ACKNOWLEDGEMENTS

In gathering information and doing research pertinent to my examination of Incarnational and Trinitarian theology, I consulted numerous resources on the internet, used a number of Hebrew and Greek Lexicons, Bible Commentaries and Dictionaries, and various translations of the Hebrew and Greek Scriptures. The works listed below are a partial list of the resources I used in preparing the material for this book.

BIBLIOGRAPHY

Athanasius: *The Incarnation of the Word of God.*

Ayres, Lewis: *Nicaea and its Legacy* (An Approach to Fourth-Century Trinitarian Theology).

Bauckham, Richard: *Jesus and the God of Israel* (God Crucified and Other Studies on the New Testament's Christology of Divine Identity).

Bowman Jr., Robert M and J. Ed Komoszewski: *Putting Jesus In His Place* (The Case For The Deity Of Christ).

Buzzard, Anthony F: *Jesus Was Not a Trinitarian* (A Call to Return to the Creed of Jesus).

Buzzard, Anthony F and Charles F. Hunting: *The Doctrine of the Trinity* (Christianity's Self-Inflected Wound).

Cary, Phillip: *The History of Christian Theology.*

Ehrman, Bart D: ***The Orthodox Corruption of Scripture*** (The Effects of Early Christological Controversies on the Text of the New Testament).

Ehrman, Bart D: ***Misquoting Jesus***: (The Story Behind Who Changed the Bible and Why).

Evans, Craig A: ***Fabricating Jesus*** (How Modern Scholars Distort the Gospels).

Graeser, Mark H, John A. Lynn and John W. Schoenheit: ***One God and One Lord*** (Reconsidering the Cornerstone of the Christian Faith).

Harris, Murray ***Jesus As God*** (The New Testament Use of Theos in Reference to Jesus).

Holt, Brian: ***Jesus: God or the Son of God?*** (A Comparison of the arguments).

Kruger, C Baxter: ***The Great Dance*** (The Christian Vision Revisited).

Kruger, C Baxter: ***God Is For Us***.

Kruger, C Baxter: ***JESUS and the Undoing of Adam***.

Kruger, C Baxter: ***Across All Worlds*** (Jesus Inside Our Darkness),

Lewis, CS: **Mere Christianity**.

Morris, Thomas V: ***The Logic of God Incarnate***.

Need, Stephen W: ***Truly Divine & Truly Human*** (The Story of Christ and the Seven Ecumenical Councils).

Navas, Patrick: *Divine Truth or Human Tradition* (A Reconsideration of the Roman Catholic-Protestant Doctrine of the Trinity in Light of the Hebrew and Christian Scriptures).

Rubenstein, Richard E: *When Jesus Became God*.

Schaff, Philip and Henry Wallace: (Editors) *Nicene and Post-Nicene Fathers,* Second Series, Volume IV, Athanasius: Selected Works and Letters.

Skarsaune, Oskar *Incarnation: Myth or Fact?*

Torrance, Thomas F: *The Christian Doctrine of God* (The One Being Three Persons).

Torrance, Thomas F: *The Trinitarian Faith*.

Torrance, Thomas F: *Atonement* (The Person and Work of Christ).

Wallace, Daniel B. *Greek Grammar: Beyond the Basics* (An Exegetical Syntax of the New Testament).

Wallace, Daniel B: (Editor) *Revisiting The Corruption of the New Testament*: (Manuscript, Patristic and Apocryphal Evidence).

REFERENCE WORKS

Arndt, William F. and F Wilbur Gingrich: *Greek-English Lexicon of the New Testament and Other Early Christian Literature*.

Brown, Driver and Briggs: *Hebrew and English Lexicon of the Old Testament*.

Harris, R. Laird, Gleason L. Archer Jr. and Bruce K. Waltke: *Theological Wordbook of the Old Testament*.

Soncino Press: *Books of the Bible (Hebrew Text & English Translation)*.

Strong, James: *Strong's Exhaustive Concordance*.

Thayer, Joseph H: *Thayer's Greek-English Lexicon of the New Testament*.

Tregelles, Samuel P: *Gesenius' Hebrew-Chaldee Lexicon to the Old Testament*, translated by Samuel P Tregelles.

Wigram, George V: *The Englishman's Greek Concordance of the New Testament*

Wigram, George V: *Hebrew and Chaldee Concordance of the Old Testament*

Wuest, Kenneth S: *Word Studies in the Greek New Testament*.

BIBLE TRANSLATIONS QUOTED FROM

New International Version: (NIV).

King James Version: (KJV)

New King James Version: (NKJV)

American Standard Version: (ASV)

Revised Standard Version: (RSV)

New Jerusalem Bible: (NJB)

New English Bible (NET)

English Standard Version (ESV)

Concordant Literal New Testament

BIBLE TRANSLATIONS REFERRED TOO

New American Standard Version: (NASV)

New American Bible: (NAB)

Moffatt Bible

Apostolic Bible Polyglot

Companion Bible

The Englishman's Greek New Testament